THE MAN WHO SAID NO

KENT THOMPSON

The Man Who Said No

Reading Jacob Bailey, Loyalist

GASPEREAU PRESS
PRINTERS & PUBLISHERS
2008

Contents

A Preliminary Note

This is not a scholarly study. This book is a personal essay in which I attempt to understand the progress of Jacob Bailey's sensibility from his youth to old age, with special attention paid to the journey he made to England in the winter of 1760. It is my telling of his life.

I have consulted comparatively few original documents, concentrating chiefly on the journals of Jacob Bailey for 1759–60 and the 1755 letterbook which are available at the O'Dell Museum in Annapolis Royal. Indeed, I have worked mostly from the handwritten transcription of Bailey's journals made by one of his descendants, R.C. Woodbury, in 1932, and subsequently photocopied. But Woodbury's transcription goes beyond the Bailey journals available at the O'Dell, suggesting that further journals which were available to Woodbury in 1932 have since disappeared. In addition, I have consulted, photocopied and included some samples of Bailey's extensive writings which are held at the Provincial Archives of Nova Scotia in Halifax.

This is not to say that scholarly work on Jacob Bailey's life is unavailable. A very good biography of the Rev. Jacob Bailey in the form of an (as yet unpublished) M.A. thesis in history by Julie Ross for the University of New Brunswick in 1975 is available at the University of New Brunswick in Fredericton, a copy of which is also at the O'Dell Museum in Annapolis Royal. Its title is: *Jacob Bailey, Loyalist: Anglican Clergyman in New England and Nova Scotia.*

Another scholarly work is the paper delivered to the Lincoln County Historical Association on 13 November 1895, by Charles E. Allen. Ross is interested in Jacob Bailey as a hardworking, dedicated Anglican clergyman. Allen shows us a Jacob Bailey who was treated very badly indeed, and unjustly, by certain people chiefly because they were different kinds of Protestant. If there is a hero in the life of Jacob Bailey, it is Allen; but special thanks should go, too, to R.C. Woodbury and George Woodbury. If there is a heroine, it is Julie Ross. But we don't want to forget Aunt Minnie.

Of central importance to this book and to everyone interested in Jacob Bailey is William S. Bartlet's 1853 publication, *Frontier Missionary: A Memoir of Jacob Bailey.* Bartlet's book is an impressive work of dedicated scholarship, and he had access to many more of Bailey's writings than have survived, but Bartlet's book is also surprisingly shifty. He conceals some facts about Bailey, but, more surprisingly, attempts to hide the identities of Bailey's enemies before and during the American Revolution. Bartlet's book, too, is at the O'Dell Museum in Annapolis Royal.

In addition, there are at least three excellent journal articles on Bailey's poetic career. In 1929, Ray Palmer Baker, an American professor who corresponded with Aunt Minnie, published "The Poetry of Jacob Bailey" in the *New England Quarterly.* A copy of Baker's article is available at the O'Dell Museum in Annapolis Royal. T.B. Vincent has also written about Bailey's poetry in the context of Henry Alline's evangelical movement in the Annapolis Valley at the end of the eighteenth century in "Alline and Bailey" in *Canadian Literature* (Summer of 1976) and in "Some Examples of Narrative Verse Satire in the Early Literature of Nova Scotia and New

A

Journal

of

a travel from Gloucester

in

New-england

to

London

in great Britain; and from

thence to Pownallborough

on Kennebeck river —

Vol: I.

Brunswick" in the *Humanities Association Review*, also in 1976. I found both articles, and so can you, at the Vaughan Memorial Library of Acadia University in Wolfville, Nova Scotia.

But I am interested chiefly in the Bailey who wrote journals. He was a conventional nature poet as well as a wicked satirist, and at least once an angry playwright. The most of his life was that of a dedicated missionary clergyman. But I am interested in the man who wrote down his life and the events around him even as they overwhelmed him. It is amazing how much he noticed and how much he endured in those tumultuous times. Moreover, I contend that his life was changed, in ways both obvious and not, by his trip to London in 1760.

That assertion can be argued, and probably will be. But I did not embark on this enquiry with the idea of proving one thing or another about Jacob Bailey. I began to look at Jacob Bailey's life because I liked him. I admired his courage. I sympathized with his plight. I soon forgave his faults, such as they were, and his embarrassments, as you do with friends. And even when I disagreed with his attitudes and conclusions, I was soon grateful to him for *writing everything down.* Not many do so well, nor do so much for our understanding of what we call, grandly, *History.* He has done well by us, and we owe him much.

A NOTE ON THE JOURNALS AND LETTERS

In dealing with Bailey's manuscripts we are almost always reading *first drafts.* The eighteenth-century letterbook was at once a first draft of letters and a record of those letters. In any event, there was no accepted standardization of grammar, punctuation or spelling at the time. Samuel Johnson's famous Dictionary (not the first, but the most ambitious) was not published until 1755, the year Jacob Bailey graduated from Harvard. Moreover, probably because Bailey was writing rough drafts, he was not fussy about consistency in spelling or punctuation. He was not thinking about publication. In addition, his handwriting is always difficult to read, and sometimes impossible. But I've made few attempts to "correct" or update his writing. I try to quote what I've found.

KENT THOMPSON
Annapolis Royal, NS
7 March 2007

Implements of Torture

Across from the public wharf, beside the grey sheds that contain the gaily-coloured Summer Saturday Market here in Annapolis Royal, Nova Scotia, right now (2008), we have a set of punishment stocks, suitable for two. The miscreants can be seated side by side on a bench with their hands stuck through holes in front of them, locked there, facing the mob.

The punishment stocks are not original, of course. In fact, these are fake. If you stick your hands in the holes, you can pull them right out again. But the supposition behind these stocks is that Tourists in search of "old-timiness" might enjoy them, as they might enjoy *Ye Olde Woole Shoppe* (which does not actually exist, but it might, although I sincerely hope not). Hubby and the little woman might fit themselves into the stocks for the purposes of commemorative photographs ("married in Nova Scotia!") of their trip to the historic village of Annapolis Royal, once capital of Nova Scotia. Look at the man and wife grinning. Haw Haw Haw.

In fact, the punishment stocks in their original were implements of torture, intimidation, and coercion, as well as gadgets for the amusement of the mob. You want always to remember the mob. The mob administered the real punishment. The stocks were simply to prevent the criminals from

escaping. The mob flung garbage and whatever else was
handy at the helpless prisoners. Dead rats were a favourite.

On one occasion—a fairly public occasion, as I recall—I
was giving vent to my disapproval of both "ye olde" desig-
nations in general and the punishment stocks in particular,
which I believed inappropriate for Annapolis Royal, which had
been French (and Catholic) when it was the seventeenth-century administrative capital of Acadia, and after the conquest
of 1710, British, and therefore not to be identified with Salem,
Massachusetts, where indeed punishment stocks were used to
enforce their theocratic government when it was not execut-
ing old ladies (chiefly—and two dogs) for witchcraft.

Turns out I was wrong.

Following my rant, local historian Ian Lawrence did some
digging around in archives, and sent me a letter in which he
noted that "after the town's transfer to British rule in 1710,
Boston held increasing sway over Nova Scotia…. Most of the
New England Planters who took up the lands of the expelled
Acadians in Annapolis County between 1759 and 1763 were
farmers and tradesmen from Massachusetts, fourth and fifth
generation descendants of its earliest settlers."

And particularly to the point:

*The earliest historical record of stocks locally is contained in
county grand jury proceedings for the April term 1788, when
the sum of £8 was allowed "to erect a pair of stocks in each of
the townships, Annapolis, Granville, Wilmot and Digby—
£2 each. [And in 1791] the stock in the town of Annapolis
being out of repair, the Grand Jury have nominated Anthony George Kyshe, Esq., Isaac Bonnett and Joseph Cousins a
committee to repair the same, and to fix them between church
and town pump, or any other public place as may seem most*

*convenient to said committee." In 1801 money from ferry rents was placed towards the erection of a new pair of stocks and a pillory, and in 1803 the stocks were ordered erected near the courthouse.**

* Ian Lawrence, letter to me, 7 May 2006. We agreed about Ye Olde Woole Shoppe, however.

I stood corrected.

In fact, it might be worth noting that when the French capital of Acadia, Port Royal (as Annapolis Royal was known then) did not quite fall to British troops—but to Massachusetts Militia, and Massachusetts was then far more independent of the British crown than is generally supposed. It was Massachusetts boys who garrisoned Fort Anne and died there of disease and cold. After the French were evicted from the Fort, and the community became Annapolis Royal, it was the capital of English-speaking Nova Scotia until 1749, when the seat of government was moved to Halifax—where life and government were dominated by the presence of the English garrison and the British Navy. But Annapolis Royal was essentially a New England settlement from 1710 to the arrival of the Loyalists in 1783—and somewhat beyond, as the dates for the purchase of stocks might indicate.

Perhaps, in fact, the Planters from New England were trying to hold onto their previous power by means of the punishment stocks after the Loyalists from all over the thirteen colonies began to arrive in 1783. So I deduce, anyway, if only because it is not unusual for groups to try to hold onto their symbols after their power has been taken away—and the Loyalists after 1783 so outnumbered the Planters that the Loyalists soon took over government posts, and patronage. The Planters were left to assert themselves as best they could—possibly with punishment stocks.

But the Planters certainly held sway in certain areas, espe-

✝ Cruise and
Griffiths, p. 36.

‡ Christopher
Moore, p. 208.

cially in the eastern end of the Annapolis Valley. David Cruise
and Alison Griffiths, in *On South Mountain: The Dark Secrets
of the Goler Clan*, explain how a Christian religious sect, the
Rogerenes, which had itself split from the Puritan Congregationalist Church, was recruited from Boston to take up the
lands of the expelled Acadians near what is now Wolfville,
and itself soon split into two mutually antagonistic groups,
one in the valley and another on South Mountain. The valley group became the more powerful, and was dedicated to
enforcing its edicts.

> *One of the first things the Planters did when they arrived was
> to erect a pillory and a whipping post—both of which were
> quickly broken in. A forger had his ear cut off before enduring
> an hour of public humiliation in the pillory and a thief caught
> red-handed with three yards of stolen cloth was whipped into
> unconsciousness.*

A father and son, prominent in the valley community, were
found guilty of stealing and butchering a neighbour's pig.

> *Solemn-faced escorts delivered them to the whipping post, set
> prominently in Horton's tiny town centre. There they shackled
> first the father and then the son to the wooden pillar and lashed
> each of them thirty-nine times with a leather bullwhip.*✝

This was in 1777.

In fact, certain New England ideas remained strong even
among the Loyalists, and at Shelburne—which was intended to be the Loyalist answer to New York—one of the first
things the settlers did was erect a "gallows, whipping post,
and pillory."‡

So it turns out that I had made a not-uncommon error when I assumed that before, during, and after the American Revolution, Nova Scotia was a loyal British colony. It was not. When I first encountered Thomas Raddall's historical novel about Nova Scotia in the time of the American Revolution, I assumed that the title, *His Majesty's Yankees*, referred to an American regiment fighting for the British during the rebellion. I was wrong about that, too.

Raddall's novel demonstrates that—except for Halifax— the Nova Scotia which was settled chiefly by New Englanders was in favour of the Revolution until Yankee privateers began looting Nova Scotia's shipping and coastal communities (including Annapolis Royal), but Thomas Raddall had to counter views to the contrary which were dearly held by Halifax historians in the middle of the twentieth century. Those views had it, he said, "that by a marvellous dispensation of Providence our fourteenth [colony] remained stoutly loyal, without a seditious thought or deed. This was precisely the fallacy I intended to attack."

And he did. He wrote:

Roughly two-thirds of the people in Nova Scotia at the outbreak of the Revolution were of Yankee birth or the sons and daughters of Yankee settlers, and their sympathies naturally were with their own people in New England.... Unlike the other colonies, they had no broad interior farmlands to which they could retreat and subsist if the king's forces dominated the coast. The Nova Scotia settlements were small, scattered, and almost all exposed to armed ships. In fact, the Yankees of Nova Scotia were pinned to the coast like a pelt to a barn door, and the result of their reluctance to commit themselves one way or another was persecution by both sides. A time came when their

§ Thomas Raddall, *In My Time,* pp. 196–7.

¶ Glebe lands are lands owned by the church for the support of the church. In 1710, after the defeat of the French, the glebe lands devoted to the Roman Catholic Church simply passed into the hands of the Anglican Church.

* Calnek and Savary, *History of the County of Annapolis,* p. 72. A somewhat different version of the event is given by Brenda Dunn, *A History of Port Royal / Annapolis Royal,* p. 123.

American brethren harassed them beyond endurance, and they turned dourly to the king. §

What a good word—*dourly!*

So when Jacob Bailey (B.A. Harvard, 1755; M.A. Harvard, 1758), Anglican cleric, arrived in Annapolis Royal in 1782, he was not especially welcome. He was a Church of England clergyman who found himself among New England Dissenters who had been doing not badly before he arrived. In fact, they had taken over the Anglican glebe lands for their own benefit some time before he arrived. ¶

Local historian Ian Lawrence is right: this was a New England town—which meant that, in turn, there was a great enmity between the New Englanders and the French and Indians which had been bubbling along for a long time—which was then altogether confused with the French and English animosities in Europe, and a British administration which seemed sometimes as much theory as fact.

In 1724, for example, there was an aboriginal raid on the fort in Annapolis Royal. A Sergeant McNeil, who had wandered outside the walls to go hunting, was shot, killed, and scalped. There was then a battle of sorts, and the Indians withdrew. But there were aboriginal prisoners held inside Fort Anne, and in retaliation for the death of Sergeant McNeil, one of the prisoners was taken out, shot, and scalped. It was later agreed that perhaps scalping was going too far and had not been strictly necessary.*

Justice—or retribution—in the New England colonies was swift and savage. In 1754, Jacob Bailey, undergraduate at Harvard, together with a friend and the friend's sister (this may seem surprising, but they didn't consider it remarkable in any way) made an excursion by horseback and carriage through

Connecticut. They stayed at inns and with friends. Bailey took note of the prosperity or lack of it in every village they passed through, and noted the churches and denominations. He was always concerned about goodness, which he equated with religion. (This has long been an American habit; perhaps a bad habit.) He noticed some astonishing poverty (half-starved, half-naked children on dirt floors), and surprising amity (a farmer's family with its workers and black slaves sitting down to eat together), and at least one instance of eighteenth-century justice. On July 11, the three young people were encouraged by their hosts "to see a man hung in gibbets." The young people "beheld an awful sight."

> *The man had been there three years already, and his flesh was all dried fast to his bones, and was black as an African's. The crimes for which he was thus exposed were robbery and murder. He was taken in the southern parts of Long Island with some indisposition, and being in a strange place, one Jackson, a leather merchant, travelling with his horse, found him and took pity on him, and being on this way to Rhode Island, bore all his expenses, and treated him with all the tenderness of a father, for near one hundred and fifty miles, till he arrived at South Kingston, where, being together about dusk of the evening, near the great Quaker meeting-house, he took up a stone, and with it struck him down. Jackson begged his life, and that he might, and welcome, take all his wealth; but he cursed and then fell upon him, and in a few minutes made full dispatch of his innocent patron; thus we have at once an horrid instance of ingratitude.†*

In many ways, the account of viewing the criminal's body is typical of Bailey's thinking: he makes a moral point, and

† Bailey, in William Bartlet, *Frontier Missionary*, p. 20. A gibbet is an iron cage, or perhaps more commonly, a set of chains in which the body of the executed criminal was hung in a tree as a warning to others.

‡ Bailey, from Julie Ross, *Jacob Bailey, Loyalist,* p. 54. Julie Ross is quoting from a Bailey journal of 1753 in the Provincial Archives of Nova Scotia.

notes the expenses. Both are understandable. He was deeply interested in *goodness,* and he was poor all his life. Money was important. The attitudes were typically Puritan.

Julie Ross, in her biography of Jacob Bailey, notes another instance of New England justice. Bailey witnessed this when he was an undergraduate at Harvard in 1753. Bailey had spent part of the day browsing among the Boston bookshops and later met up with his friends Goodhue and Miss Salley Clerck. All three "wore a dreadful countenance."

Bailey recorded:

> *great numbers of people began to flock here of all degrees and ages and sexes about 12 all King street from the Town House down to the middle of the street was crowded about ¼ after 12.0c. was exposed to publick view on a large Scaffold near 7 feet high just by the Royal Exchange tavern in King Street hanah dilly a notorious bawd or procuress upwards of 60 years old ... one who had follow'd such practices for above 40 years She opend upon the stage drest in a striped cotton Gown a Canlaek cap a check apron.... she had a large ... piece of paste board fastened to her breast upon which was written in great capitals a procuress and keeper of a bawdy house ...*‡

Julie Ross writes that Bailey noted that little happened for the first fifteen minutes. "The rabble made no disturbance." But then they threw "lemon peels, old turnips, onions, stones, cats dead and alive and old rotten rats upon the poor criminal." Bailey wrote that not all in attendance acted as the mob acted, and some showed their anger at the mob's behaviour. But, he wrote, he had not before seen the "rage, disorder, and tumult of an ungovernd mob" which he compared to the "raging of the sea." Julie Ross remarks, "It was not the last time."

But Ma Dilly was not exactly a stranger, even to the somewhat prissy young Jacob Bailey, and was surely well known among the Harvard undergraduates. Bailey was to mention her in his poem about the Husking Bee, which is contained in his letterbook of 1753. The rural husking bee was a gathering in which the youth of the community met to rip the husks off the corn, and when a young man happened upon a red husk or a couple of red kernels in the cob, he was entitled to kiss the girl on his right.§ In Bailey's poem, they go beyond kisses. Bailey (or the narrator) does not necessarily approve.

So the punishment stocks in the Market Square of Annapolis Royal had Massachusetts origins, as Bailey did. It is worth remembering that Massachusetts, from its founding as the Massachusetts Bay Colony in 1629–30, was a Puritan theocracy rooted in the Congregational Church. Church membership was a requirement to vote in elections until 1684, when the British government objected. Thereafter, the vote was given to property owners. But the property owners were almost always members of the Congregational Church, so the church continued to control virtually all of the culture and government. The Salem Witch Trials took place in 1692, and Bailey (born in Rawley, Massachusetts, not far from Salem, in 1731) was to devote a chapter to them in his never-published "History of New England."¶ In 1895, Charles Allen was to write of the Massachusetts Puritan stock that they were "a people which, when pious were very pious, but seldom very good."*

I think Allen's comment is insightful. Resonant, too.

The term *mob* and its near-synonym, *rabble*, will recur in this story.† It was the mob who pelted Ma Dilly with refuse. (And how could she have practised her trade without patrons?) It was another which attacked British soldiers

§ Or so I was told by a Bill Casselman website explicating the French word *l'épluchette*. Casselman refers to the practice in a context of nineteenth-century Acadian farming communities.

¶ The manuscript of Bailey's "History of New England" can be viewed on microfilm at the Provincial Archives of Nova Scotia.

* Charles E. Allen, "The Rev. Jacob Bailey, His Character and Works," a paper read before the Lincoln County Historical Society on 14 November 1895.

† I admit it: I always keep a copy of Ambrose Bierce's *The Devil's Dictionary* close at hand. His definition of rabble is: "In a republic, those who exercise supreme authority, tempered by fraudulent elections. See 'soaring swine'."

in Boston in 1770. The British soldiers fired upon the mob and killed five of them. Much was made of this by the genius propagandist of the American Revolution, Samuel Adams. It was he who originated the term, "Boston Massacre." Which it might have been, but not in the view of Samuel Adams' younger second cousin, John Adams. Adams, classmate of Jacob Bailey at Harvard, and second president of the United States, *defended the British soldiers*, and largely got them off.

But John Adams was always uneasy with the mob. His break with his longtime friend, Thomas Jefferson, came when the French Revolution became controlled by the *mobs* and transmuted itself into the Reign of Terror. It is fair to say that a *mob* is one step from *anarchy*.

But a mob could also become the tool of religious zealots. Something very like this happened in the Salem Witch Trials. It was not only the judges and young girls who condemned the innocent citizens of Salem, Massachusetts. Crowds attended the curious trials and executions. And it is no accident that the great American playwright, Arthur Miller, conflated the political and zealot history in his response to Senator Joe McCarthy in the play, *The Crucible*.

It's fair to say that there was always a mob nearby throughout most of Jacob Bailey's life.

Performing His Person

The most famous earthquake of 1755—in the books of cultural history, at least—was the Lisbon Earthquake of 1 November 1755. The destruction caused by the Portuguese earthquake was immense, and it quite literally (please excuse the expression) shook the Faith of Europe. How could a loving merciful God, it was asked—a Discriminating God, a Judging God—cause such death and destruction among the innocent as well as among the others who may well have deserved such damnation? It was the indiscriminate destruction of the Lisbon Earthquake which led to the awkward question: What if God did not interfere in human affairs at all? What if God had nothing to do with it?

Those who believed that God had nothing to do with it included some prominent people—like Benjamin Franklin and Voltaire—and many of them were called Deists. The Deists were of the opinion that the Creator generally called God was very like a Clockmaker who made the clock, wound it up, set it going, and walked away from it—out the door, as it were.* To the Deists, Jesus Christ was a significant teacher but perhaps only that. The Deists were great doubters, and most of them (like Franklin) were very interested in scientific enquiry.

* The curious reader might want to look at the opening of the great comic novel of 1760, *Tristram Shandy*, in which the hero's conception occurs with his mother querying his father about winding the family clock. The author of this wickedly funny, wildly ironic, often improper novel was Laurence Sterne—an Anglican cleric. Sterne was being feted in London in the winter of 1760 when Bailey arrived there to be ordained.

But there was also a major earthquake much closer to home—to Jacob Bailey's home—in 1755. Seventeen days after the Lisbon Earthquake shook European society, on 18 November 1755, the Cape Ann Earthquake struck the New England coast.

Jacob Bailey, recent graduate of Harvard College, employed (unhappily) as a schoolmaster at Kingston, New Hampshire, was near the middle of it. With a great deal of excitement, but nonetheless with care, Jacob Bailey describes the effects to a friend back at Harvard in a letter of 24 November 1755.

The present terrible dispensations of providence engage the attention of everybody in these parts. I have often thought that among all the errors of nature none are so calculated to inspire the minds of people with such fearful apprehensions as Earthquakes to feel the ground trembling beneath, and all nature to be thrown into the most horrid convulsions must needs affright the most hardened mortal into some consideration. I must give you some account of these amazing dispensations here and desire you to write me word of how it was in the place where you live. On Friday morning, Nov 18, the weather being perfectly serene and clear about 10 minits after 9 o.c., we felt an amazing shock of an earthquake. It lasted about 2 minits and an half. The shock seemed to be repeated several times without intermission. I was not sensible of much rocking or any great motion to and fro but a prodigious quivering which made the whole house and everything seem alive. The tops of several chimneys and part of a house were shaked down and some stone walls. At Exeter it was smarter where several chimneys and part of a house were thrown down. We have had near 20 shocks since the first tho none very considerable except the 1st which happened between 8 and 9 o.c. at night on Saturday last.

I was at a house near the borders of Haverhill. We were sitting by fire and perfectly still (the weather being somewhat stormy) when we perceived a heavy rumbling at a distance which kept approaching nearer and nearer. At length it gave the house a long heavy jar....

P.S. Miss Molly Robinson is in a terrible condition on account of....

These comments are found in Jacob Bailey's letterbook of 1755, which is among the documents which arrived at the O'Dell Museum, Annapolis Royal, in the winter of 2001. We have no idea what Miss Robinson's terrible condition was—only that Jacob Bailey noticed it.

The letter is valuable as a record of what happened, but also because it demonstrates the duties of an educated person at the time. He gives an account of the event, and asks for information in return. It is a practice noted in Benjamin Franklin's *Autobiography*. This is how young men of the colonies educated themselves formally and informally, with observations which might lead to deductions which, in turn, would discover empirical truth. Unless, of course, religious belief was injected into the process. In this thinking, as in so many things of the era, Jacob Bailey was caught in the middle.

But he was very good at observation. Examples are given, and the verbs are lively and precise. It is not only that houses are shaken or that the verb "jar" is exact, but that "the whole house seem[ed] alive."

Here is a more recent account of the Cape Ann Earthquake of 1755, taken from the website of the New Hampshire Department of Safety (Division of Emergency Services, Communications, and Management, Bureau of Emergency Management, Natural Hazards, Earthquakes):

The earthquake, with an estimated magnitude of 6.0, caused wide-spread damage along coastal New England on the night of November 18, 1755. The crew of a vessel sailing 200 kilometers offshore thought they had hit a rock. They "hove-to and cast the lead," only to find plenty of water under the keel. In Boston twelve to fifteen hundred chimneys toppled, gable ends of brick buildings broke off and the streets were blocked by fallen bricks. According to John Hyde, a Boston writer, carnage was particularly heavy "on the low, loose ground made by encroachments on the harbor...." This earthquake caused damage well into the interior of Massachusetts ... New Hampshire coastal communities reported the same types of damage. In Portsmouth crew aboard vessels anchored in the harbor scurried on deck thinking they had run ashore when the seismic wave stuck their hulls. In Greenland, the Weeks House, a brick home built in 1710, suffered cracking and bulging of its southern wall. This house, located just off Route 108, can be seen today, its damage intact. [A FEMA *study of the 1980s estimated the effects on Boston if this earthquake took place today] ... if this earthquake took place at two o'clock in the afternoon, there would be approximately 365 deaths, thousands of injuries, and over five billion dollars in damage. Some authorities consider these findings conservative.*

But Jacob Bailey's observations came to a moral conclusion about the earthquake, and he was harsh in his condemnation of his neighbours in Kingston, New Hampshire. His was the religious interpretation. After a winter's thought, on 2 March 1756, he wrote to another friend at Harvard:

I know of no place in N.E. [New England] where igno-rance stupidity and profaneness of mind so abound as in the

place where I now reside, yet in that dreadful morning Nov.
18 numbers of the most profligate and wicked whose knowl-
edge in things either sacred or humane scarce exceeded the
brute creation came flocking with their miserable offspring to
their minister's house expecting it seemd to find shelter under
his roof who they had upon every occasion treated with the
utmost scorn and contempt. They began with the greatest con-
cern to beg his prayers and to intreat him for a discourse suit-
able to the awful occasion. Accordingly we had meetings for 3
or 4 days succession but alas I must tell you in a fortnight after
everything returned to its former position, the earth grew in
some measure still, taverns were crowded as before the seats of
many in the place of divine worship left empty, the education of
children neglected and in short swearing, imodesty and rude-
ness of all sorts comited both by young and old.... They take
these things as punishments inflicted for sin and not as turn-
ing to repentence.

Bailey's moral position is not perhaps as clear as it might
at first seem. The townspeople, in his opinion, look upon the
earthquake as punishment for their sins, and having survived
it, and taken their punishment (as it were), they seem to find
the slate wiped clean and continue as before. But Bailey, on the
other hand, believes they should take the event as a *warning*
to repent. They believe the punishment is over; he believes it is
yet to come. It is clear that he disapproves strongly of swearing and immodesty and rudeness—and includes "the education of children neglected" among the errors of their ways.
His position is clearly that of a Puritan of his era. Jonathan
Edwards would be proud of him. Jacob Bailey is a prissy, censorious young man. His interpretation is entirely religious—
and he is not yet a clergyman of any kind.

He concludes his letter with a poem which, in part, reads:

With fear adore! Let us with reverence sing
The spreading grandeur of that allmighty king
One frown of his can make a nation fall
lean, swel the seas or shake this solid ball
At his rebuke the vast Atlantick roars
And rolls destruction round her spacious shores....

Jacob Bailey likely did not know that back at his beloved Harvard, a strikingly different attitude was on display. John Winthrop, the Hollis Professor of Mathematics and Natural Philosophy, "gave two lectures in Holden Chapel on earthquakes, following the famous Lisbon quake of 1755."

In proving that earthquakes were purely natural phenomena, and not manifestations of divine wrath, he attracted the unpleasant attention of some of the clergy, and demonstrated to the laity the value of experimental research, untrammelled by theological considerations. Thus academic freedom was established in at least one department of knowlege.†

In fact, Samuel Eliot Morison, the famous historian who provides the story of Winthrop's lecture, is likely mistaken in attributing the occasion to the Lisbon Earthquake. Winthrop would have had much better scientific information from his own laboratory and the evident destruction in Boston from the Cape Ann Earthquake. But Morison also remarks that Winthrop's equipment came from his lifelong friend in London, Benjamin Franklin, and tells us that Franklin was awarded an honorary doctorate by Harvard in 1753—when Jacob Bailey was still an undergraduate there.‡

† Samuel Eliot Morison, *Three Centuries of Harvard*, p. 93. It is interesting that the eminent Harvard historian draws a larger conclusion about academic freedom from the incident. But it would seem to mark a moment where the definition of "truth" shifted from religion to science.

‡ Bailey will visit Franklin's house in London in 1760 on more than one occasion, but will say nothing about the great man. Much later, Franklin—and Bailey's Harvard classmate John Adams—will both be targets of Bailey's harshest satire.

But if Jacob Bailey cared little and knew less of the scientific progress at the Harvard from which he had just received his Bachelor of Arts degree, he was devoted to everything else which Harvard represented. Harvard was the embodiment of everything which Jacob Bailey respected: good manners, wit, learning, scholarship, tradition and excellence.

Until he visited London in 1760, Harvard was the high point in Jacob Bailey's life, and it is impossible to exaggerate its importance to him. No sooner had Bailey left Harvard than he was writing back to friends still there to enquire about the earthquake (if he was told of Winthrop's lecture, we don't know about it)—or the names of the entering first-year students. Leaving Harvard, Bailey felt he had been sent into a kind of intellectual exile. He wrote about his feelings to his classmate John Adams on 29 December 1755. Bailey's draft reads:

Sir: I have sent these characters to wait upon you from the most solitary regions of rusticity, from a place where Minerva never entered and from whence the Heliconian Virgins never received any addresses. Ignorance is the goddess to whom all devotion is paid and those on whom she smiles propitious ... To tell you the truth, sir, I am deprived of all humane society as much as if I liv'd in the moon or any other planetary world and shold never know what passes among mankind did not some former acquaintance favour me now and then with letters. Our classmate Goodhue is become extremely popular in these parts and bids fair to make a second W—d [likely Whitefield]. He preached at Eping in a room of Mr. Cutter who was lately dismissed the place for his too open and familiar behaviour toward the fair sex. Pray sir excuse my boldness, my inelegance and abruptness and if you will take the trou-

ble to write me a line by the bearer you will greatly oblige one who remains yours, etc.

It is very much a letter from a lesser member of the Harvard Class of 1755 to the acknowledged class leader—although Bailey was older than Adams. Bailey was a mature student when he entered Harvard at twenty years old. By contrast, John Adams was a more usual new student at sixteen, and the other eminent classmate, John Wentworth—who was to become both governor of New Hampshire and, later, governor of Nova Scotia—was only fourteen when he entered Harvard.

The likely reference to the famous evangelist Whitefield is worth noting, as is Bailey's concern for the relationships between a teacher and pupils of the "fair sex." Note the classical allusions.

Adams replied. He knew exactly how Bailey felt. Adams was then teaching (also unhappily) in Worcester, Massachusetts. Adams' letter is dated "January. I know not what day, 1756."

I received your favour of Dec 29 about 3 or 4 days after it was wrote. The bearer left it at the tavern and proceeded on his journey. So that I despair'd of ever getting an opportunity of answering it, till this moment. I heartily sympathise with you in your affliction, which I am the better qualified to do as I am confined myself to a like place of torment. When I compare the gay, the delightsome scenes of Harvard, with the harsh and barbarous nature of sounds that now constantly grate on my ears I can hardly imagine myself the same being that once listened to Mr. Mayhew's instructions and revelled in all the other pleasures of an academical life total and com-

plete.... However, one source of pleasure is left me still. That is the letters of my friends.... I should be extremely glad therefore of a correspondence with you.... If you see any of my old friends, tell them I am well and should take a line from them very kindly—But I can add no more now than that I am your friend....

> J. Adams
> *Pardon all our epistolary sins* §

§ The Adams letter is found in facsimile form in William Bartlet's 1853, *Frontier Missionary*, facing p. 34.

Adams is clearly the more confident of the correspondents—there are no verbal flourishes or classical allusions—and it is clear also that Adams and Bailey were at best acquaintances at Harvard. Adams asks for news of *"my* old friends," not *our* old friends. But if the correspondence did develop, and likely it did not, we do not know of it. Adams would visit Pownalborough when Bailey was an Anglican cleric there, but there is no record of them meeting, although Pownalborogh was a very small place. Within fifteen years of the tentative correspondence, the two men would have completely incompatible views.

My interest in Jacob Bailey began with a wig. The wig was important to Bailey's era because it noted the wearer's status, and its condition said much about his affluence or lack of it. Bailey's wigs were often in poor condition, which demonstrated that he might be a gentleman, but he was poor. And of course the wigs tell us that it was an age of artifice, and, as the wigs fell out of fashion, that artifice was also falling out of fashion. In Richard Brinsley Sheridan's 1775 play, *The Rivals*, an old coachman greeting a younger in the spa-resort-town

¶ In a recent U.S. Public Broadcasting System television biography of John Adams, Adams is shown wearing a modest iron-grey wig. The fops—the British sorts—wear dapper snow-white wigs.

of Bath laments the passing of the wig. For the old fellow, the wig meant stability. You knew where you were when the fellow wore a wig. Now that wigs were going out of fashion, why, the past was no longer safe. Everything was changing.

Benjamin Franklin was notable for not wearing a wig. ¶

When I was asked by John Kirby, then Executive Director of the Annapolis Royal Historic Restoration Society (headquartered, as it were, in the O'Dell Museum) to read from the recently acquired journals of Jacob Bailey, I agreed—and quickly telephoned Charlie Glover of Bear River Costumes. Bear River Costumes was a chiefly mail-order costume shop which provided costumes for various purposes all over the world. It was odd to find it in nearby Bear River, but then, life is often odd hereabouts. Charlie Glover's mother had been a wardrobe mistress for a Hollywood film company some time back, and retired to Bear River. I asked Charlie if he had an eighteenth-century wig. "Of course," he replied. "Early eighteenth century or late eighteenth century?"

"Er … late, I suppose."

So I had a wig—with two little rolls over each ear. I wore it with my academic regalia, which suggested something about rank and learning, if not much more. In fact, my regalia is almost gaudy: burgundy with green shot-silk facing. University of Wales. Flashy, rather than sober. Not perhaps entirely appropriate for a performance of Jacob Bailey. He was an educated man, but no one ever spoke of him as *gaudy*.

But I found myself in a dilemma. After I read the recently acquired journals, I found myself interested in the fellow who was Bailey. He seemed very human, especially in his weaknesses, and I soon found myself wanting to understand him. But, over a distance of some 250 years, it wasn't going to be easy.

Perhaps theatre offered an opportunity. Perform a man's

words and quite often you understand what he meant—you understand his feelings as well as his thoughts. So I took Jacob Bailey into the theatre, as it were. In fact, it was the church hall attached to St. Luke's Anglican Church, Annapolis Royal.

For the performance I had two chief sources. One was a primary source—the Bailey 1755 letterbook (containing what I came to call the "Harvard Letters") and the 1759–60 journal in the form of the 1932 handwritten transcription by R.C. Woodbury, a descendant of Jacob Bailey. The other was the *History of Annapolis County*, begun by W.A. Calnek, edited and completed by A.W. Savary, and published in 1897. Calnek's *History of Annapolis County* is a wonderful fund of stories, but few of them are documented in any way, which does not mean that they are inaccurate. Stories told for a hundred years in the barber shop or pub or coffee shop are as likely to be true as not, but admittedly they are not supported by a more independent source—preferably a written independent source. Still, for an actor, they can be quite sufficient.*

So I used Calnek's version of Bailey's offence in Pownalborough on the Kennebec during the American Revolution. That is: Bailey was charged in an American Revolutionary court with preaching a sermon which threatened the (self-righteous) revolutionaries with divine punishment. He was responding to the text for the day, which was Numbers 26:26. *Depart, I pray you, from the tents of these wicked men, and touch nothing of theirs, lest ye be consumed with all their sins.*

The revolutionaries believed themselves accused as "wicked men." Was the invocation to "depart ... from the tents" a criticism of recruiting for the cause? Were they to take it that Bailey's sermon was a warning to his congregation that further association with the Patriots would result in divine punishment? And the punishment might take a particularly

* As I came to know more about Jacob Bailey, I found that Calnek's accounts of Bailey's life were in fact confirmed by Bartlet's scholarship and Bailey's own journals. So, in my opinion, Calnek and Savary can be trusted—at least in the narratives about Jacob Bailey.

nasty turn. (If we continue the scripture, verse 30 of Numbers, Chapter 26, describes it: *But if the Lord make a new thing, and the earth open her mouth, and swallow them up, with all that appertain unto them and they go down quick to the pit; then she shall understand that these men have provoked the Lord.*) Six-point-0 on the Richter scale! He knew about earthquakes, didn't he? The earth would open up and swallow them!

Did he threaten them with an earthquake? They thought he did. And clearly, he was guilty of reading from scripture. The revolutionary court did not like that one bit. Scripture was inadmissible, and he was so informed, forcibly.

I also read scripture to the assembled group (you could not honestly call it a *throng*) at the Spring Meeting of the Historic Restoration Society. And I read from some other entries in Bailey's journal of 1759–60 pertinent to his trip to England to be ordained. These entries were perhaps a tad discomforting, or at least un-clerical. It seemed almost indecent to bring them up at St. Luke's—although this was merely in the church hall and not the church proper, and what's more, this was not the church building he came to in 1782. And some of those entries I was sure were fictitious. Bailey was writing fiction. I'd stake my wig on it.

He and I did not exactly bring the house down. There were no questions afterwards.

But there were cakes and tea and coffee; all good.

THREE

The Box & What Was In It

It was a very ordinary cardboard box, somewhat less than a foot square and perhaps three inches deep—probably purchased from Canada Post—but it contained some real historical goodies—or *artifacts*, if you prefer. In the winter of 2001, George Woodbury, of Osoyoos, British Columbia, used the ordinary box to convey certain eighteenth-century documents written by his ancestor, the Reverend Jacob Bailey, to the O'Dell Museum in Annapolis Royal, Nova Scotia. Besides the documents—Bailey's letterbook of 1755 and his bound and unbound journals of 1759—there were the remnants of Charles Bailey's watch, carefully wrapped in tissue paper. Charles Bailey was the eldest of Bailey's children to survive to adulthood. At least one child was left behind in the graveyard by the church in Pownalborough on the Kennebec when Bailey and his family fled the American Revolution in 1779.

Charles Bailey was apparently singled out as a promising lad by the Duke of Kent (later father of Queen Victoria) when the Duke visited Annapolis Royal, and it was the Duke of Kent who secured a commission for the young man in the Grenadiers.* Charles Bailey was a captain in the Gren-

* Edward, later Duke of Kent, visited Annapolis Royal on several occasions at the end of the eighteenth century, and might well have taken Charles Bailey under his wing on the 1797 visit, when Edward also—well, legend has it—fathered a son by a Mrs. Maria Walker Williams, who already had several children by her husband, barrack master Thomas Williams. Williams also rose in the world somewhat. The son became Sir William Fenwick Williams, hero of the Crimean War ☞

sanctify'd as not to feel some re-
ant inclination, when in such a
posture with his dearest delight
let [...] will not anticipate[...]
designs, but with humble expectab[...]
request a speedy answer til whi[...]
time I remain Dear sir yours [...]

P.S. y evening Dec, 19 we ha[...]
leut three quaters of an hour a[...]
y.o.c a shock of an Earthqua[...]
y roaring continued near a min[...]
in some houses y pewter was p[...]
ceiv'd to jar

VIII.

King: of N.H. Dec: 29 175[...]
To John [...]ums [...] of [...]
Sir
I have sent these caracters [...]
wait upon you, from y most sol[...]
ny regions of rusticity, from a pla[...]
where Minerva never enter'd, a[...]
from whence y Helviconian virgi[...]
never receiv'd any adress, [...]
name is y godess to whom all [...]
votion is pay'd, and those on[...]

the humble propositions & only deal
horses in these parts, to tell you
[…] but sir I am deprived of all
humane society as much as if I
liv'd in y moon or any other pla
netary world, and [those] news that
that passes among mankind, did not
some former acquaintance favour
me now & y with their letters —
my class-mate god has it become extremly popular in these
parts, and will pass to make a secon
[…] — I he preaches at epping in
room of Mr Cutler who was last
y discharg'd y place for his too open
familiar behaviour towards some of
the inviting sex — pray
excuse my boldness my uneloquence
a lumpishness, and if you will take
trouble to write me a line by y
bearer you will greatly oblige one
who remains your &c

IX

King: dec 30 1755
[…] he had hung at H C
dear sir

and a lieutenant-governor of Nova Scotia. See Brenda Dunn, *A History of Port-Royal/Annapolis Royal, 1605–1800,* p. 231.

† The alert reader may recognize the reference to the British singing wits, Flanders & Swann, who played upon the legend that Henry VIII had written the lovely English air, *Greensleeves,* and the use of the long-s, which looks so much like an f.

adiers during the war of 1812, and was killed in the Battle of Chippewa (on the Niagara Peninsula, Ontario) on 5 July 1814. George Woodbury was especially proud of the watch, which was smashed by a bullet. In a romantic story, the watch would have saved Charles Bailey's life. But this isn't a romantic story, and it didn't.

The Woodburys of British Columbia were descendants of the Reverend Jacob Bailey through Bailey's third daughter (sixth child), Elizabeth, born in January 1792, who married John Whitman of Annapolis Royal on 14 January 1816. The Whitmans married into the Woodburys. It was George Woodbury's grandfather, R.C. Woodbury, who in 1932 made the handwritten transcription of Jacob Bailey's eighteenth-century journals and letters. According to Aunt Minnie, the task nearly ruined R.C. Woodbury's eyes. This handwritten transcription was also in the box.

The eighteenth-century journals would certainly have been difficult to read in 1932. The ink was fading and the handwriting was often cramped, to say nothing of the use of the 'long s' ($\int$), which, to the contemporary eye, looks much like an f with the missing crossbar and was used when the s came in the middle of a word, as in *Greenſleeves*.† The eighteenth-century documents are even more difficult to read today, in 2008. Moreover, Bailey was often writing hastily and in draft, and was not overly particular about spelling or punctuation—nor was the age. Samuel Johnson's 1755 dictionary was intended to "settle the orthography," but had not had time to succeed, if it ever did.

The two bound journals match in part the two unbound journals of Bailey's trip to London in the winter of 1760 to be ordained an Anglican priest. The bound journals suggest that Bailey might well have been preparing a fair copy for possible publication. If so, it would have been a prose form also used by two famous contemporaries. As the English novel developed in the middle of the eighteenth century, one of the forms it took—as in Tobias Smollet's *The Expedition of Humphrey Clinker* (1771)—was that of a kind of travel book. Laurence Sterne (like Bailey, an Anglican clergyman) was to use a similar form in his *Sentimental Journey* in 1768. Both Sterne and Smollett (who disapproved of one another) included much fiction. Sterne, apparently, did not visit some of the places he described. Bailey in his use of the technique (we cannot call it a *tradition* yet) wrote several "Adventures" in his travel journal—"adventures" which were somehow overlooked or omitted by William Bartlet when he came to compile *Frontier Missionary: the Memoirs of Jacob Bailey* in 1853. I think Bartlet disapproved of them.

Also in the box were some letters from Aunt Minnie in Annapolis Royal to Reginald Woodbury in British Columbia from 1924 through 1927. It was Reginald Woodbury, as R.C. Woodbury, who copied the journals in two notebooks, also included in the ordinary box.

Aunt Minnie was more formally Maria Cooper Whitman, and a descendant of Jacob Bailey through the Whitmans. She was a wonder—a schoolteacher by profession (in Round Hill, and then later in Granville Ferry)—and a vigorous and forthright correspondent. She could have a sharp tongue. She was proud of her pupils. She was (not surprisingly) outspoken in her views on education. Brains were inherited, she insisted, but work was required. She saw the necessary combination in her best pupils—and cited Jacob Bailey as an example of what she meant. He had grown up in a narrow-minded place (Rowley, Massachusetts), she said, but had overcome its influence.

‡ One can easily imagine that for over a hundred years it would be difficult to find a copy of *Frontier Missionary*. But the internet has changed the difficulty of the search, at least. I was in Jim Tillotson's The Odd Book, a rare book establishment in Wolfville, NS, and mentioned to him that I wished I had a copy of Bartlet's book on Bailey. Before I left the store, Jim looked up from his computer and said, "I've found three—which one do you want?"

Aunt Minnie was in possession of some of the Bailey materials, and she worried about their survival. An Aunt Dorinda, for example, had been known to throw out Bailey manuscripts as so much old paper. Aunt Minnie knew that her copy of Bartlet's *Frontier Missionary* was a valuable book, and believed it was not likely to be reprinted because, she had heard, the printer's establishment had been burnt to the ground and the type used to set *Frontier Missionary* had been melted.‡ She was willing to lend her copy for research purposes and genealogical interest, but she was very firm when she said she wanted it back. She worried about the manuscripts disappearing, and made arrangements to deposit them in the Provincial Archives of Nova Scotia before Aunt Dorinda did anymore wicked housecleaning. Aunt Minnie knew the value of Bailey's writings if no one else did.

Aunt Minnie (as she always terms herself in her letters to British Columbia) retained some of Bailey's library, and one of the books, James Thomson's *Poems*, was included in the box from British Columbia which returned the Bailey artifacts to Annapolis Royal in the winter of 2001. All the rest of Bailey's library has disappeared.

But Aunt Minnie (bless her heart!) made a list of Bailey's books in her possession in January 1926. She also had his snuffbox and ordination papers. Heaven knows where they are now. But her list of books is given below. For a scholar, a critic, or even a literary browser, like me, the list is pure gold.

First, however, some provisos. Dear reader, you should be aware how much accident may be involved. These are the books that survived the expulsion from New England, the trip to Halifax, to Cornwallis (Kentville), to Annapolis Royal, and Aunt Dorinda's housekeeping. Some of his books were lost even to Bailey for two years after the family fled the

Kennebec. Who knows what other books—which might tell us much about Jacob Bailey's sensibility—have disappeared? Who knows how much he valued these books? At least one of them seems quite surprising. And did he acquire these particular books because he admired them, or wanted to use them, or wanted to inveigh against them?

> *Shakespeare, 1771*
> *Alexander Pope, 1776*
> *[Laurence Sterne] Tristram Shandy, 1769*
> *David Hume, Hume's Essays, 1760*
> *A Poetry Collection by Several Hands, 1758*
> *Cowper's Poems, 1812*
> *Homer, The Odyssey*

Sometimes the dates seem important; sometimes not. It might be a good guess that Bailey bought *A Poetry Collection by Several Hands* in 1760, when he arrived in England. He records that he went to a bookstore immediately upon his arrival in London. But whose work was represented in the anthology? We have no idea. Bailey might well have enjoyed the *Poems* of William Cowper (1731–1800), but if the date of the edition cited is accurate (1812), the book would have had to have been added to Bailey's library after his death in 1808, so its value to our understanding of Jacob Bailey is nil. And was Homer's *Odyssey* in Greek? We know that Bailey could read Greek, not only because Greek was expected of an educated gentleman of his era, but because it was required for his ordination examination in London in 1760. He passed. Or was it a translation, possibly by Alexander Pope? For all her virtues, Aunt Minnie doesn't tell us.

Well, Shakespeare is Shakespeare, we might think—except

§ Arthur H.
Cash, *Laurence
Sterne*, Vol. 2,
p. 8.

that he wasn't, not then. Jacob Bailey saw David Garrick perform in *King Lear* (and remarked upon it, on 27 March 1760), and perhaps the edition Bailey acquired was something like that used by Garrick—but Garrick had no hesitation in altering or improving Shakespeare for fashions of the time, so we cannot be certain of *which* Shakespeare Jacob Bailey was reading.

But a 1769 edition of *Tristram Shandy* would likely indicate that it contained all of its sections (which were published serially), although likely bound in one volume—interesting chiefly (to me) because when Bailey arrived in London in the winter of 1760, so did Laurence Sterne. Sterne was the toast of the town and feted everywhere by royalty and celebrity alike (by Garrick, for example, and the two were friends for a time) because of the hullabaloo occasioned by the publication of the first two sections of *Tristram Shandy*. Did Bailey hear of Sterne in 1760? It would have been difficult for him *not* to have heard of Sterne that winter in London. Moreover, both men saw the same play at Drury Lane—*The Siege of Aquilla* by John Home (who was sometimes dubbed the "Scottish Shakespeare"). Garrick starred, along with Mrs. Cibber. Unfortunately, Bailey and Sterne were not present at the same performance, much as I'd love to have them in the same building at the same time in the same audience. Sterne was in the audience on 6 March 1760;§ Bailey saw an earlier performance, on February 21. Bailey thought very highly of the play and the acting.

But the truly surprising book is that by the great religious skeptic, David Hume, and the date. Did Bailey acquire it in London that important winter? He records buying books, although he doesn't note their titles. So there is no telling what he thought of the Scottish philosopher. Bailey does note that on the morning he was ordained, he and the other new Anglican priests were given copies of an anti-Deist book. Did Bailey have a skeptical turn of mind, even as he was committing himself to lifelong Christian service?

The presence of a book of Hume's essays raises a small question, but gives no answer.

It is from the draft letters in Bailey's letterbook of 1755–56—the Harvard Letters we might term them, because the majority of them are addressed to Harvard friends and classmates back at Cambridge—that we begin to glean some idea of the scope of Bailey's personality. For Bailey, Harvard exemplified the perfect life, and it would be difficult to exaggerate his devotion to the university. He not only kept in touch with old friends, but wanted to know of the new students. He writes twice to a Daniel Noyes for a list of the entering freshmen. On 14 May 1756, Bailey writes from the family home at Rowley, Massachusetts, to Mr. J. Emerson at Harvard College:

> *Dear Sir: Excuse a line from one who lately enjoyed the happiness of living with you at the seats of the muses. It is needless to tell you that your pleasantest moments are just expiring and that you're about being delivered into the wide world where a thousand anxieties and perplexing concerns will arise to your portion.*

A month later, on 17 June 1756, Bailey writes from Rowley to E. Sparhawk at Harvard:

Dear Sir: Your pleasant moments are now almost at an end. The happy season the delight and the innocent amusement you have lately enjoyed at the very point of vanishing away. you are now soon to be delivered from a thousand pleasurable scenes, from a multitude of gladening influences into a world restless with anxietys full of bustle and disorder and crowded with endless vicissitudes of fortune. When you shall no longer enjoy those streams of satisfaction which enlived the sons of Harvard. You shall no longer indulge yourself in the sweets an evening or morning walk among groves of locust nor anymore be saluted by the wanted signal to matin devotions. But sir, the thought of being made useful in the world and the prospect of benefiting mankind in some station of life agreeable to the divine will must some measure alleviate these heavy considerations. I wish you a situation after as pleasant as mine and one that will give you twice the profit. I must acknowledge the favour I had of receiving your last. I hope to see you at commencement.

It was apparently the custom for recent Harvard graduates to return to attend subsequent graduation ceremonies. There were great Homecoming parties. But notice Bailey's objective in life: "benefiting mankind in some station of life agreeable to the divine will ..."

His wishing that Sparhawk might find after graduation "a situation as pleasant as mine" was more polite than accurate. Bailey's teaching position at Kingston, New Hampshire, was not pleasant at all. He did not like the people of Kingston, and disapproved of them. He found them rude, ignorant, and profane, as he noted in his earthquake report. Moreover, the teaching was difficult and the day extremely long. On 6 January 1756, Bailey writes to J. Jewet at Rowley, mentions the earthquake of the previous November, and describes his working day:

> *From 9 o.c. in the morning to the same at night I am contin-*
> *ually in my school ... except 2 hours viz from 12 to one and*
> *from 5 to 6 and this will no ways seem incredible if you only*
> *consider the numbers under my inspection. My constant atten-*
> *dance in the day are between 45 and fifty and not to reckon*
> *divers others who come and go as the weather permits. In the*
> *night season I have no less than thirty so that the whole num-*
> *ber of my scholars are at present at least 75, among these I have*
> *3 Latin scholars, 16 cyphers and 32 writers....*

Nor was his first teaching post a rewarding experience in a financial way. From a draft letter of 8 March 1756, to a Dr. J. Row of Kensington, it would seem that his further employment at the school was to be dependent upon his taking a cut in pay.

> *I would inform you that the selectmen of this town have been*
> *together and agreed to persuade me to tarry among them pro-*
> *vided I would keep for less than I had the year past, but having*
> *considered of the matter and finding that it will by no means*
> *answer I have a return to Esq. Sanborn who is to give my*
> *answer to the selectmen some time next week—and look upon*
> *myself as in no way engaged to the place at present.*

"By no means answer." That's tart. I like that. It was a favourite rebuke of Bailey's.

So he was not to be put upon nor taken advantage of. It's another part of his character.

Reading was central to the new graduate's life. Another draft letter is to booksellers in Boston, Edes & Gill, re-directing his periodical subscriptions to Rowley, as he was to re-direct them again at the end of May, when he had evidently accepted his next teaching position at Hampton, New Hampshire.

The Harvard Letters demonstrate much of Bailey's relationship with Harvard, but by no means all of it. For example, although the Class of 1755 had a total number of graduates of only twenty-five, the number does not reflect the number of students at Harvard, or even a quarter of the number. Jacob Bailey writes to members of his class, but also to others who seem not to have graduated—John Xehung, for example. (Moreover, there is no clue whatsoever to explain the odd Oriental suggestion of the name.) Harvard, in common with Oxford and Cambridge of the time, welcomed people who simply hung around to sop up the atmosphere, some learning, and to make (influential) friends. Some were enrolled as students, but just as likely, some were not.

Classmate Robie Morrill receives the most confiding as well as the most literary letters from Jacob Bailey. Bailey addresses him with the Latin name of *Fidelis*. It would seem that at the time of the letters, Morrill was a physician in Salisbury, Massachusetts, not far north of Bailey's birthplace of Rowley. At one point, Bailey and Morrill are interested in buying together the library of an acquaintance recently deceased. Bailey makes the suggestion in a letter of 5 November 1756.

It is to *Fidelis* that Bailey sends two formal stories and a letter of sexual concern, which in turn seems to have some bearing on a rude longish poem in rhyming couplets which is included in part among the papers which are generally the Harvard Letters. The copyist, R.C. Woodbury, notes in 1932 that the first portion of the manuscript volume is missing, and the first page illegible. Internal evidence (see below) suggests the poem was written shortly after Bailey left Harvard, while he was teaching at Kingston, New Hampshire. Ray P. Baker, who in 1929 seems to have other sources of information which have not survived, says that it is dated 6 November 1755, and gives its title as "A Description of a Husking Frolic Lately Celebrated by the Beaux and Belles of Kingston." ¶

It's a lively poem about a lively evening. A party. It might be termed a wild rural party—and Dear Reader, it would be good at the moment if you disabuse yourself of all notion of pastoral innocence—which, in any case, is chiefly a construction of William Wordsworth, whose notion of rural life was gleaned almost entirely from the seat of a carriage, and carried forth by the popular twentieth-century painter Norman Rockwell, resulting in the widely-held view that cities are wicked and rural communities innocent and good. Not in my experience, and I've lived in rural communities for a good part of my life. The people who actually tilled the soil, certainly in the eighteenth century, were not the innocent rustics who were postulated later. Remember, in fact, that Shakespeare's term for illicit sexual conduct was "country matters." Everyone knew what that meant.*

But, too, Dear Reader, consider that in many eras, the prohibition of talking about sexual matters is stronger than the prohibition of the activity. Everyone knows what is going on; but polite people agree not to talk about it. It is an attitude which grew strong in the nineteenth century and prevailed in much of the twentieth century, and continues, hilariously, in contemporary schools.

In "The Husking Frolic," the narrator (Ray Baker presumes the poem is autobiographical and Bailey is talking of himself)

¶ See Ray Palmer Baker, "The Poetry of Jacob Bailey, Loyalist" in *New England Quarterly*, Vol. 2, No. 1 (Jan. 1929) p. 67.

* The novelist Ernest Buckler, who devoted a career to depicting rural life in the early twentieth century some twenty kilometres from Annapolis Royal, demonstrated something of the sexual aspect in *The Mountain and the Valley*. Local people were shocked—not at what he said, but that he said it.

† The boy, if he
found a red ear of
corn, was allowed
to kiss the girl
on his right. Mol
and Nab intend
to make sure he
knows what to do
and does it.

is a guest at the rural communal activity of husking ears of corn, sometimes called a "husking bee." The girls are not shy; indeed, they seem quite forward.

> *I'll try what he's made [of, she cried]*
> *And that we'll do gently Mol quickly reply'd*
> *But I know he's a dumb sot as ever was made*
> *"No matter," says Nab, "if as dumb as a brick,*
> *I'll find out a way to play him a trick*
> *We'll set him down by us as red ears we will show*
> *And if he won't use them we'll soon let him know"* †

The poem is, perhaps, a somewhat surprising guide to rural entertainment. The party is soon heating up. Others appear.

> *A few minits after came in a great crew*
> *With Tom Joe and Jenny Kate Dolly and Sue*
> *The chorus completed we all set away*
> *As frolick as lambs on a sunshiny day*
> *Being seated together black Letty came near*
> *To welcome our coming with hearty good cheer*
> *To handle this damsel some have a great knack*
> *some hug her while others must give her a smack*
> *The ladys in these parts to lads are so kind*
> *That eager embraces discover their mind*
> *The sparkling red ears soon invited to play*
> *With damsels are shining as roses in May*
> *When down on the husks with dear Jenny I lay'd*
> *As her bosom heaved softly I whispering said*
> *How sweet are the kisses of a country maid*
> *Kate seeing what was acted with a simpering eye*

A shot of five ears among us let fly
They told me the meaning tho I guest by her look
Mol cryed you've the bait but beware of the hook
I neglected their smiling despised all the charms
While I'd a heaven of pleasure with Dol in my arms
And squeeze her soft bubbys and play with her hair
Count over her beautys and call her my dear
But alas it was transient. All human delight
Is like birds that we read forever in flight ‡

‡ Professor Ray Baker quotes most of the last four lines cited here, but does not mention the soft bubbys. Indeed, later in his 1929 article he cites other things in Bailey's writing which are too "improper" to quote. Which indicates a considerable difference between what might be said in 1755 and 1929.

At this point a supper is served and Dol and her softy bubbys are abandoned. It's a scramble for food. The boys are stealing from one another, like "crows round a carcass," and the girls—Jenny and Kate—finger the pie like harpies and "with hunger they fall ... rather like scholars in old Harvard Hall."

Then the party moves to new levels. "Here father and daughter wife brother and son / In heaps of disorder promiscuously run.... While others.... Lay tusling the Girls in wide heaps on the floor."

Loud cursing and swearing o'erwhelmed me with fear
For an Athiest might tremble such profaneness to hear
How a foolish young fellow so awkwardly swore
That a sailor would have doom'd him for a son of a whore ...
While scenes of vile lewdness so forward they push
That 'twould make Mother Dilly of B—n blush
... Quite sick of confusion dear Dolly and I
Retired from the hubbub new pleasures to try.

The poem ends there—and invokes some problems, certainly in 1853 for William Bartlet (who ignored it) and Bishop Burgess, but for us as well. We've met Ma Dilly two years pre-

§ Baker, p. 69.

¶ For the American, and especially for the New Englander, there has always been a problem of Christianity and sexuality. Its pathology is brilliantly depicted by Nathanial Hawthorne in the story, "Young Goodman Brown." The contemporary writer John Updike has confronted the problem in his novels, *Couples* and *A Month of Sundays.*

viously, guilty of running a brothel and pelted with garbage and dead cats in 1753. And our narrator—let's call him just "the narrator"—seems not very censorious. It is a very naughty party, but Bailey does not seem to think it was *wicked, evil, wrong.* He is much more broad-minded than we might have supposed, although Baker quotes a comment by Bailey which offers an observation dear to my own heart. "From many of these indecent frolics which I have seen in these parts, I must conclude that rustics are not more innocent than citizens." §

Which is not to say that Jacob Bailey was not concerned. He was. He wrote back to Eben Sparhawk at Harvard: "I must tell you I have satisfaction of finding several blooming young creatures under my inspection, something inclined to virtue and modesty, but alas, dear souls, I must leave them in a few weeks and am afraid they will be after all ruined by bad examples." See Kate, Jenny, Letty, and Mol, above. Bailey's attitudes were ambivalent. He believed in goodness, but the girls were, after all, quite blooming, and there were "indecent frolics."

And he was worried. ¶ There were terrible temptations. Most of the Harvard Letters are polite and somewhat distant, frequently with antique verbal flourishes which are the equivalent of the leg-forward bow and the doffing of a hat, but his friend *Fidelis* (Dr. Morrill) receives a cry of anguish. It is dated 15 December 1755. It begins with a question posed as if in formal debate.

> *I remembered one of the sacred writers letters we are to shun all appearance of evil. Now, sir, I don't intend the question shall demand whether it be absolutely an evil for a Man to lye on the bed with a Woman but whether it is possible even in the nature of things for a Lover to lay entangled in the arms of his mistress, to be encircled in her fond embraces, to feel the soft melt-*

ing impressions of her heaving bosom, to hear the complaining
interrupted sighs, and in short to read in her languishing the
living I might also say the dying countenance 10,000 longing
expectations and amorous wishes murmured at every breath
with as many blushings of modesty, now I say is it possible for a
composition of flesh and blood to perceive all this without some
inclination to Evil, without some secret pantings after forbid-
den pleasure. I will not determine to what a degree of sacred
refinement some persons may arrive by the more immediate
influence of heaven, tho I am confident but few are so sancti-
fied as not to feel some secret inclination when in such a pos-
ture with his dearest delight but sir, I will not anticipate any
design but with humble expectations request a speedy answer
til which time I remain dear sir yours, etc.

And it ends coolly enough. But in between? And it was likely not an abstract question. He was now twenty-five years old.
He had noted the "blooming creatures" in his class. He had
also noted the dangers. See his letter to John Adams, p. 39.

Had he been bundling? From the letter to *Fidelis* it would
seem so, or something very like it. And bundling is yet another paradoxical rural activity, like the husking frolic—a necessity which offers an opportunity.

The best account of bundling which I have read is from
Nova Scotia writer Thomas Raddall, in his novel about Nova
Scotians in the American Revolution, *His Majesty's Yankees.*

Bundling is an uncomfortable business … I had been obliged
to bundle a number of times, usually with the child or children
of the house, sometimes with men, once or twice with women—
one of them a crone of sixty who made a prodigious noise in
her sleep. The warmth of two bodies close in a blanket is not to

* Raddall,
*His Majesty's
Yankees,* p. 379.

† Julie Ross is
especially helpful
concerning
New England
education in
the seventeenth
and eighteenth
centuries. See
Ross, pp. 28–9.

*be despised when bedding is scarce and the weather cold. But
you must lie in each other's arms, and there lies discomfort also,
despite the rhymes of our country wits and the ranting of the
preachers. In the first hour there is warmth and blessed ease
after the long day's march, and if you can get to sleep then, all
is well. But as the night grows there comes a cramp in the bones
from long lying in one position, and the arms begin to prickle
and pain from shoulder to finger tips, and from then on it is
one long wish for daylight. With a stranger for whom you care
nothing it is ordeal enough. But with Fear in my arms … soft
breathing on my neck, so near and yet so very far…. with all
these things the night was torment.**

Reading was considered a necessary skill in the Massachusetts colony, and the towns were ready to support that aspect
of children's education—although, as we have seen in the case
of Bailey's first employment, with a hard eye on mean economy. It was necessary for people to learn to read in order to
read the Bible. Writing was not so important because there
was less need for it.† And it is not clear if the Writers to
whom Jacob Bailey referred in his letter to J. Jewett of 6 January 1756 were studying penmanship or simple communication or effective prose, although likely the two former rather
than the latter.

On the other hand, among those young men who sought
to better themselves, effective writing was important. Benjamin Franklin, in his *Autobiography*, notes that a serious reader of books was soon sought out by other serious readers, and
a young man might well advance in the world thereby—but
Franklin also takes seriously the task of writing well, and cites

as his example, the essays of the British writers, Joseph Addison and Richard Steele. Franklin writes that he took examples of their writing, turned them into verse, and then back into prose as an exercise.

Jacob Bailey, too, was an admirer of Addison and Steele, and on 3 November 1755, Bailey writes a letter (no recipient is noted) which was likely an exercise which attempted more than simple communication. It raises the question of the value of dreams and then recounts one the writer had in which he confronts a vast wilderness—handy enough in North America—into which seem to be cut mazes and paths through which multitudes are struggling while others are returning with stories of failure. The wilderness seems emblematic: life is like that. Then a beautiful creature appears. The beautiful creature is female, but not further described. She promises to guide him to a land of perfection, which seems much like the Garden of Eden before the Fall, and the dream seems to have echoes (not surprisingly) of John Bunyan's *Pilgrim's Progress*. A "dangerous road" is passed by—and then some noisy person under his window wakes the narrator before nirvana can be found. (The essay might profitably be compared to Joseph Addison's "Vision of Mirza," which you can find, as I did, in the Harvard Classics.)

Perhaps more pertinent to any understanding of Jacob Bailey are the two stories which he sends to *Fidelis* in Salisbury. The first, featuring two young ladies, Rustitia and Rustina, is written 12 April 1756, at Rowley, and the second, about Rigida, is dated 20 July 1756, from Hampton, where Bailey is now teaching. Both are social, educated commentaries, and in both cases, the names of the female protagonists tell us much.

The earlier story, featuring Rustitia and Rustina, begins as an essay on small-mindedness and narrow-mindedness, which

Bailey suggests all too easily slip into superstition and big-otry. The story of Rustitia and Rustina exemplifies this. Both are country girls born in the same neighbourhood, but at the "blooming age of 15" (Bailey's words), Rusitia happens to be taken to her uncle's house in the city. He is a Merchant Adven-turer and with his knowledge of travel teaches her much of geography and the extent of the world. Moreover, while in the city, she reads both Addison's *Spectator* and Fielding's *Romances*. Then she returns to her former home, where she is met with "coldness and indifference." Indeed, Rustina calls Rustitia a "proud fool." It's a nice term and a nice bit of writ-ing. But the story/essay demonstrates a truth about small towns then and now: one is not forgiven for leaving, and cer-tainly not for becoming educated, and most certainly not for a wider view of the world. Rustitia is not welcomed home; nei-ther, likely, was Jacob Bailey.

The second story, featuring Rigida, is not quite a rever-sal of the first, but demonstrates instead that, in Alexan-der Pope's famous dictum, "a little learning is a dangerous thing." Or perhaps Rigida learns nothing when "at about 14, she had a sight of the town." After her return to the country, "she became intolerably haughty and never failed in all pub-lick assemblys to exercise a tyrannick air over her former associates."

There's worse:

> *I have known her to criticize even upon the performances of scholars and enter warmly into the merit of their profoundest disputations, and sometimes dictate to a Harvardian in the prosecution of his studys.*

Oh! Was he serious? I think he was.

No one can please Rigida: not other women, not soldiers, sailors, Divines, nor lawyers.

Her constant employment is to communicate disagreeable sensations to all her acquaintances and her capital virtue seems to be an obstinate refusal upon all occasions to be pleased.

Where this essay differs from the first is that—in the first, the subject of education being brought back to the countryside is abstract, and aside from the "proud fool," the topic is merely exemplified by the tale. But Rigida, in the second story, seems real. You have the feeling (well … I do) that Bailey had met her, and that it had not been a happy experience. I wish he'd used her name.

The model Jacob Bailey had before him in writing these stories was not necessarily either Joseph Addison or Richard Steele—but Fielding of the *Romances.* That is not the more famous Henry Fielding (of *Tom Jones, Joseph Andrews, Jonathan Wilde* fame), but Henry's younger sister, Sarah, author of what is sometimes claimed to be the first book written expressly for children, *The Governess or The Little Female Academy.* It appeared in 1749, and, I discovered, is still available. It is written especially for the education of young women, and features a sequence of didactic tales. What might be a little surprising, however, is that the morals invoked are not religious, but secular. The girls in Sarah Fielding's stories are not above brawling, but, led by the oldest pupil, they learn to hold their tempers, and become generous, kind and reasonable. They learn civilized conduct.

From the mention of Fielding's name in the first story, and the term "romance" (a fairy tale is central to the moral tales), it would seem certain that Jacob Bailey had read *The Governess.*

He was to order a copy of it from London in 1785, which suggests he had lost the copy he first read, or had read it in a borrowed copy. Moreover, the Governess herself, who keeps the school for the girls, is a "Mrs. Teachum," widow of an Anglican clergyman. When Bailey came to write his play about his appearance before the Committee of Correspondence in Pownalborough, he calls himself "Parson Teachum."

All this is more important, I think, to an understanding of Jacob Bailey—and his conversion to the Anglican Church—than it might first appear. When I was searching, more or less unsuccessfully, for some information about William Bartlet, who compiled and wrote *Frontier Missionary: Memoirs of Jacob Bailey*, a googling turned up a story by Jonathan Edwards which featured a Phebe Bartlet. Nothing but coincidence, as far as I can tell, invoked by the random searching of the Internet. But Phebe Bartlet, daughter of William Bartlet (same spelling) is a little girl who is converted to Christianity and is born again over and over again with increasing gloom and visions of damnation. In short, it is a Puritan tale of the sort common to Jacob Bailey's youth. Jonathan Edwards was a very popular preacher, famous for damnation, for his image of man as a spider dangling over a fiery pit of hell. The moral of his little-girl story is plain: goodness is one form of one religion. Feel it and be saved; reject it and be damned. It would seem that Jacob Bailey, just out of Harvard, foolish as he might seem to be sometimes, preferred another form of goodness.

There is one more story in the letterbook of 1755–6. One hesitates to mention it. In it, the narrator is an official attached to Lord Anson, and he is writing to Dear Madam to tell her that Lord Anson has met with the leader of the Chinese to tell the Chinese fellow that if any of Lord Anson's "Britannick Majesty" are so much as detained prisoner, the Chinese will have to answer to cannon. The Chinese immediately give in to the threat. The narrator remarks in concluding that he is pleased to have the happiness of "rescuing a young creature."

Boy's Own fiction.‡ But a story which supports the majesty of the British Empire, and suggests cannon as an answer to disagreement— which would be tried twenty years later against the rebellious colonies, and fail.

‡ Baron George Anson (1697–1762) had an impressive naval career. In his flagship, the *Centurion*, he was the first British officer to enter Chinese waters, where he sold a captive ship in Canton. His sailors, however, suffered terribly from scurvy, and on return to England he inspired James Lind to find a cure—lime juice. As a member of the Board of Admiralty, Anson introduced new uniforms into the British Navy, established the British Marines (1755), and created new categories of ships.

The Conversion of
Jacob Bailey

J acob Bailey taught school for two years in Hampton, New Hampshire, before taking another teaching position in Gloucester, Massachusetts, in the spring of 1758. We do not know why he left one teaching position for another. While in Hampton, however, he had formed an important friendship with the Weeks family. Colonel Weeks was a physician as well as an officer in the New Hampshire Militia, and his daughters were Bailey's pupils. The family adhered to the Congregational Church, although a son, Joshua Wingate Weeks, would later become an Anglican clergyman. William Bartlet remarks that no reason for Bailey's move from Hampton to Gloucester is known, but that Bailey visited the Weeks family in Hampton on several occasions.

But Bartlet also notes that the journals for the period were already missing in 1853, so that we have little enough information for this crucial period of Bailey's life, when he left a possible future in the Congregational Church and opted for the Church of England.* It was a decision which put Jacob Bailey right in the middle of the major events of his time: the Enlightenment, which he largely ignored, the great evangelical movement associated with the Great Awakening which

* What's more, William Bartlet's chronology of events is none too clear. Bartlet—I conclude, from this example and some subsequent instances—seems somewhat uncertain when confronted with awkward circumstances.

† Bartlet, p. 39.

swept across New England and England itself; and the American Revolution—and it is one of his signal virtues that, having made his decision, he never wavered in it, even when it might have been not only easier, but to his advantage, to do so. Bailey was a steadfast man.

There are many possible reasons for Bailey to have left the church in which he was raised for the official religion of the British empire, but all of the reasons are open to interpretation, and it is likely that more than one came into play. Bartlet seems surprised at how quickly it happened. But it was not, perhaps, as sudden as Bartlet thinks.

Jacob Bailey's objective in life was clear. As he wrote to Harvard friend Eban Sparhawk on 17 June 1756, it was to benefit mankind "in some station of life agreeable to the divine will" (see p. 52). But it is clear that this did *not* necessarily mean becoming a clergyman: "some station in life." He was always interested in goodness, and he was always interested in the various religious denominations—as he demonstrated on the undergraduate tour through Rhode Island and Connecticut, when he noted every church in every village—but he did not see himself at Harvard preparing for the church. If he had, he might easily enough have stayed on in residence after his bachelor's degree to obtain his master's, as Samuel Eliot Morison suggests this was the usual course for those intending a career in the church. Instead, like John Adams (who was to become a lawyer), Bailey taught school and *returned* to Harvard to fulfill the requirements for an M.A., in 1758, which seems chiefly (and perhaps entirely) to have been to debate on a set topic. Bartlet quotes Bailey as recording on 19 July 1758, "About four o'clock in the afternoon meeting began, when I had ... to dispute from this question: *Imperium sive hominibus prorsus neccarium sit?* † Morison provides the translation and further information: "Is Civil Government absolutely necessary for Men? John Adams argues the affirmative."‡ It is not recorded if the debate was in English or Latin. Probably Latin.

In fact, very shortly, Jacob Bailey was "approved" to preach in Congregational churches, although he held no specific pastorate. The approval came while he was still a teacher at Gloucester. In the late spring of 1758 he left Gloucester, visited Colonel Weeks and family in Hampton, and "went to the printer's, where I engaged him to print a little book for children."§ Some time shortly after that, Bailey is in Exeter, New Hampshire, where, Bartlet says, "the association of [Congregational] ministers were assembled," who, Bartlet quotes Bailey, "came with an expectation of hearing my approbation discourse."

But Bailey was shy; "… it was with the greatest difficulty I was prevailed upon to overcome my bashful humor so far as to read my discourse. When I had finished, I had the satisfaction to find it well received, and accordingly … they gave me an approbation to preach the Gospel."¶

Throughout that summer of 1758, he preached at various meeting houses, including one in Plymouth, in the Puritan heart of Massachusetts. He was not impressed with the Sunday behaviour of the Plymouth children:

> *I beheld a vast number of boys and girls diverting themselves in the most noisy manner. At length they entered a ruinous building on the opposite side of the way, and spent the remainder of the day and part of the evening, in playing hide-and-go-seek. This is the more remarkable, as the Plymouth people have always been the most zealous pretenders to religion, and still are the greatest sticklers in the country for orthodoxy.* *

I would call that prissy. But the notation also demonstrates

‡ Morison, p. 91.

§ Bartlet, p. 38. We have no idea what it was—although it would seem that Bailey's "textbooks," in his papers in the Provincial Archives of Nova Scotia, are in his own handwriting. That is, he had to write the textbooks he needed for teaching. Or did the "little book for children" include the secular moral tales in his Harvard Letters?

¶ Bartlet, p. 39.

* Bartlet, p. 43.

✝ Horton and Edwards, p. 41.

‡ www.first churchrowley .org/history .html. However, this information should be treated cautiously, not least because the author of it seems also to believe that George III was King of England at the time. Truly the web is a wonder, but the authenticity of its content can be iffy.

that the prevailing religious attitudes were helpless when confronted by youthful energy—and perhaps we would be wise to question the history which notes official restrictions which might have been simply ignored by the populace. One authority notes that "at the best of times only twenty per cent of the early settlers were members of any church."✝ Consider also, for example, the corn-husking bee.

But Bailey's response to the children playing outside his window was quite in keeping with the history of his home town, Rowley, Massachusetts—at least as that history is recorded on the contemporary website of the town's First Congregational Church, which notes that church and town were founded together in 1639 by a Reverend Ezekial Rogers. Rogers was the assistant pastor of St. Peter's Church of England in Rowley, Yorkshire, when "the leaders of the English church sent down a decree telling the pastors of their churches to encourage their parishioners to play ball and in general to engage in sports on the Sabbath Day." Rogers refused to read the decree from the pulpit, and was suspended from his duties in the Yorkshire church. Shortly thereafter, he led some of the congregation across the Atlantic to found the town of Rowley on Puritanical lines.‡

Or perhaps the young Puritan Jacob Bailey was simply offended at the disparity between official attitudes and actual conduct. When on his undergraduate trip by horse and carriage through Rhode Island and Connecticut, Bailey could be amazed at the conflict between individuals over seemingly minor matters of dogma, but at the same time be himself unsettled by a mixing of the genders in the congregation.

I am greatly astonished when, upon travelling, I find the people of this country to carry their resentments against each other so high, on account of the differing sentiments with respect to a few unessential modes and trifling circumstances in religious worship, at the same time, all of every persuasion, indulge in a custom, not only notoriously indecent, but the most subversive of the reverence due to the Grand Object of adoration, and this is a practice they have in all their assemblies of persons of both sexes meeting together, by which practice they utterly overthrow the design for which religious societies were established. §

§ Bartlet, p. 26.

¶ I, of course, hold the belief that an actor learns from the character he performs. But the character of Scapin, the clever servant, goes back to the Roman playwright, Plautus, and *The Menachmae*. You can find him later in *commedia del arte*, in *A Funny Thing Happened on the Way to the Forum*, and in the character of Bugs Bunny.

Had his attitudes changed by the summer of 1759? Or was he asking himself some serious moral questions? Certainly he was horrifying William Bartlet one hundred years later. Jacob Bailey was playing cards socially, and on 30 May 1759, he was performing in a play! He was playing Octavian in a Rowley amateur performance of Moliere's *Scapin*. French! Bartlet in 1853 is so outraged at Bailey's behaviour that he adds a footnote: "The gentleman who sustained this character became a clergyman afterwards, if, indeed, he was not one at this time," which tells us more about Bartlet than it does about Bailey.

But the production of Moliere's *Scapin* is worth some small examination. A production of a play written originally in French was perhaps a bold gesture in Rowley in 1759. The French and Indian War had been underway since 1754 and would not end until 1763. Moreover, the French were Catholic, so there was a religious dimension to consider. And although the play *Scapin* is little more than a pointed farce in which the young gentlemen are saved from their rash behaviour by the clever servant, Scapin, the fact is, the young gentlemen are disobedient, and Bailey played the part of one of the young gentlemen.¶ He was going to be disobedient to his upbringing. And what in the world would the neighbours think if they knew that the playwright, Moliere, was also the author of one of the great mockeries of religious hypocrisy, *Tartuffe?*

* Bartlet, p. 45.

William Bartlet lets posterity know what *he* thinks:

*That a religious man, and more than all, a minister, should in these, our days, play cards, engage in private theatricals, drink wine and punch, and occasionally dance, would destroy his influence and subject him to discipline. But the very fact that these things were done without any concealment, and with no apparent consciousness of their impropriety, shows, in the absence of all other proof, that public opinion in these matters was different then.** *

As indeed it was. Does Bartlet realize, in fact, that in his emphatic statement he was counselling hypocrisy?

Jacob Bailey was recruited not only for the Church of England, but for a specific post: that of missionary in the small community of Pownalborough in the Kennebec Purchase, which was then in eastern Massachusetts, in what is now the vicinity of Wiscasset, Maine. He was part of the ambitions of Dr. Sylvester Gardiner (who gave his name to Gardiner, Maine), a very wealthy European-trained physician who made his fortune with a chain of apothecary shops (that is, a chain of drugstores), and who wanted the community to be Anglican rather than Congregational or anything else. There had been another, earlier convert to the Church of England who had been a missionary on the Kennebec, but he left. In Gardiner's view, the position had to be filled immediately. It could only be a missionary posting because there was no Anglican ecclesiastical hierarchy established in America; consequently, there were no bishops. Indeed, to be ordained, the person chosen would have to travel to England. Friends of Gardiner looked about for a likely candidate. Some of them approached the teacher from Gloucester who was preaching in a few Congregational churches in Massachusetts near Boston. Bailey had in fact never seen the inside of an Anglican church nor experienced an Anglican service until he attended one in Portsmouth at the behest of one of the recruiters in the early summer of 1758.

† Bartlet, p. 38.

‡ Bartlet, p. 40.

§ Bartlet, p. 40.

We reached Portsmouth just as the bells were ringing … and came to Col. Warner's, where we met with exceeding handsome treatment. In the afternoon I went to church, but was so overcome with the extreme heat, the fatigues of the journey, and the want of rest, that I should have certainly fallen asleep, had not the novelty kept me awake. At evening I returned to the Colonel's, and spent some time in conversation with Mrs. Warner, on the ceremonies of the church.†

Later that summer he meets with other Anglicans, one of whom, a Mr. Brackett, "had an invitation to Portsmouth, which he imagined might be greatly for my advantage, as there was a mission vacant for a minister of the Church of England." And Bartlet records that on the same trip Bailey stopped at Hampton, where "I relieved their impatience to hear of my success at Portsmouth," and also visits "a classmate at Salisbury"—who would be Dr. Robie Morrill—"and acquainted him with designs of visiting England."‡

Then he returned to Rowley.

I visited my parents, where I found my Aunt Bailey, who all cried out upon me when I discovered my resolutions of visiting London for orders; and after all, I found it extremely difficult, with all the arguments I could use, to gain them over to any favourable sentiments concerning the Church of England. §

We may safely take "all cried out upon me" as an understatement. He was denying his family's church and his communi-

¶ Samuel Eliot Morison details at some length the controversies ignited at Harvard by Whitefield, and Harvard's response. One undergraduate was thrown out when he accused one of his professors of being too easy on secret sinners. He tried to recant later, to no avail. In fact, the faculty seemed insulted by Whitefield's belief that Harvard was full of sinners, and answered him in the academic manner with pamphlets and wit. Just who, one professor noted, was going to meet whom in hell? See Morison, pp. 84–7. The Whitefield controversy took place just before Bailey entered Harvard.

ty's history. What he does *not* mention was that he was also denying the teacher who not only prepared him for Harvard, but likely supported Bailey financially while he was there, the Reverend Jedadiah Jewett, Congregational minister in Rowley.

Were there other religious options? Certainly not the scientifically-minded Deists of the Enlightenment. Bailey wanted nothing to do with the thinking of Benjamin Franklin and his circle, then or later. If the Deists admitted to a Creator, they were offhand about the Gospels, and Bailey was a committed Christian.

He was equally dismissive—although not quite so easily—of the Enthusiasts, the evangelists who preached emotional conversion to Christianity: the Wesley brothers (the Methodists), for example, and George Whitefield. All were gaining adherents throughout North America and Great Britain. The Great Awakening was under way. But Whitefield, who was initially welcomed at Harvard, was later denied an opportunity to speak.¶ Even Jonathan Edwards, accepted at Yale, was denied at Harvard. Bailey was not likely to opt for what Harvard rejected.

But Whitefield and the Wesleys presented problems for the established religions. Chiefly, they claimed to be more Christian than thou, and valued emotion over reason or tradition. The presence of the evangelical strain in eighteenth-century religion was cause for a great deal of concern. Tobias Smollett, in *The Expedition of Humphrey Clinker*, raises it with the character of the title, a servant who becomes an evangelical preacher. The evangelists of the time, the Wesleys and Whitefield, attracted large crowds. Smollett suggests they were chiefly of impressionable women and the lower classes. In his later career, writing in Annapolis Royal, Bailey was to write satires blaming the Deists for invoking free thought which opened the way to emotionalism. He was specific in his satires against Benjamin Franklin, and, in "Jack Ramble," the Methodists and other Enthusiasts.

Rejecting the church in which he was then "approved," was likely more difficult, and there are few clues to guide us to an understanding. We can only speculate. One might have been the Witch Trials of Salem, Massachusetts, in 1692. Rowley was not far from Salem, and the events took place only forty years before Bailey was born, and under the auspices of the Congregational Church. Perhaps, too, seeing the self-righteous mob in action at the punishment of Ma Dilly in Boston in 1753 made a lasting impression on Bailey. A fervently self-righteous congregation all too easily became a mob. The election of leaders by the Pilgrims (who were absorbed into the Puritan Massachusetts Bay Colony) is commonly cited in America as the first steps toward popular democracy, in which leaders are chosen from below, as it were; but mobs can also create demagogues, and become their own justification, as Bailey may have sensed, and would certainly experience later on the Kennebec in the Committees of Correspondence.

So what was he choosing in the Church of England? For one thing, England. For another, top-down authority allied with the state. The head of the Church of England is the monarch; the bishops of the church (some of them) sit in the House of Lords. For a third, academic excellence. He would have to pass an examination to be ordained as an Anglican clergyman. He would be by definition (someone who might conceivably have a seat in the House of Lords) a gentleman, as befitted his education as a gentleman. He was poor, and there was no other opportunity for advancement. He would be paid (chiefly, sometimes entirely) from London, not from the local congregation. So the Church of England offered him tradition—stretching back to Henry viii—authority and empire, all at once, and in *The Book of Common Prayer*, a set guide to ecclesiastical ceremonies.

He knew from the start that he was going to a missionary outpost at the edge of what was then Massachusetts. It would be a hardship post. He had no illusions that he was going to be a gentleman-vicar sipping port with the local landed gentry and their ladies. But the ordination offered something more: a trip to London to be examined and, if successful, ordained by the Bishop.

Jacob Bailey had only just arrived in London when he wrote an impassioned autobiographical essay which included the following:

> *In my childhood as soon as I was able to read I was seized with an insatiable desire of travelling and a boundless curiosity to visit foreign regions.... This inclination I was obliged to suppress since such numerous obstacles arose to check my ambition and to prevent me from indulging those desires which all my acquaintance looked upon as the most extravagant and romantick.*

First Steps in a New Life

On 13 December 1759, Jacob Bailey set out to fulfill his childhood dream of travel, his quest for his new life, walking from Gloucester, Massachusetts, to Boston to take ship for Britain. The very first evening out, at a tavern, he met a veteran of the French-and-Indian War, which was still under way. Bailey was stunned by the fellow.

> *We had among us a soldier belonging to Capt Hazen's company of rangers who declared that several French were barbarously murdered by them after quarters were given and the villain added I suppose to show his importance that he split the head of one asunder with his hatchet as he fell upon his knees to implore mercy. A speciman of New England clemency!*

We'll meet the same savagery in Thomas Raddall's 1942 novel, *His Majesty's Yankees*, in the character of the protagonist's father, a fierce old man who is also a veteran of the French-and-Indian War, who served with "Gorham's Rangers." As the rebellion which became the Revolutionary War was heating up in Nova Scotia, the old man tries to explain to his neighbours just what war means. They are reluctant to hear. So he tells them in fine detail about scalping the Indi-

* Thomas Raddall, *His Majesty's Yankees*, pp. 28–9. Raddall's novel raises the question of history and historical novels: was Raddall, in this case, building his character off Bailey's journal entry? It is quite possible Raddall was doing just that. He did a great deal of research in the Provincial Archives of Nova Scotia, and therefore had easy access to Bailey's journals. So Bailey records an incident, but Raddall in fiction demonstrates the feelings of the time.

ans, and how the scalp of a Micmac could be divided in three for thrice the bounty. The neighbours are horrified. As for the French, well—they were heathen, weren't they?

> *Bowed down to graven images, didn't they? Worshipped a Woman and set God—our God—back somewhere about the head o' the saints, didn't they? Murdered all the Protestants in France one time, hadn't they? All that ought to count for something now.... Yes, by God, by the Protestant God ...*

Later, after more details than any of his listeners want to hear, the old man says, "But you can't think of everything—not in war. It *was* war you wanted to hear about, wasn't it?"

"Not that kind" shouted several men together.*

Perhaps some further context might be helpful as we follow Jacob Bailey on his walk to Boston. It was in the summer of 1755, when Bailey graduated from Harvard, that the British General Braddock wandered into an ambush near (what is now) Pittsburgh, and was routed by a force of French and Indians. It was in 1755, also, that the Acadians were expelled from the Annapolis Valley. At the time when Bailey (and John Adams) were receiving their M.A. degrees from Harvard by disputing the question of a government necessary for men in 1758, Fortress Louisbourg in Cape Breton fell (for the second time) to British and American forces. And only three months before Bailey began walking to Boston to set sail for England, General Wolfe defeated General Montcalm on the Plains of Abraham (Quebec City) in September 1759.

But while all these events were taking place for the history books, Bailey was demonstrating some everyday characteristics of the age. For example, that it was a very social age. His journal notes over and over that he called upon this person or that one, and "took a dish of tea" here and there. The tea will soon become a political symbol, but not quite yet. Most of Bailey's friends were new, and found in the circles of the church he was off to join, but some were known from his youth. It was after all a familiar route to Boston. Jacob Bailey's brother followed a couple of days later, bringing Jacob's linen.

There were pretty girls to be noticed, and he did. On December 17, at Parson Hooper's, "I was mightily pleased with the conduct of his beautiful daughter, a young miss of about twelve years old." On the same day, however, he met another woman of whom he disapproved. "She is a great talker, a person of considerable education and indifferent good sense— but is very tenacious of her own favourite notions, but this is not a miracle in a woman." Humph!

On December 22, he dined at Mrs. Renkins'.

> *I spent the afternoon with an agreeable company of young ladies. I think that Miss S exceeds any person I was ever acquainted with in the strength of her memory and the agreeable way of turning everything into innocent ridicule yet the fine sense and pretty remarks of her younger sister I think are much more entertaining as well as instructive.*

On the 26th he spends some social time with a young lady impressive enough to cause twinges of uneasiness.

> *She behaved with so much unmeaning innocence and modesty that I was a great deal more than indifferent towards her. But forgive me Almina [Almira?] I cannot think of another unless you hate me!*

But it is on New Year's Day, 1760, that he has a more private meeting with two young women:

> *I returned to my lodgings about ten, when I found all the peo-*
> *ple gone to repose except Miss Jenny and Polly.... I have been*
> *considerably taken with the pretty modest behaviour of Miss*
> *Jenny and not less with the agreeable vivacity of Polly her wit*
> *and humor being as sparkling as her eyes.*

The spouse of a Dr. Bulfinch also impresses Bailey on 5
January 1760.

> *This lady tho far from being a beauty has something exceeding-*
> *ly agreeable in her countenance. She resembles Dorinda more*
> *than any person I ever saw both in person and behaviour....*
> *After dinner took a dish of tea in company with Florinda and*
> *Orinda (Miss Debby Thompson and Sally Clark) and passed*
> *away the evening in a very agreeable manner.*

And it was his landlady in Boston, Mrs. Mecom, with her
"courteous and obliging" daughters, who gives him a letter of
introduction to the "famous Mr. Franklin" in London.

So Jacob Bailey liked girls. His interest seems to have followed him for nearly 250 years in Annapolis Royal, where
gossip lives on and on and on and rumour becomes history. He liked young girls, although "young" then and "young"
now are different measures. As he noted in his letter to the
young John Adams, girls in the classroom—"blooming creatures"— could be a dangerous attraction for a young teacher.
He was in fact later to marry one of his former pupils, Sally
Weeks, who was fourteen when he met her in Hampton. He
valued grace, modesty, innocence, and good manners, which
is certainly understandable in light of his experience with
the aggressive, raucous girls in Kingston. But in his impassioned autobiographical sketch, written two months hence in

London, he was to reveal that already in his childhood he was frightened of the opposite sex.

At the age of ten ... I was bashful to the extremest degree.... This disposition had taken such a possession of me that I was even afraid to walk the streets in open daylight and frequently when I have been sent abroad in the neighbourhood of an errand rather than be seen, I have gone a mile about the fields and bushes—a Female was the most dreadful sight I could possibly behold and till I was 18 I had never courage to speak in their presence—whenever I had the misfortune to meet one of these animals in the street, I immediately climbed over the fences and lay obscured 'till they passed along.... And if a young woman happened to come into a room where I was sitting I was immediately seized with a trembling, but if she spake my confusion was so great that it was a long time before I could recover ...

At various stops on the route to Boston he meets religious people for whom doctrinal differences are not abstract in the least. Some are "bigoted" (Bailey's word) against the Anglican church. Others are "bigoted" against the Dissenting sects. Bailey remarks that he doesn't like bigotry even when it supports his decision to leave one Christian denomination for another. His new associations with his new friends seem to have opened up his mind considerably within the space of only a year. But "bigotry" wasn't the half of it: some looked upon membership in the Church of England as treachery.

So it is one of the virtues of Bailey's writing that he records that anti-British attitudes were common in New England well before the Stamp Act of 1765, or the Boston Massacre of 1770, or the Boston Tea Party of 1773, or the armed conflicts at Lexington and Concord in 1775. Before he even sailed for England he was sailing in troubled seas.

And it is possible that his religious decision was also a political decision, and seen as such everywhere.

It would seem that when Bailey visited Harvard in the last days of 1759, his beloved *alma mater* did not return his fond affection. Was it religion or politics or both which resulted in the cold reception at his beloved Harvard? Or was it something else?

At first there seemed to be nothing wanting. Bailey needed testimonials to his conduct at Harvard, as well as letters of recommendation from local persons of note, if he were to be ordained an Anglican priest in London. When he first approached President Holyoke of Harvard, Bailey was greeted cordially.

I waited upon the president—he kindly invited me into a parlour and behaved towards me in a genteel and obliging manner. Not only before but after I had manifested my request—when I desired some testimonials of my moral conduct at college he answered with a mildness and told me that a diploma would be the most advantageous thing I could possibly carry from that society and added that it should cost me nothing for the seal.

If it were not for the date of the above comment, 15 December 1759—had it been in 1765, for example, at the time of the Stamp Act controversy—we might take President Holyoke's comment ("nothing for the seal") to be ironic or even sarcastic, but it seems unlikely at the time that any sort of criticism was implied. Still, when he returned ...

*About three I waited again upon the president who behaved
towards me not only with incivility but a kind of barbarous
roughness. Not withstanding the weather was excessive cold
he caused me to tarry in an outer kitchen for near half an hour
without any fire to mitigate the prevailing severity and finally refused to give me any testimonials altho it was well known
that I was never punished for the breach of any college laws.
He however signed my diploma and sent me to the gentlemen
of the corporation for the like favour.*

Bailey was astonished. He knew he had done nothing wrong
when he was at Harvard. He had at worst suffered the most
minor of penalties. Of course, it would have been difficult to
use one of the punishments available to the college authorities, of dropping him a few places on the class list. Members of
the class were listed in order of the importance of their families, and Bailey could not have been dropped because he was
already at the bottom.

Perhaps President Holyoke's change of attitude might have
been due to nothing more than a quick look at that class list of
1755. A chap named Charles Cushing was at the top, and John
Wentworth—later governor of New Hampshire and lieutenant governor of Nova Scotia after the Revolution—was fifth,
just ahead of a Jonathan Bowman (who was to play a later role
in Bailey's life) at sixth, and John Adams was fourteenth; Bailey was last at twenty-fifth.

Perhaps it was just that he was viewed at Harvard, even
by President Holyoke, as a person of no account, a farm boy.
Perhaps the very term Bailey himself applied to another was
applied to Bailey himself: he was a "plough jogger."

Did he think he was as good as someone like John Wentworth, whose family owned significant chunks of New Hamp-

† He also begged money in Boston from two gentlemen, Cushing and Newman, and I hoped it might actually have been "Cushing and Bowman" because of later events, but it was in fact Cushing and Newman. I checked the original notebook, a very small book with pages perhaps two inches wide by five long, where Bailey's writing was very cramped. His entry for 13 April 1753 is difficult to read even with a magnifying glass, but if Newman was clear enough, "Cushing" seemed a bit of a guess on Bartlet's part.

‡ And not so different, when you stop to think about it, from applying for scholarships and grants in more recent times.

FACING PAGE

An Attempt to land a Bishop in America (London, 1769)

shire, and who passed around the offices of the government of that colony among themselves? As Bartlet notes, Jacob Bailey had begged money of John Wentworth's father in order to stay in Harvard, and been given some, too!† But he begged money of many eminent persons; it was the way it was done, then.‡

Did some incident take place which, though not illegal, might have caused talk among students and faculty at Harvard? If so, we have no evidence of it. But at least two of his classmates became his lifelong enemies. Why?

Was it his personality that might have offended the Harvard president? Bailey had been a mature student, so not really one of the others, who were young and from good families; and he was somewhat prissy and flourished his good manners. Was he "getting beyond himself?" Was he committing that American sin of "giving himself airs"? If he was so smart, why wasn't he rich?

The very afternoon of 15 December 1759—after he has met initially with President Holyoke, but before he returned to be treated with "barbarous roughness"—Jacob Bailey dined with a group of men at Harvard. One was a Mr. Jackson, and Bailey remarks in his journal that "I must acknowledge that he hardly treated me with common civility," from which Bailey concludes, "I observed that it is possible for a narrow bigoted soul to animate a huge overgrown body ..."

Jackson was fat.

Or was it simply the times. Consider the cartoon.

So when Jacob Bailey reported to one of his recruiters, a Dr. Caner, that he was obtaining no testimonial letters but only signatures on a copy of his Harvard diploma, Caner was in despair. Bailey would need testimonials if he were to be accepted as a candidate for the priesthood. But all was not

An Attempt to land a Bishop in America.

1768

§ It was the Boston area which was to provide the "Planters" who replaced the expelled Acadians in the Annapolis Valley. The Planters were evangelical and did not welcome Anglicans like Bailey who came with the Loyalists.

lost. It seems that Dr. Caner himself had written some testimonials for Bailey on behalf of some eminent members of the Anglican community, and Jacob Bailey was sent round to get them signed, which he did successfully, although one fellow complained that he ought to have been consulted earlier.

Anger on one side or another of Bailey's decision was evident. A Dr. Cutler endorsed the letter of recommendation which Mr. Caner had prepared, but, as Bailey remarked, "I could discover in him the remains of a rigid spirit against the Dissenters." Further, "there is nothing I so sincerely detest as the spirit of bigotry, let appear in my own or an opposite party."

On December 18, Bailey is at Parson Hooper's (he of the beautiful twelve-year-old daughter), and after Parson Hooper and another guest, an English officer, "are obliged to retire after dinner," Bailey is left with the ladies. He had an agreeable afternoon, he notes, not least because "One thing observable in this family is their aversion to bigotry." Again, Bailey concludes, "Moderate principles render a person extremely agreeable even to the most rigid and severe."

On the 19th, Bailey

> took a dish of tea with a certain old maid who having outlived all hopes of gaining a husband now applies herself violently to religious disputations. I was here a witness to abundance of impertinence and those reflections that are very common in the mouths of certain people called new lights, tho I think with a great deal of impropriety.

He then remarks that quarrelling about religion seems general among all classes in Boston, and that very evening at his lodgings found a "Mrs D almost as rigid as the ancient virgin above mentioned on the opposite side of the question."§

Jacob Bailey seems here to see himself as a rare temperate person in an intemperate age.

Something else to put Bailey and his era—even his sense of time—into perspective. Bailey arrived in Boston on December 14, and hoped to see his patron, Dr. Sylvester Gardiner, immediately, but found that Dr. Gardiner was ill—too ill to receive anyone. On the 17th, he spent "a considerable part of the day with Jemmy Gardiner which was the last time I had ever an opportunity of seeing him." Jemmy Gardiner was Dr. Gardiner's son. On the 18th, "heard the disagreeable news that Jemmy was taken extremely ill. This considerably affected me as I had been several times in his company and found not a little civility in his behaviour." Civility was important to Jacob Bailey.

On the 23rd he hears the "sad news that Jemmy Gardiner was drawing near his end." On the 25th he learns of the death of Jemmy Gardiner "after a week's illness."

Bailey was ready to leave for London, and his recruiters secured passage for him on the British warship, *The Hind*, Captain Bond commanding. As nearly as I can tell, the passage cost him nothing—and so demonstrates the one-ness of church and state which so upset the revolutionaries. There were objections. On 7 January 1760, Bailey notes in his journal that he had been informed by Dr. Gardiner and Mr. Paxton that "some passenger on our ship ... had endeavoured all in his power to prevent my free and generous treatment from Captain Bond." There were other enemies, too. Waiting to board his ship, Jacob meets his brother "upon the change, who gave me a most shocking relation of the meanness and injustice of Epes Seargant, Esq. of Gloucester towards me."

¶ Bartlet,
pp. 59–60.

However, the conditions allotted him on board *The Hind* were not those of a gentleman. William Bartlet in 1853 is outraged by the lack of respect shown Bailey in 1759.

Although [Bailey] found friends who had sufficient influence to secure him passage in an armed ship, yet, it would seem, he could not obtain decent accommodations on board, and that he was even obliged to share his hammock with the man servant of one of the passengers. The captain treated him with a superciliousness little to be expected from one of a profession with which civility and politeness are uniformly associated. The petty officers of the ship, including the surgeon, appear to have been almost brutes in human shape, who bore the royal commission. Their passenger was an educated man, a licensed clergyman of the Congregational denomination, and the object of his voyage to England was to obtain orders in the Established Church. Yet their profaneness appears to have been unrestrained in his presence; they sought to tempt him into some fashionable excess; they made severe reflections on his native country; and … they criticised his pronunciation and manner of speaking.

… We are sure, that a person of similar standing with Mr. Bailey, who should now take passage in an armed ship, would not suffer as he was compelled to do. The naval service has gentlemen for its officers, and among them are bright ornaments of the religion which they profess.¶

Bright ornaments! And the passage (again) tells us much about Bartlet and the attitudes of 1853—but it is also accurate enough about shipboard life in 1759. Captain Bond, of *The Hind*, does seem to treat Jacob Bailey as a lesser being, even as he sends Bailey viands from the captain's table. (But so had the president of Harvard treated Bailey badly!) And the ship's surgeon was an unbeliever, and all of the crew, sailors and lesser officers included, swore something awful and ignored the Sabbath, both of which bothered Bailey initially.

What he found below-decks was about as far from the genteel life as can be imagined: it is Bailey's value that he records it in some detail.

* Bartlet, pp. 52, 54.

† Bartlet, p. 54.

> *In the middle stood a table of pine, varnished over with nasty slime—furnished with a bottle of rum and an old tin mug with 150 bruises and several holes, thro which the liquor poured in many streams.... lobscouce [was] a composition of beef, onions, bread and potatoes mixed and stewed together, then served up with its broth in a wooden tub; the half of a quarter cask.... there were two pewter plates, the half of one was melted away, and the other full of holes more weather-beaten than the sides of the ship. One knife with a bone handle, one fork with a broken tine, half a metal spoon, and another wooden one taken at Quebec, with part of the bowl cut off.**

And the boy, sent to fetch the "lobscouce"?

> *Nothing in human shape before did I ever see so loathsome and nasty. He had on his body a fragment only of a checked shirt, his bosom all naked and greasy—over his shoulders hung a bundle of woolen rags which reached in strings almost down to his heels and the whole composition was curiously adorned with little shining animals.*†

Bailey does not say *animal skins*; he says *animals*. Not likely alive, but still ... and likely rats because rats would be in abundant supply. Mummified rats, then.

Rough Crossing

Jacob Bailey boarded *The Hind* on 10 January 1760. He was immediately put in his place by both the captain and a junior officer, who spoke to him briefly and rudely. It is fair to say that his experience with British military men was not good, and it was more than evident that he was to receive no special treatment; it was a favour from the Navy to the Church to take him at all. He was little more than an ecclesiastical parcel.

The Hind immediately unmoored and "drifted down to Nantucket," where it lay at anchor until January 19, waiting for favourable winds. The fleet consisted of *The Hind*, a twenty-gun ship, the *Maria*, the *Ruby*, the *Molly*, the *Genoa Packet*, the *Galley*, and the *St. Paul*.

On 10 January 1760, Jacob Bailey describes his messmates. I have taken the most of his account from William Bartlet's version.

The persons present were: first, the captain's clerk.... He was born in Northampton, about sixty miles from London, and was educated to the stationery employment. I found him a person of considerable reading and observation, who had fled his native country on account of a young lady to whom he was engaged; but his parents, for certain reasons, appeared so vio-

* Bailey much
admired Samuel
Butler's 1660
satiric epic, *Hudi-
bras*, which Bailey
"continues" in
his own satiric
poem, "America."
See Thomas B.
Vincent's article
in the *Humanities
Association
Review*, 1976.

*lently against the match, that he was prevented from marrying.
He would sometimes get drunk, and at other times behave in
a most unaccountable manner. Second: Another was one John
Tuzz, a midshipman, and one of my messmates; he proved to
be a good-natured, honest fellow, was apt to blunder in his
conversation, but too frequently gave it a dash of extravagant
profaneness. Third: another of my messmates, named Butler,
was a minister's son, who lived near Worcester, in England.
His mother was a Bailey, and himself a descendant from Butler, the author of Hudibras.* He appeared to be a man of fine
sense, considerable breeding, a stiff Jacobite; his language, upon
all occasions, was extremely profane and immodest, yet nobody
seemed a greater admirer of delicacy in women than himself. My fourth companion was one Spears, one of the mates,
a most obliging, ingenious young gentleman; he informed me
that the captain had recommended me to him, and that he
should endeavour to make the passage as agreeable as possible, and accordingly he treated me, upon every occasion, with
uncommon civility and kindness, and was as tender of me in
my cruel sickness, as if he had been a brother, and what I most
valued him for, was his aversion to swearing and obscenity.
Fifth: One of our company, ths evening, was the carpenter of
the ship. He looked like a country farmer, drank excessively,
swore roundly, and talked extravagantly. Sixth: Another was
one Shephard, an Irish midshipman, the greatest champion of
profaneness that ever fell under my notice. The sacred name,
at every word, was uttered with the strongest emphasis, and I
scarce ever knew him to open his mouth without roaring out a
tumultuous volley of stormy oaths and imprecations. After we
had passed away an hour or two together, Mr. Lisle, the lieutenant of the marines, joined our company. He apeared about
fifty years old, of a gigantic stature, and quickly distinguished*

himself by the quantities of liquor he poured down his throat.
He also was very profane.†

Much of Bailey's account seems to have been written after the
voyage (he remarks of Spears, that "he was as tender of me in
my cruel sickness as if he had been a brother"), which suggests
that William Bartlet was working from the copied version of
the O'Dell journals of 1760. The sickness has not yet taken
place. But Bartlet omits the continuation of the scene featuring Mr. Lisle, the gigantic Irish Lieutenant of the Marines,
and simply summarizes it by noting, "He also was very profane." Bailey's original account is much more dramatic.

*Having made himself a little warm he turned about, and
begin to address me in the following manner—"God dam my
blood I have the honour of bearing a commission under King
George. The devil take me the very best of kings—Understand
me blood and zounds I have a commission signed by his own
hands and that I will assure you is more than everyone in the
ship has besides." He sends for the commission. "There," continued he, "in George's own handwriting—that dear name, by
heavens, I have often and often kissed it. But blood and furies
it is a thousand pities he should be imposed upon—Did he
know what villains he has on board this ship!—but no matter
thank God we are going home now and I will protest it will be
to some of their confusion. God blast them—we shall quickly
know how it will be every tub upon its own bottom."*

This is one of my favourite pieces of Bailey's writing in the
journals of his crucial journey. Look at the huge man kissing
the king's signature! Great theatre. Concealed wickedness!
Villains on board!

‡ When he was
at Pownalbor-
ough later, Bailey
controlled a
married couple
who were his
indentured ser-
vants, but they
ran off. Later,
when Bailey was
in Annapolis
Royal, a Captain
Mowat of the
Royal Navy sent
his son to Bailey
to be educated,
and a slave to
look after the boy
and serve Bailey.

§ Bartlet, p. 55.

Another scene is much understated, and the more interesting for it. On January 12, Bailey notes,

> *This day began to reconcile myself in some measure to my new
> method of living. Nothing remarkable happened except that
> the Captain and officers endeavoured to conceal a Negro ser-
> vant belonging to Capt. Ellis at Beverly, but Mr. Ellis under-
> standing his business recovered his servant by authority.*

The town of Beverly was not far from Bailey's birthplace
at Rowley. It is not difficult to imagine the scene. The negro
slave pulled from his hiding place as reclaimed property. To
my mind it would be a silent affair; perhaps the sound of bare
feet on the deck, water slapping on the hull. And look who
attempts to conceal him—the arrogant captain and his officers. Perhaps we have misjudged Captain Bond, or judged
him too quickly.‡

But Bailey is yet finding it difficult to separate virtue
from convention. The next day, January 13, a Sunday, Bailey records:

> *This day spent in a very disagreeable and scandalous manner,
> without any kind of divine worship. Our people, instead of
> keeping the Sabbath day holy passed it away either in diver-
> sions or quarrels.*§

Then, with scarcely a pause (Bartlet gives it three asterisks), Bailey recounts the following story:

> *This evening the barge returned from a cruise to one of the
> neighboring islands, when Mr. Glover, the lieutenant, and
> Mr. Pearson, gave an account of the following adventure.*

They came to a house where lived a man, who, in our coun- ¶ Bartlet, pp. 55–6.
try dialect, is called a substantial farmer; he had several pretty
young daughters, whom he had taken great pains to educate.
They could not only read and write, but understood letters
to a considerable degree of perfection. Every lady admired
their innocence, modesty, and decent behavior, but the neigh-
boring youths, in general, imagined themselves too inferior
to offer their addresses to these excellent virgins. Mr. Glov-
er and Mr. Pearson, however, had the happiness, by means of
laced cloathes, and loud, rattling oaths and imprecations, to
get introduced to their company. They followed their suit with
all expedition, and in less than two days, seduced and ruined
a couple of fine creatures, the one about sixteen, the other about
eighteen years old. That this was really true, the following
accident discovered. As Mr. Pearson was taking something out
of his pocketbook, he dropped a paper that I took up and read,
which was as follows:—

> *"Dear Sir:—'Tis with the utmost regret I am forced*
> *to part with you, and shall have many a sorrowful hour*
> *till you return.*
>
> *"I cannot think you will ever be so cruel as to forget*
> *one who has sacrificed my innocence, and, I fear, my hap-*
> *piness, to your pleasure.*
>
> *"Pray let me hear from you before you sail.*
> *"I am, sir, yours forever,*
> *"Sally"* ¶

In his notebooks, Bailey usually makes no distinction among
different types of writing, except that he does indicate poetry in stanzas and rhyme. But what seems to be a personal
account can easily slide into narrative, or drama, or fiction.

For example, the scene in which the Irish Lieutenant of the Marines sends for his commission (omitted by Bartlet), is dramatized by Bailey. Was that straight reporting, or was it an imagined dramatization? Such distinctions were not always definite even in published work of the time (in the familiar essays of Addison and Steele, for example), and forms of fiction often conflated the real and the imaginary (in Smollett's travel fiction, *The Expedition of Humphrey Clinker*), and here Bailey is writing in his notebook and paper is scarce and expensive. He does label it "An Adventure." (Bartlet ignores the label.) So is this story truth or fiction or both?

My feeling—my interpretation—is that it is moral fiction. On the one hand, in certain of its aspects, it does challenge belief. It is the dead of winter, a cold winter, and the young officers are amazingly quick in wooing and ruining the farmer's daughters, even considering "laced cloathes … and loud, rattling oaths."* In addition, Bailey seems to understand things which he could not have personally observed: "Every lady admired their innocence, modesty, and decent behavior, but the neighboring youths … imagined themselves too inferior to offer their addresses …" This is the narrative imagination at work, and moreover, reflects Bailey's preferences for female innocence, modesty, and decent behavior. The innocent girls are exactly those of his pupils who, he fears, will be ruined by bad examples.

But what about the letter?

I might say that it is the sort of detail added by a fiction writer to give authenticity to a story which he or she feels lacks verisimilitude. Consider the urban ghost legend of the sweater found in the car after the driver has brought the girl-hitchhiker home. The driver later attempts to return the sweater, only to be informed by the girl's mother that the

* We might imagine big black Harley-Davidson motorcycles and black leather jackets.

girl was killed long ago in an automobile accident. Or the 'folk' song "Scarlet Ribbons." A physical detail added to an account in words validates the words—or, as we shall see later on this crucial journey, invokes a surprising if ambiguous truth. In short, I don't believe the story is fact; I believe it is moral fiction.

The voyage from Nantucket to Portsmouth in England took twenty-eight days, and Bailey was sick for most of it. Not that we should be surprised. Any crossing of the North Atlantic in winter is likely to be rough, and this was worse than usual— much worse. There was a bad storm while they were still at anchor off Nantucket, and when they set sail for England, one storm followed another, each more severe than the one before. Bailey was usually in his hammock. Notations in his journal are brief: squalls and distances. The distances are sometimes given in "leagues" and sometimes in "miles."

He notes profanity several times; profanity is general. On January 29, "several of our petty officers were excessively drunk which caused them to utter the most horrid oaths and blasphemies …" However, when it seems the ship might go down at any moment, some of the crew exhibit greater devotion to God. On February 2, the captain's clerk, Mr. Archibald, sits with his prayer book until the storm abates somewhat. Then he cries out, "I thank God with all my heart, and if it pleases God that I should arrive safe at Portsmouth, I swear I shall get devilish drunk the first night." (When they arrive in England, Archibald is too exhausted to fulfill his vow.) In the same storm, Midshipman Shepherd is "remarkable for braving death after he thought himself out of danger."

A few hours' respite for the fleet (Bailey gets on deck and sees some whales in the sea) is followed by further squalls and storms. What's more, there is a war going on, and when two sails are sighted, directly on *The Hind's* course, "the decks are cleared of everything," and Bailey endeavours to hide his money in his shoe, and every moment "expects a broadside."

But the ship turns out to be a British man-of-war, the *Fowey*. Its captain comes aboard and is ordered by Captain Bond of *The Hind* to follow it to Spithead. On the terrible 15th of February, they meet another British ship, the *Ramilies*, from which they are signalled to engage a ship which the captain of the *Ramilies* believes to be a French privateer. However, when shortly thereafter they approached the suspected ship, "she hoisted Danish colours." "We attempted to hail her but were prevented by the storm," which "began dreadfully to rage."

The *Ramilies* had a history. Bailey says:

> She was a large three-decker carrying ninety guns and having on board 743 men. She was one of the most stately and beautiful ships in the British navy. And is the same in which Admiral Bing formerly sailed and on which he was afterwards shot for his cowardly behaviour in the Mediterranean.

Bailey was not quite right about the notorious case of Admiral Byng (the more usual spelling), who was not executed on board the *Ramilies*. He was executed by firing squad on the deck of the *Monarque* in Portsmouth harbour not quite three years earlier, on 14 March 1757.

It was a famous case at the time. The *Ramilies* was Admiral Byng's flagship of the fleet when the British fleet was sent to relieve the garrison at Minorca in the spring of 1756. The French fleet attempted to intercept the British fleet, and the two fleets encountered one another just off Minorca on 20

May 1756. For various reasons, Admiral Byng decided on a tricky manoeuvre for which he did not have adequate signal flags, and the operation came to nothing but disarray, and Byng ordered the ships of his fleet to regroup for another attack days hence. However, it was too late for the garrison at Minorca, which was captured. Admiral Byng was assumed to have retreated, which was not allowed by the Twelfth *Article of War,* which read "Every person in the fleet, who ... shall not do his utmost to take or destroy every ship which it shall be his duty to engage ... every such person ... being convicted thereof by the sentence of a court-martial, shall suffer death." And so it was. There was great public outcry on behalf of Byng, but to no avail. The article of war seemed clear enough; he was sentenced to death. To prove he was no coward, Byng asked to give the execution command to the firing squad himself, and this was allowed. He also asked not to be blindfolded, but this was refused because having to stare their target in the face might put the men off their aim. It was Voltaire who remarked, "Ah, the English—they shoot one admiral to encourage the others."✝

✝ Most of this I have taken from my 1969 *Encyclopedia Britannica.* Voltaire depicts the scene in his 1760 novel, *Candide,* Chapter Twenty-three.

There was at least one Deist on board *The Hind.* This was the ship's surgeon. On January 24, Bailey recorded that he dined with the surgeon,

> *after which I had a long conversation with him upon the subject of revelation, which he stoutly denied affirming likewise that he imagined there is no difference between vice and virtue. And that all people after death will be equally happy.*

During the terrible storm of February 15, after *The Hind* has been buried by a monster wave, the surgeon turns to the bottle for comfort.

The doctor, in order to disipate all uneasy reflections, which are extremely apt upon such surprizing occasions as these, to intrude upon the most hardened mind—applied himself to the bottle with great eagerness—till the effects of the liquor began to appear, at length addressing me—he crys out—"Don't be frightened, we shall in a few minits be safe moored in Hell.

Bailey's account of the terrible storm of February 15 is by far the longest entry in the journal about the voyage. A sample:

The ship thro her violent rolling opened her seams, from whence the water gushed in on every side. And she presently grew so leaky, that both pumps could scarcely keep her above water: and yet every soul were ordered to leave pumping notwithstanding the ship had 5 feet of water in her hold and immediately to ply the task with axes in their hands expecting every moment they should be obliged to cut away the mast.

The poor seamen were in a situation which demanded the utmost compassion—they had for several days before been perpetually wet, and for the most part entirely deprived of sleep—and now death inevitable death with all its alarming consequences, threatened every soul.

The greatest part of the evening I continued in the gun room with the doctor, who could not help discovering some emotions of fear in his countenance, notwithstanding all his heroick infidelity.

About eight the whole ship was entirely buried under water, an enormous wave tumbled over us from head to stern, when the sea remained for some minuts several feet above the quarter deck. By this eruption our men were suddenly washed up in heaps, and some of them bruised in a terrible manner—among

*the rest our Boatswain was struck off the forecastle and driven
with the utmost fury against the companion door.*

The officers realized later on February 15 that *The Hind* was
likely doomed. They knew they were near land, and if the ship
did not founder under the waves which washed over them, it
would be dashed to pieces on the shore. There was thunder,
and lightning—and snow, even hail.

Then the next morning (February 16) they found themselves still alive, the storm abated, and, not far off, the Isle of
Wight. They had survived.

*When the first emotions of joy began to subside the poor sail-
ors quickly discovered how much they were weakened with the
prodigious fatigue they had lately undergone and it was really a very moving sight to see with what difficulty they handled
the rigging. 30 men were not able to manage a rope, which formerly six men could govern with the greatest facility.*

The safe conclusion of the terrible voyage is notable for
some evident changes in Jacob Bailey's attitudes. Where the
earthquake of only five years before had invoked a feeling of
God's warning for misbehaviour and anger at the unrepentant
tavern-patrons who returned to their former ways, now there
are no warnings taken from this storm. And by the time *The
Hind* reaches Portsmouth, the sinners are at worst blasphem-
ers and drinkers, and neither behaviour is taken seriously.
There is no angry God at play here; no punishing *Jahweh*. No
hell provided by Jonathan Edwards for poor helpless man.

Instead, there is a recollection of hypocrisy.

Deceiving is an art practiced in some measure by all mankind, tho some regions are more famous than others for producing a generation of hypocrites—and New England is commonly esteemed one of these ...

One day while we were upon our passage, as I lay in my hammock extremely sick, an old man called Daddy Wilson came to visit me, and kindly offered to give all the assistance in his power. After a little conversation he told me that he was born in Boston, New England, where he had kept a barber's shop for several years, that he had buried his wife and all his children, after which he ventured at sea, till he was pressed on board a man of war—since which, continued he, "I have never enjoyed myself perfectly—the horrid oaths and curses which are continually sounding in my ears fill me with the utmost terror—and you are sensible that whoever has any regard for the honour of his maker, or esteem for religion, has but a very poor opportunity of improving and that it is exceeding difficult to find places for devotion. I however enjoy many pleasant hours ... in communion with God—which I would not be deprived of for all the riches of the world. 'Tis that bears up my spirits amidst such dreadful profaneness as I am hourly witness to— I always put my trust in God and hope that he will some time or other deliver me from this unhappy situation."

About an hour after this conversation as I was talking with Mr. Spears I heard, on a sudden the following exclamation— "God eternally damn you, you lousy cursed rascal to hell!"

In a few minutes Jack came in and informed us that the person who had expressed himself in that terrible manner was Daddy Wilson.

The celebration of their safe arrival was subdued. They were too tired to celebrate. The captain's clerk, who had promised himself he would get devilish drunk, had one drink, and left.

The ship's company had entered into a resolution of consuming the night in diversion, but this merriment was the most awkward and restrained that I ever saw. Wet, fatigue and perpetual watchings had so effectually deadened their spirits that nothing lively or agreeable appeared in their behaviour. One after another withdrew to silent repose till not a soul was left to carry on the frolick ...

‡ Bartlet, p. 58.

The next day (February 17), Jacob Bailey caught a ride ashore with a fellow who had come to pick up an unaccompanied trunk, and was at last to set foot in England. His last remark has none of the tones of his remarks when he boarded *The Hind*. Nor was Bailey's response to the terror of the sea anything like his response to the Cape Ann Earthquake of 1755. He was a more subdued and thoughtful man than he was before he left America; even before becoming an Anglican. He wrote:

Having taken my leave of all my friends in the ship, I left it with the greatest satisfaction but not without a strong inclination of seeing again those who had been my companions in so many dangers.‡

The prissy young man who wanted to do good and be good was now a veteran of life. He had no more answers in advance of experience.

An Introduction
to England

So it was that on 17 February 1760, a Sunday, Jacob Bailey stepped ashore into the Old World at Portsmouth, England. He was safe, sound, and amazed.* He had with him letters of introduction to ecclesiastical authorities and others who might assist him in various ways; as well as some recommendations for lodging from friends on *The Hind* (including notably Mr. Spears)—and his chest.

> *While I stood staring around me in the wildest disorder, a young lad came down to the water, and offered to carry my chest to any place I should direct. I, in a moment, recollected that it might be proper to have it reposited in some wagon-house, till it could be conveyed up to London. Accordingly, he put it down at the Blue Anchor, where I was informed that it would be put into the wagon the next morning.†*

As well, Bailey had with him new experiences and stories from new friends which were to prepare him for England. Some of these stories were cautionary tales. One was curious, considering its source. Bailey noted that it was told him by Rev. Mr. Caner, then Rector of King's Chapel, Boston, one of the group

* William Bartlet, in *Frontier Missionary*, omits all of the journal entries (although Bartlet summarizes some information) from the arrival of Bailey at Portsmouth until he meets the Archbishop of Canterbury on 28 February 1760.

† Bartlet, p. 58.

‡ This story
is *not* included
in Bartlet, but
is provided in
transcription
from the O'Dell
Journal of 30
December
1759, by R.C.
Woodbury.

§ Thomas
Rowlandson
(b. 1757) took
great delight in
embarrassing
moments,
often featuring
nakedness, and
usually hypocrisy,
as well. Many of
his cartoons are
frankly, rudely
sexual.

of Anglicans who recruited Jacob Bailey for Pownalborough and the Church of England. It is about robbers.

A certain highway collector having discovered a coach filled with genteel people rode up and with a great deal of complaisance demanded their loose change but the passengers not being disposed to part with their money sorely affronted the collector who immediately ordered them out of the coach and stripped every soul perfectly naked even to the driver. They were obliged in this manner and to their prodigious confusion to enter the city.‡

It might be noted that a story is as much baggage as a chest, though more portable. It's a funny picture which the Rev. Mr. Caner gives to Bailey's busy pen. The eighteenth-century cartoonist Thomas Rowlandson would have done great justice to it, though to be fair, Rowlandson would depict a somewhat later era.§ And here we have a story told by another Anglican clergyman. Was the story prurient (not really) or amusing (and broad-minded) or simply a wry warning? Does it tell us about highwaymen in the eighteenth century or naughty fun in the eighteenth century? More the latter, I believe; it is a wry comment.

But there is another story recorded by Bailey on 8 January 1760, the day before he boarded *The Hind* on the way to change his life forever.

Bailey writes it as if told to him by a certain Deacon Woodward he met at a boarding house, saying, "I cannot forbear however to relate a story of this rich Deacon to show his generous soul."

As he was travelling one morning from his habitation to Boston, in company with a young gentleman, they arrived togeth-

er in sight of a house of publick entertainment, when the spark desired the Deacon to alight and take a breakfast, but the latter being of a more prudent disposition told him that he had a friend not far distant, where they would presently stop. At length they came to a little hut, inhabited by a poor lame old man who had no other way of gaining a living but by making brooms. He and his consort happened to be at breakfast upon porridge, upon which they invited our travellers to partake of their fare to which the Deacon and his companion readily complied. After this refreshment they travelled on till dinner time, but hunger approaching they were compelled to call at a tavern where they satisfied the cravings of nature. The bill was sent for when the generous Deacon addressed himself to his companion in the following manner.

"Sir, I hope you will pay for both our dinners, since I was the means of procuring you a breakfast at my friend's." Upon this the young gentleman discharged his reckoning and took the first opportunity of quitting his company.

Ambiguous little tale, isn't it? The Deacon supposedly tells the story with a purpose. Are we to understand that he thinks himself a clever fellow because he has bested the young gentleman? The young gentleman seems innocent enough and certainly does not complain at the breakfast porridge. But he is called a "spark," and the term might suggest a fellow who thought himself livelier and more fashionable than others might describe him.¶ So has the Deacon given the young chap his comeuppance?

Or has the Deacon been shown to be a grasping mean old man who at once takes advantage of the courtesy of the old broom-maker and the naivety of the young man? And if so, what does this say of the Deacon? Moreover, what does this say of the Church which the Deacon represents?* Would the

¶ Such characters are common in plays of the seventeenth and eighteenth centuries. See the character of Sparkish in the Restoration era play, *The Country Wife*, by William Wycherley.

* There are of course deacons in many Christian denominations, including both Anglican and Roman Catholic. But this deacon is almost certainly a representative of the Congregational Church in which Bailey had been raised. My old *Webster's Third New International Dictionary* gives interesting meanings for the verb form of "deacon," among which are sharp practice, the packing of fruit with the good fruit on top, and the shifting of boundary lines.

Deacon's grasping manner explain why Bailey, an approved Congregational minister, was teaching school in Gloucester?✝

Do the two stories together explain (unintentionally, perhaps) why Bailey was leaving one church for another?‡ One is cruel and crass; the other is broad-minded and amusing?

Portsmouth overwhelmed Jacob Bailey. All the activity! At the Blue Anchor, Bailey learns that there are no horses to be had for hire to take him on to London. A disease among the horses, he was told, had played havoc among the usual supply. And, not liking the look of the Blue Anchor, Bailey set out to find the lodging recommended by Mr. Spears, who had looked after Bailey so well on *The Hind*. He was soon lost. He turned for help to an "honest looking tar," who, in sea-going language, navigated the streets to the recommended establishment of Miss Harris.§ (There has been a literal sea change in Jacob Bailey: when he boarded *The Hind* he found the sailors profane, blasphemous and often drunk; now a sailor is an "honest tar," and a fellow to be trusted.) Mr. Spears had been quite taken with Miss Harris, it seems, and considered that their friendship had promise for the future, but, to Jacob Bailey's surprise, it seems Miss Harris has changed her name. She has gotten married. Spears has been superseded. Bailey remarks that women as a group are inconstant. The lodging house, however, is clean and well managed by the former Miss Harris and her mother.

Reflecting further on women, Bailey notices that the former Miss Harris is "a woman of pretty accomplishments," and generalizes that women are more engaging than men.

✝ There is a great deal of irony in the story, where the character thinks one thing about himself and the author thinks quite another. We ought not be surprised at the method or the skill. Jacob Bailey was to become a reader of the great master of irony, Laurence Sterne. See *Tristram Shandy*.

‡ Charles E. Allen, in his most excellent study of Bailey's life, thinks that the young spark of the Deacon story was Bailey himself, and clearly enough assumes the story is autobiographical. I myself am inclined to think of the Deacon's story as an ironic moral fiction.

§ The sailor who lives always in nautical terms will appear also on the Flying Machine to London—and in fact a version of him can be found in Roderick Random's youthful benefactor in Smollett's novel,

Men seem devoted to argument and splutter. Women talk, converse, tell stories.

And are prudent. When Bailey determines to go on foot to see the town of Portsmouth, the mother volunteers her son to accompany Bailey for protection. One doesn't stroll the town in the evening by oneself.

Certainly Bailey is surprised by the number and aggression of the street whores. They are numerous, loud and predatory. He is convinced that they are quite capable of dragging a fellow into their lairs where, if he should fail to satisfy them (he does not specify how), they will strip him naked and turn him out of doors. More nakedness.

However, he and his young protector make it safely to The Three Fighting Cocks, where Bailey reserves a seat on the stagecoach to London, termed the "Flying Machine," for the 19th, the day after the next. A deposit of half a guinea is required.

The next day (February 18) is given over to unaccompanied observation and education. The observation takes in the overwhelming might of the British Empire and its navy in Portsmouth, as indicated by the thousands of cannon, the piles of cannonballs, the forests of masts and ships in the harbour, and the impressive buildings pertinent to the Royal Navy.

One of these buildings is a school for the children of Royal Navy officers, and it possesses a cupola which promises a fine view of Portsmouth and the harbour. Bailey would like very much to take in that view, and enquires of a serving girl if such would be possible. She thinks it likely, and goes off to ask her mistress. But does not return. After an hour, Bailey repeats his enquiry to a passing carpenter. The carpenter indicates that Bailey ought knock on the headmistress's door. Bailey does so.

Roderick Random, to which Bailey refers on a subsequent occasion. It is quite possible that already fictional characters are appearing in Bailey's travel account.

¶ It was a phrase used as late as the twentieth century by my grandmother, who, in her old age, decided to read the Old Testament and was shocked.

He is open, innocent and guileless—which we may take as already established American traits. We may also deduce that these traits exasperate beyond measure the English who demand recognition of the elaborate nuances of British society, which demands in turn second thoughts and a little reticence for heaven's sake. The headmistress answers the door, listens to his request, denies it in short, sharp terms, and slams the door in his face.

Bailey is at first furious—and then reflects on the state of his clothes. Not very good, he concludes. Well, he's been at sea since sometime the previous December. And women are very serious about clothes. He holds no grudge.

Then, walking among the cannon, he is attacked by a dog—and saved by a passerby. Shortly thereafter, Bailey notices again the women of Portsmouth, who are "no better than they ought to be." ¶ The violence shocks him. A woman's body, cut into quarters, is pulled from the harbour. Another is led through the streets with her hand hacked off and bleeding. He doesn't know why.

Bailey moves to The Three Fighting Cocks, and takes a room to be ready for the early departure of the stagecoach the next day. He finds The Three Fighting Cocks a dirty establishment, but he hasn't much chance to rest in any event because he is called for the departure of The Flying Machine at 2:30 a.m.

The Flying Machine is an amazing conveyance, pulled by a team of six horses. The trip to London will take one day. Horses will be changed at stations along the way. The stagecoach holds four to six passengers inside at one price (first class, or business class, as it were), and several more outside at a lower price. The outsiders travel in a "basket" attached to the back of the stagecoach, open to the weather. It soon begins to rain. This is the middle of February, in England.

Inside are (besides Bailey) a gentleman from New York, a "young and pretty lady," a lieutenant of a man-of-war, a Welch [Bailey's spelling] "captain of transport," and a country clerk on his way to a position with a London merchant.

Outside in the basket are a sailor (who is given to shouting out nautical comments on the progress of the stagecoach, a "Jew, somewhat disordered in his mind," a farmer's son, a ship's steward, a poor widow, a "lady of the town," and two beautiful girls from Drury Lane. The girls will later explain that it's chiefly accident that finds them in the basket. They were obliged suddenly to return to town because of the unexpected death of a relative, and could only find transport in the basket of the Flying Machine. They are invited inside the stagecoach, and respond with several entertaining songs. The Welch captain seems especially charmed.

The passengers breakfast at Petersfield, and the journey continues in bad weather. A rider is encountered who just might be a highwayman—a Flying Machine was robbed only the day before—but, other travellers appearing on the road, the passengers save their valuables (and possibly their clothes), and they pass by the chasm of the Devil's Punch Bowl before stopping at a lonely country inn to change horses again. Here Bailey witnesses the value levied on the smallest of services.

The poor widow had the evening before (presumably at The Three Fighting Cocks) been allowed to sit by the fire to warm herself. Now the coachman informs her that the warmth was not free, and she must either pay him for the privilege she enjoyed or give up her miserable little bundle of clothes. She gives up the clothes.

* The walnuts are different. The English walnut, or the Persian walnut, or the Syrian walnut—all the same thing, apparently—is a thin-shelled walnut which in North America is associated with Christmas. One authority suggested that it came to Great Britain from the Romans. It is comparatively easy to crack. The North American walnut, however, has a tough craggy shell, and the tree is grown chiefly for its salty-smelling lovely tough wood. "English walnuts," however, are now grown in California.

And the Drury Lane beauties are denied a return to the inside of the coach unless a fee can be paid. The other inside passengers (perhaps only the men) take up a subscription of five shillings, and the entertainment continues. Bailey notes that the girls sing beautifully, and he has never heard before several of the songs which they perform. So they are certainly legitimate performers, if not quite actresses, and their abilities alter, although not quite entirely, other suspicions about them.

Bailey describes each community as they pass through it, the landscape by soil type and topography, and seems much taken with the gracious "gentlemen's seats," with their long tree-lined drives and imposing dwellings. He includes a list of tolls charged to maintain sections of the road. The entire length from Portsmouth was not apparently a toll road, but parts of it were fenced and travel was restricted to those who could pay. The tollgates might be eight to ten miles apart, and the coach and team of six is charged sixpence at each tollgate.

At Guildford:

We called here at a public house to change horses when I ventured out of the coach in search of some fruit for the company—I rambled about ten doors down the street till I came to a fruiters shop, where seeing some English walnuts I had the curiosity to enquire what they were—the honest shopkeeper upon this told me staring at the same time with the utmost earnestness—

He continued some time in a posture of admiration—then suddenly breaking his silence cryed—pray sir did you never see any walnuts before—I returned him an answer in the negative* —pray replied he with increasing surprize where have *you lived in what part of England was you born? In no part of this kingdom, but that I was a stranger just arrived from N England in America.*

Upon this he started New England! bless me! is it possible for a person educated in New England to speak such good English—why sir, you speak as plain English as we do.

The man by his earnest manner of expressing himself, had drawn all the neighbourhood around us—who instantly began to ask me a variety of questions concerning my native country. Does America, says they, look anything like England.

I told him that our inhabitants both in their manners language and method of living very much resembled the English of Great Britain—that our towns generally bore the names of theirs—and that among others there was a Guildford in New England.

This still raised their admiration and excited their curiosity—twenty questions were now proposed at once by multitudes of men women and children who flocked from every quarter.

In the midst of these puzzling interrogations, I saw the coach ready to push off—upon which I hastily withdrew from my greedy admirers who doubtless looked upon me as the greatest wonder they had ever seen.

Upon my return I acquainted my companions of this comical adventure which promoted among us a very hearty laugh.

Hmmmmmm. It's quite possible that the people on the street were indeed amazed that an American could speak as plain English as they did. Or were both of them referring to accent, not syntax or vocabulary? Probably yes. And it seems clear (embarrassingly clear, perhaps), that Jacob Bailey wants to be mistaken for an Englishman.†

But Guildford was on the main road from Portsmouth to

† To this day, an English accent—an Oxbridge accent, if you please—is accepted by the general North American public as a mark of refinement. You can see this exemplified in television commercials, hustling goods. And every English department in every university in North America has at least one member who changed planes at Heathrow and returned with an Oxbridge accent.

London, and American travellers were likely common. A fellow passenger in the Flying Machine was from New York, after all. There were enough Americans in London for there to be a New England coffee house (which Bailey visited the next week), so it is unlikely that Americans were very exotic. In fact, it is more likely that the Guildford folk were having a bit of fun, a good bit of fun, with the passing American.

The Flying Machine passes through Leatherford, Epsom and Tooting ("no considerable place," but it was too dark to see much), and then in the distance appear the lights of Westminster Bridge, and shortly,

> *We reached London bridge I was agreeably smitten with the grandeur of the streets and the magnificence of the structures.... The houses were extremely uniform four stories high, and all the shops adorned with productions of every climate. The several commodities and manufactures were distinguished in a most conspicuous manner by the vast number of lamps which were burning before every door.*

The coach deposits them on Grace Church Street at the Spread Eagle Inn.

> *All our fellow travellers entered the tavern except the Welch captain, who was diverted from waiting upon the two town ladies by some extraordinary event which has since slipt my memory.*

An extraordinary event which has slipt his memory? Not, then, a very extraordinary event, if an event at all. And so much for the Welch captain. He disappears.

And the Nymphs of Drury Lane? "These females after taking their share of a bottle, gave us directions to their lodgings, and then retired—leaving the American gentleman, the steward, and the young married lady with me."

What, now that we have arrived in London with Bailey, are we to make of his companions in the Flying Machine? Real or fictional? Some real and some fictional?‡ The Welch captain gives Bailey the opportunity to try his hand at regional speech when the captain swears he would "pe revenged upon the tam tog of a coachman for his tevilish impudence."

If we turn our attention back to the journey of the Flying Machine, we find that the characters come to life just after breakfast in Petersfield.

During the fury of the storm our sailor found himself a little uneasy, and remembering the danger to which he was lately exposed, threw out his extravagance in sea phrases to the no small diversion of the whole company. When the coachman drove hard he would bawl out a dam ye mr son of a bitch take in a reef or we shall all be overset—when we passed by a tavern he was always for throwing out anchor to take in a little ballast—when the storm blew full in his face he crys out lay to lay to!

Whenever the coach stopped he would curse the driver, bid him in all strength go fore and aft and heave ahead—when we were going up hill it was nothing but unfurl the maintop, and crowd on all the sail boys—

In this manner he proceeded till the wind and cold had almost stiffened his tongue. Our poor widow went on to relate her adventures till she was nearly chilled to death, and at length became exceeding ill.

The steward of the man of war swore that their bread was very bad, and that their provision behind was cursed mean,—

‡ I regret having to address this issue, but the fact is, some readers find it difficult to believe that a writer can imagine a person real as life. Some readers insist on a factual origin. Some readers will believe that everything a writer pens is autobiographical—and some writers are very autobiographical, or somewhat autobiographical and on occasions not autobiographical at all. Reader, I beg of you: grant the writer the power of imagination.

the young farmer wished himself in his father's chimney cor-
ner. The Jew began to rave and deal out his imprecations in a
most liberal manner, upon which the sailor accosted him in the
following strain—

"Make yourself easy messmate we shall soon arrive at a
good harbour where we shall make ourselves merry with a nip
of toddy, and have a good dinner upon a leg of bacon—"

This immediately threw the son of Abraham into a tremen-
dous rage, and they were with no small difficulty restrained
from fighting.

The Lieut sat in a sullen posture and said nothing, but now
and then looked upon the silver hilt of his sword that we might
not forget his dignity and importance.

While the two Nymphs of Drury were practicing all their
arts upon the honest welchman who was entirely ignorant of
their designs; he engaged their chief attention—the country
clerk however was frequently the subject of their merriment.

To avoid their observation he had drawn himself up into
the most distant corner. Silence closed his lips, continual blush-
es bespoke his confusion—and his downcast eyes were turned
towards the floor.

The married lady and I passed away the time very agree-
ably in conversing upon America.

In many ways the companions in the Flying Machine are
stock characters distinguished by occupation (sailor, naval
lieutenant), race (the Jew), nationality (the Welshman), and
social roles (widow, nymphs of Drury Lane). The narrator is
presumably Bailey, conversing with the young married lady,
but if there is an autobiographical character in the coach, it
might be the country clerk who is terrified of the women and
what they imply.

So is Jacob Bailey reporting real people or writing a fiction? He's good at it—so at first I considered them as facts. Upon reflection, however, I am not so sure.

The account of the journey in the Flying Machine, as well as the "History of Mrs. R"—presumably the "married lady" had to have been written upon his arrival at the Spread Eagle Inn on Grace Church Street on the evening of February 19. He records that:

> *About 12 at night I called for a bed and was conducted thro a long gallery into a bed chamber.... But it was a long time before I could compose myself to sleep, notwithstanding I was so fatigued with my journey and the busy scenes of the day.*

He wrote, and wrote, and wrote some more. It was a frenzy of outpouring—fiction and autobiography and reportage, one after the other, overwhelming one another.

A prefatory note to the "History of Mrs. R":

> *The young lady tho married was extremely sociable and pleasant and before we parted gave me a concise History of her life and adventures which was delivered nearly in the following words.§*

So Bailey takes up the first-person narrative.

> *I was born in Chester where I passed away my childhood without anything remarkable till I was eight years of age, at which time a wealthy Aunt residing in London sent to my parents and desired that I might be permitted to live with her.*
>
> *I was pleased at the notion of going up to that fine city, and accordingly went. My aunt received me with great satisfac-*

§ There was a literary model for the form. In Tobias Smollett's *Roderick Random*, the young adventurer has been thrown out of his lodgings and happens upon his former beloved, from whom he had parted in some animosity after discovering her in bed with another man. But now—it's quite a tender scene, really—both on their uppers, they look after one another while both are waiting out a cure for their venereal disease, and she tells him her history.

tion and spared neither labour nor expense to give me a genteel education.

I continued her darling and seemed daily to gain upon her affections till I was about fifteen.

I happened then one evening to fall in company with an agreeable Gentleman, an officer in his Majesties army.

He quickly found means to insinuate himself so far into my affections that I consented to marry him, contrary to the advice and inclinations of my friends—and having discovered by every relation as well was thrown out of my Aunts favour I was reduced to an entire dependence upon my Husband and his friends who treated me upon all occasions in a very generous and obliging manner. Soon after our marriage the Regiment to which my consort belonged was called into America—I immediately determined to accompany him, and to share his fortune in all the fatigues and dangers of a campain.

After a safe passage we arrived at Virginia, and were constrained to follow the Army—

I travelled with general Braddock over the vast mountainous deserts which separate the English settlements from the Ohio.

Here I saw the rash general killed and his army cut to pieces and entirely defeated—After this unhappy Expedition I returned to England with my companion who ever treated me with the kindest affection.

We afterwards attended Loudon's sham expedition to America—where I was a witness to all his shameful and stupid conduct.

I now returned a second time to Europe, and again crossed the Atlantick when it was my misfortune to lose a most tender Husband under the walls of Louisbourg. I was not however left without a pretty fortune to render my life comfortable in those remote regions.

I here acquired considerable acquaintance with several field officers and other Gentlemen of the Army, who treated me with great civility. By their influence I was recommended to lodgings in the city of N York—here the Master of a man of war, a young fellow happened to see me quickly professed a violent passion—he by his obliging behaviour gained so far upon me that I gave him some encouragement to continue his addresses—

Which he did in the most obsequious manner—till he was forced to make a voyage to England—at parting I entered into a kind of engagement to marry him after his return—

I had during his absence heard so much to his disadvantage that I was almost tempted to break my promise—I treated him when he visited me with a coldness which had such effect upon him that he became entirely incapable of business—this constrained the capt and some of the others to interest themselves in the affairs—who overcame me by their intreaties and persuaded me to marry the young Man in order to save him from ruin. His only fault, (tho I confess this is not a small one) is drinking to excess, and I have been so happy as almost to break him off.

He has considerable estate and powerful friends, able to advance him whenever his good behaviour shall merit their esteem and notice.

At this point Bailey drops the first-person narrative and says, "The lady further informed me that her consort was shortly to be in town, when she promised an opportunity of seeing him." Moreover,

When the steward left us he invited me to his lodgings and told me he should do himself the pleasure of waiting upon me frequently at mine—this young fellow was of wealthy parents

> *and took only this voyage to Africa which effectually satisfied*
> *his desire of roving—*

And then it's off to bed, except that Bailey cannot sleep and embarks on his autobiographical sketch and an account of life in Hampton, and more—but, as Woodbury notes, "several pages at the end of volume are here missing."

The next day (February 20), Bailey records that the lady sent for him to join her at breakfast and "gave me the History of her life which in short was as follows"—except that he's already written it. Then he and the lady part, promising to see each other frequently, "but, unluckily I never enquired her name—and not making a memorandum soon forgot her lodgings by which means our acquaintance was entirely dropped … She had a fine set of features and was but little more than twenty."

So she (of no name) is gone the way of the Welchman and the Nymphs of Drury Lane. But her story allows us to infer quite precisely Bailey's writing habits. That is: she probably existed. She was almost certainly in the coach. She might well have been married to a soldier who served in Braddock's campaign, and Loudon's. Her husband might well be dead. But it also seems clear that Bailey extrapolates from her personality a story which interests him and might indeed interest a possible reader. His understanding of the character is fictional, and what he is writing are notes for fiction. If the sailor becomes a Popeye cartoon figure bawling out nautical terms as the Flying Machine heaves through the storm out of Petersfield, the lovely young lady's account of her upbringing by a wealthy aunt is suitably romantic—both for Bailey's interest and ours. It might be noted how much the story has in common (rustic beginnings; urban civilization) with the stories in the Harvard Letters to Dr. Morrill about Rustica. Notice, too, that situation with the young officer of the man-of-war is very like that of Mr. Spears and Miss Harris, who did not wait for him.

So there seem to be two lives going on in Jacob Bailey's head while he travels: one is the observer of events; the travel writer, as it were. The other is the imaginative writer, the fiction writer, who takes a voice, an attitude, a happenstance, and construes it into fiction.

And thereby, I might suggest, into understanding—which is the business of fiction. The very first thing he does the next morning (February 20) is hustle off to a bookseller.

Prepare to be (Somewhat) Embarrassed

No question about it: life for Jacob Bailey in his first days in England was a whirlwind. Five days earlier, on the 15th, he was almost drowned, and indeed, expected to die with all the hands on board *The Hind*. He landed in Portsmouth and was much impressed by the evident might of the British Empire on display, frightened by the aggressive street whores, rudely rebuffed by a headmistress, attacked by a dog, and, on February 19, mistaken (or so he thought) for an Englishman, and became a member in good standing of a most merry crew on the journey from Portsmouth to London in the Flying Machine. All of it invoked writing—including a most valuable autobiographical sketch.* All, it would seem, written during the prolific night of the 19th.

When Bailey arrived in London on that evening, he was ready to embark upon a new life, knew it, and welcomed it. No sooner had he completed a sampler of "The History of Mrs. R," when, without any discernible pause, he turned to an autobiographical sketch. It will turn out to be the key to an understanding of Jacob Bailey's life. Consequently, some of it bears repeating.

* Bartlet uses the sketch in the first chapter of his book on Bailey, so we know that Bartlet read the accounts contained in the previous chapter. Yet he omitted all mention of them. Bartlet was not interested in stories, nor, it seems, in improper people.

I now reflected with transport upon all those schemes and adventures which I had laid and passed thro. Upon all those hardships I had sustained with the dangers and almost impossibilities I had surmounted to obtain a sight of this ancient city.

In my very childhood as soon as I was able to read I was seized with an insatiable desire of travelling and a boundless curiosity to visit foreign regions ...

This inclination I was obliged to suppress since such numerous obstacles arose to check my ambition and to prevent me from indulging those desires which all my acquaintance looked upon as the most extravagant and romantick—

When I had completed my tenth year I found myself an inhabitant of a place remarkable for ignorance, narrowness of mind and bigotry—

An uniform method of thinking and acting universally prevailed, and nothing could be more criminal than for one person to be more learned religious or polite than another—

For instance if any one happened to make advances in knowledge beyond his neighbours, he was immediately looked upon as an odd unaccountable fellow, was shunned by every company and left to drink his mug of flip alone, on a lecture day night he was sure to draw upon him the contempt and ridicule of the other sex and always became the banter of the young females not only at the frolic and the dance; but at the washing tub and spinning wheel.

Whenever a person began to make a figure in religion or had the boldness to be more virtuous than his companions he instantly drew upon him the envy of all the old professors, who branded him with the various names of upstart hypocrite or new light—

As for all politeness and every kind of civility except what

their great grandmothers taught them, it was esteemed a cry-
ing sin—thus I have known a boy whipped for saying sir to
his father when he came from school—a young fellow severe-
ly reprimanded for drinking a health—and a very pretty girl
obliged to live a virgin ten years for once preferring a Gen-
tleman to a plough jogger—and for saluting every body with
a curtsy—

Reflecting on his life to that point, Jacob Bailey is angry—
angry that he could be mocked for considering the larger
world in terms of learning, virtue, or courtesies. Who would
have thought that the notions of uppitiness, or being "too big
for yer britches" would hold sway in American life as early as
the first years of the eighteenth century? Consider the implications of the phrase flung about in Alice Munro's short stories, "Who do you think you are?" or the damnation conveyed
by the term "conceited." The young Jacob Bailey felt himself
damned for being smart and condemned for using courtesies
associated with a Gentleman, and notes that a girl could be
condemned to remain a virgin for "preferring a Gentleman."
And demonstrates by using the word "virgin" that the eighteenth century was different in its attitudes and language
from the nineteenth century (and even much of the twentieth, come to that).

Bailey then turns to a description of the community, and
bit by bit, the description becomes more detailed.

The old people were so tenacious of the customs of their ances-
tors that no consideration could prevail upon them to deviate
in the minutest instance—This stupid exactness might be dis-
covered in the field, at home—at the tavern and even at the
meeting house. Every man planted as many acres of Indian

† See the novels
of Sinclair Lewis,
especially *Main
Street, Babbitt* and
Elmer Gantry.

*corn and sowed the same number with rye—he plowed with
as many oxen hoed it as often, and gathered in his crop on the
same day with his grandfather—with regard to his family
he salted down the same quantity of beef and pork—wore the
same kind of stockings, shirts and Garments—and at table
sat upon his bottom, and said grace with his wife and children around him—just as all his predecessors had done before
him.*

*At the tavern the same regulation obtained—where it was
esteemed impious to venture except upon a training or lecture
day—upon the former occasion the good man always bought a
piece of sweet cake for his spouse and a roll of gingerbread for
each of his children—upon the latter you might see the fathers
of familys flocking from the house of devotion with a becoming gravity in their countenance to the house of flip.*

So it would seem that in Jacob Bailey's youth in the village of
Rowley, Massachusetts, the rule was: *there shall be no changes whatsoever in anything, ever.* Anyone who has ever lived or
grown up in a small American town will find this strikingly familiar.†

Soon Bailey becomes more specific.

*The young sparks assemble upon this evening to divert them-
selves where after two or three hoarse laughs at some passage
in the sermon they proceed in the following manner—*

*They send for an old negro, who presently makes his appear-
ance—with the parish fiddle—part of the head is broken it is
glued together in several places with rosin—has three strings
and c—*

*Now the music begins which instantly inspires the youths,
who haul out the willing fair to mingle in the dance—they*

hold this violent exercise till sweat and fatigue oblige them to desist—in this interval one is dispached to the tavern for a dram, which revives their spirits till midnight—then they separate when each jolly fellow leads home his bonny lass and sleeps quietly in her arms till morning.

They have one excellent custom here, and that is their constant attendance upon publick worship—upon the ringing of the bell on Sundays every one repairs to the meeting house and behaves with tolerable decency till prayers are over.

As to singing the greatest number have renounced their prejudice to what is called the new way, but others continue to place such sanctity in a few old tunes that they either hang down their heads in silence or run out of the meeting, while their neighbours are singing one of a more modern composition.

When the sermon begins every one has the privilege of growing drowsy about the middle many catch a nod, and several sleep quietly during the Application.

These people would esteem it a great hardship if they were denied the privilege of taking a nap once a week in their meeting house.

Bailey then returns from the community at worship to the boy he once was.

Thus at the age of ten I found myself among these people— without any education, without money and to increase my misfortune, I was bashful to the extremest degree.

This disposition had taken such a possession of me that I was even afraid to walk the streets in open daylight and frequently when I have been sent abroad in the neighbourhood of an errand rather than be seen, I have gone a mile about thro fields and bushes—A female was the most dreadful sight I could possibly behold, and till I was 18 I had never courage to speak in their presence—whenever I had the misfortune to meet one of these animals in the street, I immediately climbed over the fences and lay obscured till they passed along.

And if any young woman happened to come into a room where I was sitting I was immediately seized with a trembling, but if she spoke my confusion was so great that it was a long time before I could recover.

But these difficulties instead of abating my thirst after knowledge, or lessening my unbounded desire for travel, only served as so many incitements to these acquisitions.

At length after encountering a variety of scenes, striving with a thousand vexations, and breaking thro all the obstacles which surrounded me I obtained a liberal education conquered my prejudices, and by the assistance of a favourable providence am safely arrived—notwithstanding the cruel dangers that threatened me, to the Metropolis of Great Britain.

It's quite a passionate confession, isn't it?—and the last paragraph convinces me that the first reason for joining the Church of England was the required trip to London. But it's not that simple. He also wanted to be good and do good (he was ambitious for virtue), and he wanted to be a gentleman. He was poor. So when Dr. Gardiner's recruiters happened upon him, he was more than ready to listen.

And it should be remembered that he kept his part of the bargain without quibble or complaint or compromise, even when he had plenty of opportunities and inducements to change his mind.

Nor has he finished his writing for the night. He next turns his attention to the more recent past at Hampton, where his heart lies.

Before I closed my eyes my busy thoughts flew over the vast Atlantick to the humble shores, where I left my dear—my fancy represented her in peaceful slumbers, her blue eyes closed now engaged in a pleasing dream, now interrupted with a smile of innocence which betokens the inward serenity of her mind—

But can I expect that her virgin charms are reserved for me, when I consider the scenes and company that surround her surely some son of rusticity supported by the rabble of females will insinuate himself into her affections and banish me forever from her heart.

The town of Hampton is an original—and its inhabitants deserve a particular consideration.

The people commonly live to a great age—are remarkably rough and honest, and esteem it impious to deviate from the customs and sentiments of their forefathers.

It was the constant practice of all the ancient men and women 100 years ago to be regular in their attendance upon divine worship, and to this day you may see them flocking to the meeting house in great numbers on a Sunday.

Upon a lecture which happens the first Wednesday in every month every person above fifty is present, the women dressed in a clean checked apron, and a Riding hood head, while the men appear in their leather aprons, and silk handkerchief about their necks.

Several ancient people make a practice of taking a comfortable nap in time of service.

One Sunday as an honest Esquire was taking his usual nap before he had fallen into a profound sleep, he kept nod-

ding over his seat till his head met a Negro wenches, who was in the same circumstances with himself.

This incident excited at once the laughter of all the young people present, which reminds me of their conduct upon other occasions—

The young people of both sexes are here extremely addicted to what in the language of New England is called frolicking by which is nothing else is meant but dissipation and nonsense, begun, carried on and concluded with the utmost indecency. And that these entertainments should be conducted in this manner is not at all surprizing, since the children are generally kept in no kind of order.

The young boys and girls are not compelled to go to school, but permitted to ramble about the streets till the day is over and then to assemble in some barn or private resort where they learn to become familiar with each other almost from their infancy—but since I have treated of these defects in education and manners in another place—I shall not enlarge but proceed to give the History of a Hampton frolick which may with as little narration serve as a pattern for the rest—

On Sunday evening as soon as divine service was concluded the young females gathered into one corner of the meeting house and presently entered into consultation the first subject that engaged their attention, was the young strange Gentleman who happened to be at meeting he had the misfortune to be severely handled by these unmerciful ladies—one certified upon his dress—"law" cries another, "I never saw such a stupid wig in my life as he had on," "how plaguy proud he looked," exclaims a third, "I don't believe he has more money than his neighbours, for all he dresses so devilish fine.—ah, cries the parson's daughter, you would (not) concern yourselves about him so much if you knew who his father was—this reflection gave their ill-nature some relief, and drew from them a laugh of satisfaction—the frolick next came onto the carpet, and having nominated a number of fellows to their liking they proceed to consult time and place, which was after much debate fixed for the following night, at a neighbour parish.

Upon this result the assembly broke up with all the tokens of joy and satisfaction in their countenances.

Several were dispached that evening to notify the young fellows to be in readiness against the next night.

Accordingly the wished for season drew on, when the young females with all the tokens of frolick and roguery in their countenances assembled in the tavern where the fellows waited their motion, about dark.

After drinking a bumper of brandy or New England rum—they held a long dispute concerning their particular partners.

A certain young miss had the misfortune to be slighted, as well by her female companions, as by all the young fellows; who refused to carry her—not indeed because she was less handsome, and less obliging, than the rest but because her modesty and decent behaviour had drawn the envious ridicule of all the pretty girls in the neighbourhood.

At length the contest is ended and the greatest rake in the company takes her for his companion.

The Multitude being mounted, leave the tavern, and drive on in a most furious manner, hallowing and screaming along the road, to the great surprize and disturbance of honest house keepers.

But now behold! a terrible accident which prudence could not forsee—nor all the daring courage and dissipation of our youthful sparks possibly prevent—

Scornelia the loftiest Nymph that ever adorned a country

meeting house whose knowledge made her despise the publick instructions of her minister, who had too much spirit to bare reproof from her parents—and was too conscious of her own dignity to admit the addresses of any neighbouring swain—

It happened that this important lady was mounted behind Pragmantius the haughty Beau of Agauam, and riding full gallop by a farmer's door in all the statliness of pride out runs a little dog, who with all the sauciness and ill manners in the world, assaulted the horse—upon which the noble animal first started forward—and then stumbling fell down and threw Scornelia headlong into a deep slough—

"Good heavens! What a sight is here," cried an impudent fellow, whom she had always refused with the utmost contempt, "I swear pride has got a confounded fall."

And indeed it afforded no small satisfaction to the envious sex, when they saw the scornful glory of all the parish lie sprawling in the mud, she who deprived them of sweethearts and engrossed all the strange fellows to herself.

But Gallantius having a little more complaisance than the rest, sprang from his horse and assisted the poor unfortunate in rising from her oozy bed.

It was certainly a moving spectacle she who was lately shining in all the distinction of self-consequence and finery—was led dripping into the farmer's cottage to be stared at by his wife and children.

What a horrid transformation was here—her new calico gown was besmeared and rent to pices. One of her stone earrings was broken, her lawn cap spotted with mud, her ruffles torn off—her red ribbon was stained—her white stockings all bespattered—her garters untied and her petticoats hung dangling about her heels—the young lady unwilling to lose her frolick borrowed some humble apparel of the farmer's

*eldest daughter and remounting arrived in a few minits to
the appointed tavern.*

*As soon as the company entered the young fellows present-
ed their sweethearts with a dram, and being all in high spirits
the frolick quickly began.*

Here were present the following couples—
Pragmantius   Scornelia
John Bawling   Tabitha Battle

And, Woodbury notes, several pages at end of the volume are
here missing.

It has been a day of some adventure in the Flying Machine,
and a night of frenzy with the pen. The alert reader may notice
that what begins as a sociological description soon takes narrative flight, and characters appear with Latinate names to
suggest their personalities. We have already met "Scornelia"
under another name in the Harvard Letters. So what began as
a tender memory of a sleeping blue-eyed girl is soon a moral
tale of "pride goeth before a fall," except that Scornelia soon
gets up and rejoins the party. And (once again it is the great
value of the diarist) we learn a good deal about a rural frolick
in New England in about 1757. We might note the recurring
use of a couple of words which play prominently in Jacob Bailey's vocabulary: *complaisance* and *frolic*. I take complaisance
to mean "accommodating" and "polite." A frolic, sometimes
spelled "frolick," is a rural party or an "adventure."

Bailey records that it was not until ten the next morning
that he "found the kitchen," and that then he was sent for by
the lady with whom he had been talking the night before, and
with whom he now talked until noon.

And then—this may surprise you; it certainly surprised
me—he and the lady part after "promising to see each other

‡ Bartlet, p. 59.

frequently, but unluckily I never enquired her name—and not making a memorandum soon forgot her lodgings by which means our acquaintance was entirely dropped." Almost as an afterthought, he mentions: "She had a fine set of features, a piercing eye and was but a little more than twenty." And away she goes into the ether with the Welsh captain of transport and the Nymphs of Drury Lane.

By which we may infer that in Jacob Bailey's journal, life and fiction are intertwined, and we are not always certain which we are reading. Which is fair enough because he was writing this journal for himself, perhaps as notes for his future writing, but not at all for us 250 years later.

We might do well to remember this as Bailey takes up his first full day in London, 20 February 1760.

He goes first to Butler the Bookseller in Cheapside—which I think is important because first stops in his new life are important, and books are important in his new life—and then to the New England Coffee House, where he happens upon Mr. Greaton, who was also in London to be ordained. Greaton was later to become the Rector of Christ Church in Boston.‡ With the bookseller's advice and Greaton's help, Bailey was soon settled in lodgings (which are rather dear), and then sought out a tailor, but the fellow was not at home, then shared a bottle of wine with Mr. Greaton, and "rambled out into the city in search of adventures."

What follows will demand some explaining. What begins the evening is unsettling enough; what follows is more so. But the initial encounter:

we quickly reached the grand piazzas of Covent Garden but the weather being remarkably dirty we had not the pleasure of seeing those multitudes of amorous ladies which in more delightful seasons frequent these seats of gallantry—it was

*not long before a nymph neatly attired fell into our hands—
she affected a great deal of that modest refinedness which is
so very engaging in young females—it not being agreeable to
our purpose any longer to ramble the streets, we left the young
courtizan to engage some other admirer—we entered the
fountain tavern a most noted place for infamous wenches—
we were immediately showed into a curious apartment by a
person who had the air and appearance of a Gentleman—the
room was hung round with the pictures of those beauties who
frequent this house.*

Bailey has added to our knowledge of the era. There is available a well-known text for comparison: John Cleland's *Fanny Hill*, which is usually taken to be the first pornographic novel in English, published in 1749. Did Jacob Bailey know it? There is no telling. But Bailey does seem to share in certain of Cleland's attitudes: that is, first of all, that "amorous ladies" stalk the streets of Covent Garden. (The opening scenes of *Fanny Hill* take place in a brothel in Covent Garden.) Both Bailey and Cleland value politeness very highly. But Bailey would seem to think the ladies lustful, while Cleland sees them as sensual—and poor.

Both Bailey and Cleland seem to agree, though, that a failure of education can lead to a lady's entrance into the world's oldest profession. Fanny, recruited to the brothel, is seduced by the good times.

*… all that frolic and thoughtless gaiety in which those giddy
creatures consume their leisure made me envy a condition of
which I saw only the fair side.… Conversation, example, all,
in short, contributed to that house, to corrupt my native puri-
ty, which had taken no root in education …*

§ Cleland,
Fanny Hill,
p. 28.

¶ Cleland,
Fanny Hill,
p. 38.

"Frolic," note. But Cleland, to his credit, notices something that Bailey does not. Fanny admits that "I made a vice of necessity, from the constant fears I had of being turn'd out to starve."§ Starve.

This next bit is embarrassing, if understandable: Jacob Bailey was innocent for his age and even for his era, although clearly enough willing to seek education, along with Mr. Greaton—later, we should remind ourselves, to become Rector of Christ Church, Boston, Massachusetts. Bailey continues:

> *My companion called for a bottle of wine, but before we had finished it we were not a little alarmed by a mournful cry in the adjoining apartment—curiosity obliged us to listen with the utmost attention and by what we could gather from circumstances and few imperfect sentences a tender innocent creature had been drawn into this scandalous house, where some villain was compelling her by the most threatening language to sacrifice her virtue to his brutal desires—this enraged me to such a prodigious degree that if I had not been forcibly restrained I should certainly have broke into the apartment in order to rescue distressed innocence—*
>
> *This adventure began to give me a shocking idea of the villainy of mankind.*

So the villainy is noted. The trip has an educational purpose, almost a field trip, if you will. But the "mournful cry" was not perhaps much heard in New England, whereas Fanny in the London brothel sees (well, she's peeking) and hears: "Oh! … oh! … I can't bear it … It is too much … I die … I am going …"¶

All of Bailey's experience would have been written up that evening. Jacob Bailey and Mr. Greaton (is Greaton as innocent as Bailey?) have found themselves drinking in a brothel where they hear unsettling cries. But back at his writing table in the evening, with pen and ink, Bailey writes a story out of his observations, and labels it, "An Adventure," as if it grew out of his personal experience.

As we were strolling down Catherine Street my companion observed one of these creatures who offer their charms to every passanger, standing between the pillars of a spacious building he looked upon her which gave her confidence immediately to accost him—pray gentlemen, says she won't you please to walk in and take a glass of wine—we never tarried to return any answer but entered without ceremony—we passed thro a stately court and were shewn into a very handsome apartment hung round with painted curtains—person who conducted us was a pretty girl neatly dressed and certainly very young—my companion being engaged with his dulcinea—she took notice that I was alone—and coming up to me she accosted me in a modest tone "Pray sir shall I introduce another lady'—being fully resolved to see a little of the town I replied in haste, "Yes my dear" ... She retired upon this and in less than two minits returned with a beautiful young creature in company.—She was of the middle size very slender and had a waist exquisitely well turned—her eyes were black and piercing her features regular and finely adorned either by the hand of nature or some ingenius painter I cannot tell which—she was dressed in a brown putty sway sack and was every way richly ornamented—at entering the room she made a low courtesy and with a little forced reluctance was persuaded to take her seat—we called for liquors which came in great plenty—this raised the spirits not only of our misses but gave us an additional vivacity—my lady began to draw nearer, and quickly proceeded to take liberties in her conversation which would have covered the face of any modest woman with confusion. She took the bowl and gave the most obscene toast that ever goes round among the templars. Both these creatures had now grown so impudent that their immodesty was no longer confined to words their actions really surprised me, for tho I had often heard high storys of the London courtizans, yet could not forbear treating them as a little romantick till this evening which exposed their wickedness in the most glaring colours—

After drinking three or four bowls of mulled wine for every one of which we were obliged to pay 3 shillings, upon its being delivered into our hands—I arose and went to the door where I found a pretty little girl dressed all in white standing, I supposed she was looking out for some game—which gave the confidence to behave towards her in this manner—clapping my hand upon her bosom, which as Milton expresses it "hove amorous to the touch," I suddenly exclaimed, "O miss I am heartily glad to see you," but how was I confused when instead of her receiving the declaration kindly, she flung herself away from me in a rage, and with the utmost degree of scorn and spirit rejected the liberties I had taken—I was so simple as to think she might possibly be a modest innocent creature—who had taken shelter in this court from the weather it being very rainy, however after walking at a little distance I returned, humbly implored her pardon, and kindly invited her to take a glass of wine. She courtesyed and silently expressed a thorough reconciliation—upon which I made a low bow and joined the company I had left.

In less than a minit the Dulcinea followed me and I must confess that I had the weakness for a moment to lose all my resolution—She had something so sweetly engaging in her countenance, took her seat with so much decency and after-

wards managed her intrigues with such delicacy if I may be allowed the expression that it was enough to stagger even virtue itself.

I presently saw indignation kindle in the eyes of my former mistress, tho no kind of resentment escaped her tongue— my friend presently with drew with his partner and left me violently beset by unequal numbers—the youngest quickly perceived by my unguarded behaviour that I was vastly more attached to her than the other, which made her earnestly press me to retire into a more private apartment, her companion stepping out she instantly rang the bell upon which the maid entered—determined to see the frolick out—says I to the maid pray can you provide us with a place of retirement it must be above stairs well furnished the windows darkened with curtains and the bed curiously adorned for I am resolved to spare no expense in this night's entertainment—being an entire stranger who have crossed half the globe to revel with the beauties of London but this dear creature whom I have the pleasure to hold in my arms has ravished my whole soul with her adorable charms and has so engaged my attention that I can think of no other. They both stared when I told them I was a foreigner and gave me to understand that they looked upon this declaration only to be a piece of artifice I passed away the time till the maid returned in pouring out a supply of nonsense and declaring how happy I expected to be in a few moments.

When the maid entered I eagerly enquired wether she had every thing prepared for our reception—she answered standing with the candle in her hand that she would engage I should find everything to my liking well miss I replied if you can conduct us to a place so retired that nothing can intrude, so remote that none can ever find us—and so dark that no eyes can penetrate I will immediately follow you—they both stared at this

*strange speech and looked upon each other—even puzzled for
an instant—at length the maid replied—for you will find
the chamber secure from every thing but the sight of him that
sees every where—well miss, resumed I, if you cannot convey us beyond his notice the scheme will never answer—and
so fare you well. I then withdrew and was instantly followed
by my companion who had carried me here on purpose to see
the inhuman practices of the town girls—which shocked me
so much that I could not for several days think upon a woman
without abhorrence—*

 This frolick cost us £1.19s.

It's embarrassing.

To whom? is a broader question.

To Bartlet, the "adventure" was embarrassing without a
doubt. The priggish nineteenth-century biographer must
have blanched when he read the account of a visit to a brothel
on 20 February 1760. Would the smarmy ending have molli-
fied Bartlet? Not likely, even if he read that far. But the story
might have turned Bartlet against Bailey; might explain Bartlet's decision to conceal information and try to hide the identities of Bailey's mortal (and I'm being careful with this word)
enemies. No proof of this whatever, of course. Consider it a
possibility.

Embarrassing to you, the reader? On moral or literary
grounds? If you believe in absolute moralities, then you might
well think badly of Jacob Bailey. If bad fiction bothers you
deeply, you might also blush.

Embarrassing to me? Certainly. I consider myself a friend
of Jacob Bailey, and I wish he'd never written the story. I'm
embarrassed at having been caught reading it and now com-
menting on it. After all, Jacob Bailey did not publish this story.

Does "History" give me the right to go prowling around in his private life 250 years later?

Yes, it does.

Embarrassing because, once again (for the second time in two days), Bailey is pretending to pass for an Englishman. But we might want to consider that there was as yet no "America," no United States, and only a quasi-defection from Massachusetts, which was, after all, a British colony. Why shouldn't he consider himself an Englishman—a colonial Englishman? And isn't he mostly trying to reassure himself?

Embarrassing because the chosen girl is clearly very young? The age of his pupils at Kingston and Hampton, in fact; the same girls he feared would be ruined by rustic lads.

What Bailey has expressed would today be a thought-crime if found on his computer.

And he is rude to the girls—if this story is true. He quotes Milton while fondling the youngest girl without her permission, and she scolds him for the fondling. Another might consider the quotation an affectation. The girl (and her maid) do their best to accommodate his peculiar demands—and to what end? He backs out of the transaction on the grounds that God will not like it, which is at best an assumption, and a poor excuse, and smarmy in the bargain. The narrator is trying to cover up his guilt and/or timidity with an unctuous moral position. Not nice. Understandable, however, especially if we consider his just-confessed pathological fear of women when he was a boy. The narrator wants to look moral and excuse his behaviour as an educational experience. He has exposed the "inhuman practices of town girls." Distasteful, I would say.*

But what if the "adventure" is nothing but fiction? He frequently uses "adventure" as a label to slide out of his own experience into something larger, and he has already visited

* Bailey's interest was not perhaps uncommon. Near-contemporary artist Thomas Rowlandson satirized a parson found with a mostly-naked young woman in a watercolour entitled "The Curious Parson," which is extremely rude.

† Nor would Bailey's presence in the brothel have been so shocking or unusual as Bartlet might think it, or we might think it. Laurence Sterne hung out with members of the notorious Hell Fire Club, which staged sex orgies, and was himself well known for sexual liaisons. See Arthur Cash, *Sterne*, Vol. 2, pp. 182–3.

‡ Arthur Cash, *Sterne*, Vol. 2, p. 8, note.

the brothel with Mr. Greaton and been unsettled by the commotion next door. Was that the total of Jacob Bailey's experience at the brothel on Catherine Street? †

Look at his methods of composition as we have seen them before—in the story of the farmer's daughters, for example, which he tells when *The Hind* is at anchor off Nantucket. In that story he asserts that he has found a letter confirming the ruin of the girls. Here he gives us a similar "real" detail. He gives us the cost of the frolick: £1.19s. It was a good deal of money. Booze in brothels is notoriously dear. At that time the cost of a box at Drury Lane was 5s, and considered expensive. A seat in the top gallery was 1s. ‡

What if the story is a fiction in which the reader is to disapprove of the narrator—as in The Deacon's Story? Or was Bailey constructing a moral story in the brothel? Was the holy light to be shone on a wicked place, and the reader's belief in the story aided by the precise cost of the frolic: £1.19s.

The next day (21 February 1760), Bailey hustles around London trying to establish his financial credit with letters (and a necessary thing, too, considering the money spent at the brothel), and goes to the Drury Lane Theatre to see Mr. Garrick and Mrs. Cibber perform in *The Siege of Aquilea.*

I found myself extremely moved at the tender part between the mother and the son—and was not less charmed with the noble struggles between duty and nature which appeared in the character of the father … acted by Mr. Garrick.

He was also much impressed with Mrs. Cibber.

So in his first two days in London, Bailey has gone to a bookseller's, to a brothel, and now to the theatre. The sequence is instructive, and perhaps suggests his priorities at the time. But it would be fair to ask the reader to remember that less than a week before, Bailey thought he was going to die in the sinking of *The Hind*.

The Hind did not go under on February 15, but as he will learn shortly (on the 23rd), *The Ramilies*—the late Admiral Byng's flagship, which came alongside *The Hind* on the 15th—sank that evening with the loss of 734 honest tars; only twenty-five survived. It was the kind of event which could focus a man's mind wonderfully.

Different Kinds
of Education

Jacob Bailey was in England for little more than six weeks—
from the time he came ashore at Portsmouth on February
17 to the time he left London to return to North America
sometime shortly after the end of March 1760— but the experience was as important to him as his Harvard education.*

He gloried in the parks of London, long social strolls, joining friends and acquaintances for tea, or dining at their homes;
meeting with them in the coffee houses or taverns. There was
the best theatre in the English-speaking world. There were
unlimited books to be read. There was the magnificence of
London itself—its buildings, its immense size, its teeming
population of well dressed and not, of the eminent and the
wicked. He felt as one with the English, although not always
in agreement with them, and not always impressed with the
titled English. The women (he noted) were often very beautiful, even if some of them were no better than they ought to
be.

We ought not minimize the importance of the peripatetic
experience even if it was not especially dramatic. Travel *does*
broaden; it *is* an education. Walking opens the eyes as much

* Bartlet skips
everything in the
journal from the
time of Bailey's
arrival in London
until he meets
Dr. Bearcroft on
February 27. To
be fair to Bartlet,
he is interested
only in Bailey's
ecclesiastical
career.

as a visit to an art gallery. (He visited private art galleries, too, and took pleasure in the pictures.) A walk through London was an experience of a kind he'd never known, and a far cry from the roads of Rowley, Massachusetts, or even Boston. It was, after all, worth risking his life for—and perhaps (although he could not know this) his future.

He did not get around to seeking out Dr. Bearcroft, the Secretary for the Society for the Propagation of the Gospel in Foreign Parts, until February 27, and was softly chided for his tardiness.

He made no excuses—nor explanations, either. He'd been busy. Leaving the theatre after the performance of *The Siege of Aquilea* on February 21, he noted,

> *I reached my lodging after having passed thro crowds of drunkard bullies and whores where I had the pleasure of supping with a couple of young ladies—these behaved with so much modesty politeness and decorum—that I began to receive a more favourable opinion of the sex than I was ready to entertain the day before.*

Clearly his education made him revise his generalizations continually—which is not a bad thing.

But he was having difficulty turning his letters of credit into cash. He discovered that servants turned him away from people he needed to see. He was clearly not treated as a gentleman, and he soon found that servants expected bribes, which was a practice which Jacob Bailey termed *corruption* "throughout the kingdom." And he had no money to bribe them! The £1.19s he'd spent at the brothel must have invoked more anguish as his funds dwindled to the worrisome and on to the deeply concerned.

On February 22, he delivered a letter (from his patron, presumably) to "Mr. Richardson, the famous American Bookseller in Paternoster Row," who "expressed great satisfaction at hearing from Dr. Gardiner and was so obliging to me as to freely offer me the reading of any book while I tarried in London." For an avid reader, what could be better?

That evening Bailey recorded another "Adventure."

About this time happened a comical affair a handsome woman genteely dressed was observed by a Gentleman walking in Cheapside—as he approached nigh her he took notice that her situation was such as the most honest women often appear in. As he passed by her she looked so earnestly upon him that the Gentleman stopped and courteously asked her pray madam have you any favour to request of me —She replied with a great deal of seeming confusion, I have sir but am ashamed to propose it —pray madam says he taking her aside to the entrance of a court be so free as to lay your commands upon me—Sir, answered the Lady believing you percieve my conditon, and to confess the truth I longed for a kiss from the moment I saw you—the gentleman pleased with the oddness of this adventure freely bestowed a profusion of kisses—and after he had lavished enough to satisfy any reasonable woman—he desisted and asked her whether her longing was in any measure satisfied—pray sir says she since you are so obliging favor me with one or two more, with all my heart replied the other and fell to kissing again—till the lady cryed out enough sir. I humbly thank you the Gentleman walked away smiling to himself but he had not proceeded far before he perceived both his Gold watch and a purse of Guineas missing—which this fair creature had certainly taken in their tender interview, that

† The "guinea" was then a gold coin, worth approximately £1.1 s., or 21 shillings. Because it was gold—from Guinea, hence its name—its value would fluctuate with the price of gold. Much later, the coin itself disappeared, but the term "guinea" remained to denote £1.1s and the term was used in pricing various commodities. Clothing, for example, was often priced in "guineas."

she might have something wherewith to remember so kind a Gentleman.

So the vanity of the gentleman (oh, men!—is there no limit to the amount of flattery a man will swallow?) costs him dear. The Kissing Pickpocket has bested him, and after he has given her "enough kisses to satisfy any reasonable woman," too. It's a nice little story, with a good bit of irony in it, although we might dispute the exact location of that irony.

By February 23, Bailey is down to sixpence in his pocket. He learns of, and laments, the sinking of the *Ramilies*, "stove in pieces" on a huge rock. In the terrible storm, "vast numbers of ships were left upon the coast of Great Britain, Spain Portugal France and Ireland—many foundered at sea." When he again presents a letter of credit, he is asked to prove he is who he says he is, and in bad temper explains that he has narrowly escaped death in the great storm of the 15th—and (having regretted his temper) after leaving and returning, is given five guineas.†

The next day, he and Mr. Gardiner (son of his patron back home, and a law student in London) sought out a tailor and Bailey was measured up for a suit of new clothes, and made some new friends in the bargain. He dined that evening with the tailor and his wife "and we passed the night extremely agreeably till the hour of twelve." Late nights in London. The following day he dined again with "my honest taylor where I was cordially treated here I found a young clergyman designed for barbadoes and a Boston Gentleman and his lady who behaved very politely and gave me an invitation to frequent their lodgings.... Spent the evening with Mr. Greaton and Captain Diamond."

The next day, the 26th, having "procured my clothes and a wig," there was more socializing. Now he was fit to be seen in polite English society, and both the proper clothes and polite society were important to Bailey. The lack of proper clothes might well be one reason, in fact, why he waited so long before seeking out Dr. Bearcroft.

Dr. Bearcroft was pleased to receive from Jacob Bailey (on the 27th) the will of a Boston lady giving £1000 to the Society, and after gently chiding Bailey for his delay in appearing to the Society, Dr. Bearcroft informed Bailey that his examination was set for the day after the next, February 29th. That evening Jacob Bailey moved to more suitable accommodations, writing up the previous situation.

> *The family where I first lodged was something peculiar—the old lady an Apothecary's widow was perpetually excused with the gout—and another terrible disease often incident to widows—I mean an avaricious disposition—her two daughters were extremely ceremonious—and together with their mother sent every morning to enquire my health. I was charged for every thing I had here excessive high.*

We might agree that there are further notes of irony in this short passage.

On February 28, Jacob Bailey and Mr. Greaton had a pleasant chat with the Archbishop of Canterbury, Dr. Secker, who concluded by saying that, "upon the recommendation I was able to produce"—Dr. Caner had done his job well back in Boston—the Archbishop saw no barrier to Bailey's ordination.

And on 29 February 1760, Jacob Bailey presented himself to his examiner, Dr. Nichols :

‡ Hugo Grotius (1583–1645) was a Dutch jurist sometimes credited with the creation of international law in the seventeenth century. He drew on both history and the Bible for his arguments. Bailey will try something similar when he is brought before the Committee of Correspondence during the Revolution, only to be told that scripture has no place in the committee's deliberations.

Requesting me to sit, he proceeded to ask me a great number of questions concerning my country, relations, and education. I observed that my answers appeared to give him satisfaction. At length, examination came on. He gave me, first, the Greek Testament, and desired me to render a portion of it either into Latin or English, according to my inclination. He likewise gave me liberty to choose what book or chapter I pleased. I happened to open about the middle of the first chapter of Matthew, and passed through this part of my examination with ease. The next book he put into my hand was Grotius de Veritate.‡ Here I was not at my liberty, but he heard me to the first section in the Second Book, where I read off that and two sections besides, into English, without receiving any correction. The last part of the examination was, to render the Thirty-Nine Articles into Latin, and then to explain it. This I had the happiness to perform, not only to his acceptance, but even far beyond what I could wish. After I had passed through the several forms used on these occasions, he dismissed me, with a declaration that he had the pleasure to find me qualified, and would recommend me for ordination the next Sunday.

The report of the examination is carried in Bartlet's edition of Bailey's memoirs. Clearly Bailey is proud of his performance, and clearly, too, he is delighted to be performing as he had at Harvard. He demonstrated that he was a natural aristocrat—insofar as he was a classically educated man. The next day he would happen upon fellow candidates, and note that three of them were educated at Oxford, three others at Cambridge, and one fellow at a "private academy in France."

But William Bartlet does not include the next "Adventure," even though it is a story told *to* Jacob Bailey by his new friend (and son of his patron), Mr. Gardiner. On March 1, Bailey notes,

This morning while Mr. Gardiner and myself were at break-fast he entertained me with several adventures he had formerly been engaged in with his fellow templars. These young Gen-tlemen who are designed for the study of law are certainly the most lawless and profligate set of men in the kingdom

It is "An Adventure of young Templars."

About a dozen of these debauchees had been drinking till after twelve when they pulled out into the street, resolved beforehand to commit all the villainy in their power—they first assault-ed the watchmen and beat them unmercifully then entered a famous bawdy house near Covent Garden the procuress at their desire presented them with a number of pretty girls these they quickly handled almost in as rough a manner as they had a few minits past done the watch—the old lady and her inno-cent attendance were extremely enraged at this conduct and began to express their resentment not in the most gentle terms, these heady young Gentlemen already bent upon mischief and not afraid of the most daring enterprises immediately rushed out of the house and dashed all her windows in pieces—the jingle of this destruction was so musical in their ears that they continued their sport and scared almost every one of her occu-pation in this manner. At length meeting with a sedan in the street they overset it and stove it in a thousand pieces but were afterwards so honest as to make satisfaction when they were constrained to do it before Justice Fielding.§

§ The story was not new. Justice Fielding—who would be Henry Fielding, author of *Tom Jones* and brother to Sarah Fielding, author of *The Governess or The Little Female Academy*—died in 1754.

So—if we may draw a moral from the story told as experience by Bailey's young friend—the lawyers-in-training saw it as sport to terrify the girls of the brothel, and to vandalize the property. Well, what rights would a procuress have? Bailey

had seen the like behaviour in a legal scene with the humili-
ation of Ma Dilly in Boston in 1753. The attitude of course is
that of "boys will be boys," and there is no harm done so long
as the lads pay for the damage. Clearly it seems that the young
gentlemen students of the law are above the law—although
not above paying damages. But this was yet another instance
where Jacob Bailey learned of the power of the mob. Here the
mob learned quickly that it could overpower the Watch, and
thereby assert power over the law. It might be thought a good
thing for a lawyer to know first-hand.

Bailey continues to use his journal as notes for travel, and,
passing through Chelsea, mentions the famous Veterans'
Hospital.

But he is on his way to the Palace of the Bishop of London
at Fulham. There he will find examples of magnificence (Boston had nothing like this; even Harvard had nothing like this),
and some "obsequious villains." More learning experiences.
To reach the palace,

> *we rode along the grandest walk I ever saw … shaded by a*
> *fine range of stately elms … on the left was seen a canal like a*
> *small river winding itself … thro a noble artificial forest filled*
> *with a number of deer …*

Ceremonies follow:

> *His Lordship the Bishop of Rochester (Dr. Zachary Pearce)*
> *soon arrived, when we were called to his presence. Here we*
> *were obliged to subscribe to the 39 Articles. We were all shewn*
> *into the Chapel, where, after taking three oaths, we were*
> *admitted to deacons' orders by the Bishop, with the assistance*
> *of Dr. Nichols and another clergyman. When we returned*
> *from the chapel, we were conducted into a vast large Hall,*

entirely composed of the finest marble. It was arched over-head and was at least 20 feet high. All the walls as well as the grand canopy was covered with the most striking figures so that this spacious apartment might truly be said to be fine without hangings, and beautiful without paint. In the middle stood a long table covered with silver dishes. We sat down with his Lordship, the Bishop of Rochester, the Bishop of London's lady, and several others, being in all 21—We had ten servants to attend us and were served with 24 different dishes, dressed in such an elegant manner that many of us could scarce eat a mouthful. The drinking vessels were either of glass or of solid gold.¶ The Bishop was very sociable at table, but was seen to behave with a very important gravity.

¶ No, no, no, cries Bartlet. Merely gilded silver, p. 63.

Jacob Bailey is impressed. A deer park ... marble halls. Gold goblets. A Bishop who is a Lord. Bailey's former Congregational colleagues would have been appalled, but Bailey loves the splendour of the Church of England and all its finery. To us it might seem a small thing, and just a bit of gawking. But to the Congregationalists, now his enemies—although he might not realize it—his delight is nothing short of apostasy.

Next, however, come the "obsequious villains."

When we arose from the table we took our leave of his Lordship and passing thro the palace we found all the Halls and entries lined with those obsequious villains which great men in this Island keep to rob their friends and dependents—Nothing less than half a crown will suffice those who are out of livery and shilling we obliged to bestow on all the rest.

It really is a pretty sight for an American to see a stately figure in lace and ruffles with several pounds of powdered hair bowing and cringing almost to his feet as he passes along

* This is almost certainly an allusion to Benjamin Franklin, who in his youth as a printer in Philadelphia gathered other like-minded workers together to educate one another in what was termed the Leather Apron Club or the Junto. It remains probably the best educational method ever.

since he has frequently seen a plow jogger assume all the state of a nobleman—and a fellow in a homespun coat and leather apron* above moving his hat to the best man in the country—but alas! upon examination he will find this altogether a deception—the one is only complaisant because he is in a state of dependence and the latter rude for no other reason but because he enjoys a freedom inseparable from the will of another. Hence we may conclude that interest is the original of politeness.

A tidy little essay, is it not? He calls himself an American, and sees that the pride of the skilled workman in a leather apron is "dependent upon the will of another." He has seen "a plow jogger assume all the state of a nobleman." Himself?

Was there ever a man caught more betwixt and between? He's an American, but delights in the pomp of the Church of England. He has always admired fine manners, but notes that they are at heart nothing but interest. You bow to whom you must. The servants, the "obsequious villains," bow with their hands out.

Jacob Bailey returns to his lodgings with nothing to do, but happens upon his compatriot, Mr. Greaton, and the two of them visit Covent Garden again. "I took notice of two little girls not more than 10 years of age, endeavouring by every sort of insinuation to draw in some humble admirer." Education, education, and more education.

On March 5, Jacob Bailey records that he

waited upon the famous Mr. Benjamin Franklin, and received an invitation to dine * * * His son dined with us, a barrister-at-law. He is a gentleman of good education, but has passed away the flower of his youth in too many extravagances.

Aspects of the era are gathering more closely about Jacob Bailey than he or we might expect. R.C. Woodbury in 1932 notes he is taking this journal entry from William Bartlet's account. Bartlet provides the asterisks denoting … what? What's been left out? Franklin's bastard son, William, was educated chiefly in Britain, and will later become Loyalist Governor of New Jersey in opposition to his father. Later still, he will (possibly) be imprisoned by the Americans in the copper mines of Simsbury, Connecticut—according to one authority, Christopher Moore, and disputed by another. The breach between famous father and bastard son will never be quite healed. William was one of Benjamin Franklin's *errata*, the term Franklin uses for his mistakes, not uncommonly with women.

On March 14, Jacob Bailey—together with his friend Mr. Greaton, and another friend to be ordained, Mr. Morton— "walked abroad."

After rambling several miles we came to Moorfields, and passing through them, we entered the lane which leads to Mr. Whitefield's famous tabernacle. We saw multitudes of people crowding along from every quarter, to hear the entertaining impertinence of that gentleman. By the calculation I was enabled to make, I am sensible there was not less than ten thousand persons in and about the tabernacle. Here were many serious people of the lower sort, several of fashion, and a great number of villains, who take the advantage to pick the pockets of the innocent rabble.

So, "entertaining impertinence," and "serious people of the lower sort," as well as pickpockets. Bailey affirms a scene in Tobias Smollett's *The Expedition of Humphrey Clinker*, and

† Bartlet, p. 29. In the drawing there is a cock at the top of the steeple. See John Updike, *Couples*.

something of its ambiguity. Humphrey Clinker is a good fellow and excellent servant who becomes an evangelical preacher and something of a success before he is warned off popular enthusiasm. The evangelical movement unsettled serious people of the middle classes and the lower classes on both sides of the Atlantic, not least of all because it was popular. It lacked the validation of excellence, authority, tradition, or scholarship. Neither Latin nor Greek was required, but chiefly an open heart and a willingness to accept Jesus Christ as Saviour. Whitefield had been both received and rejected by Bailey's beloved Harvard. Whitefield was to leave his name to a community not far from Bailey's future missionary pastorate at Pownalborough. He is in fact buried at Newburyport, Massachusetts, as noted and depicted even by Bartlet in Bartlet's book on Bailey.† But Bailey was always wary of the evangelical enthusiasts, and would later attack them in the Annapolis Valley by way of satirical poetry. He was deeply suspicious of, and eventually opposed to, emotional Christianity.

❧

On 17 March 1760, Jacob Bailey was ordained a priest in the Church of England by the Bishop of London, Thomas Sherlock. Before the candidates met the Bishop, however, they received their licenses to preach, in return for £1.18s 6d. It would be churlish to note that the license was 6d cheaper than the adventure in the brothel.

But Bailey is at his best in showing us the Bishop.

We had the honor of being introduced to His Lordship's presence. He was sitting with his consort in a beautiful parlor, with his hat upon his head. When we approached him, he endeavoured to move, but with the greatest difficulty. We came around on the other side of the table, and saw, in the face of His Lordship, an object which at once excited horror and compassion. His face was swollen to a prodigious degree, and his tongue, infected with some terrible disorder, hung out of his mouth, and extended down his chin. The good Bishop, unable to speak, looked earnestly upon us, as if he meant to convey us a blessing.

‡ Remember the Irish Lieutenant of the Marines kissing the King's signature on his commission on *The Hind?*

Quite a scene. The holy moment; the disfigured bishop; the silence; the inferred blessing. In the right light, mixed with shadow (see Rembrandt) the occasion could mark a man for life, and perhaps did.

Two days later (on March 19), Bailey and Mr. Morton, "dressed in our robes and went, first, to wait upon Mr. Franklin." Wearing the robes was not, perhaps, tactful, and the occasion seems something of a challenge to the great man, but, "We found him and his son at breakfast, with several ladies, who prevailed upon us to take a dish of tea." Nothing more is noted except plans to return to dine on the following Thursday. If Bailey talked to Mr. Franklin, it is not recorded. Then Bailey and Mr. Morton attend St. Martin's and meet with many ranking ecclesiasticals. It turned out to be a most profitable day.

*From the chapter house we went directly to the treasury * * * there to the chancellor's house. Here we received £19 7s 6d, the royal bounty to all American clergymen after ordination. The king himself signed the order for the delivery of the money.‡ I cannot but thankfully acknowledge the goodness of Providence, this day, in succeeding my concerns, and so happily finishing the business for which I made this dangerous voyage to*

*London. I had the pleasure to be informed that the generous
Society had appointed me their missionary, with a salary of
£50 per annum, to begin last Christmas.*

Poor no more! Have we realized just how poor Jacob Bailey
was, only the week before? Why, he could never have married without some sort of income. And how was a gentleman
with no income to live like a gentleman? Alas, he never quite
solved this problem.

On March 22, Bailey rode to "the upper part of Bond Street,
and bought a number of books." Wealth, I would argue, is
best measured in books. A man of much money is poor without books. A man with several fine books is rich beyond measure. It is a personal measurement, I admit, but one reason
why I like Jacob Bailey.

Later the same day, Bailey spent some time "collecting articles I designed to take with me to New England, having first
visited the New England Coffee House, and agreed with Capt
Watt for a passage, first paying for it ten guineas."

He could pay his own way! He could *buy* books! Wealth!

On March 23, Bailey and Mr. Morton set out for the Royal
Palace in order to see his majesty—not, however, in a private
audience. "We arrived about eleven and were obliged to wait
amidst a prodigious throng of people who were assembled
there upon the same occasion." A bribe was paid (by a companion) to a Yeoman of the Guard, and they could now wait
in the guardroom until noon.

*Precisely at this hour the prince of Wales passed by with his
brother prince Edward—the former wants no advantag-
es either of person or fortune to render him extremely agreeable—his stature is what in Britain is called midling, tho in*

*New England he would rather be esteemed shorter—he carries
an open countenance expressive of mildness and humanity.*

*Prince Edward is of the shortest size and one of the great-
est rakes in Britain....*

*In another Gallery his Majesty passed along preceded by
the mace-bearers—and a large train of Gentlemen officers—
then followed the royal family—after which moved in slow
procession ... the Tripolitan Ambassador and his train—this
representative ... was covered with a long robe thrown carefully over his shoulders his bosom appeared all naked — his
chin was smoothly shaved but a long black beard on his upper
lip pointed to the right and left—with a white turban curled
like a serpent—this caused him to make an appearance awful-
ly majestick ...*

In the afternoon, he and Mr. Gardiner walk along the Mall.

*It is very diverting to take notice of the great variety of faces
and the splendid appearances of the ladies and pretty faced
beauties that are exposed at this season.*

*Among the persons of distinction I had an opportunity of
seeing was the famous Lucy Hooper the illustrious courtezan
her charms if ever she had any are now extremely blasted by
disease and age.*

A day of much pomp and some circumstance and an implicit
lesson that beauty does not last. Which does not seem to dim
its immediate effects.

*Such shining beauties never before struck my eyes as now
crowded along the spacious walk. A Gentleman was so smit-*

*ten by one of these fair creatures that he could not help discov-
ering the effects to every body present.*

We have some idea of what that must mean. Was the "dis-
covery" draped or undraped, do you suppose? Nor does Bailey seem much surprised. There is no moral horror expressed.
Who would have thought that an afternoon stroll could be so
adventurous or so theatrical.

On Tuesday, March 25, Jacob Bailey finds himself right in
the middle of some of the great issues of the day. In the morning he, Mr. Greaton and Mr. Morton all meet with Dr. Bearcroft of the Society, who gives them each a copy of *Leiland's
View of the Deistical Writers*, a present from the Prince of
Wales, and "several other excellent pieces." We can take it
that the Leiland book is exactly the kind of book which the
young Benjamin Franklin, setting it in type, said convinced
him to the contrary.

In the afternoon, Bailey and Mr. Morton call upon Mr.
Franklin at Craven Street.

*We had four ladies at table among the rest a very pretty young
one who with the others behaved with the utmost ease and
propriety.*
*They all dined in full dress without so much as taking their
hats from their heads. Nothing could possibly be more agreeable than the conversation, behaviour, and entertainment of
this afternoon.*§

So his visit to one the great figures of the Enlightenment is
devoted to women who wear their hats while they dine. Bailey was never much interested in the Enlightenment; women
were more interesting. Especially pretty young girls with
good manners.

Now follows another "Adventure," which features an "acquaintance."

As one of my acquaintance was walking Ludgate Hill, late in the evening, he espied one of those impudent females who frequent that region. She came up—accosted him with usual familiarity and desired that he would walk to her lodgings, he seemed readily to consent and followed till coming to a door she attempted to enter whence the gentleman seizing her by the hand, cried "Stop! I have walked with you a while and now you must accompany me. Where? replied the girl. To Bride-well," answered my countryman. This struck the infamous wretch with the greatest surprise and made her to entreat him for God's sake to forgive her, he took advantage of her conster-nation and extorted from her a promise to forsake her pres-ent way of living.

This from Abigail Adams' letter to Lucy Cranch; of course it was much later (1784) and in France. Cited by Jesse Lemisch in his edition of Benjamin Franklin's *Autobiography and Other Writings*, Signet Classics, New York, 1961, pp. 312–313.

Not a very nice story, but, taken together with all his other London experiences, shows Jacob Bailey was determined to write fiction which demonstrates virtue. It has again the problem from which he may never have escaped—the notion that women were lustful creatures bent on corrupting men. Only by calling on the resources of religion, or (here) the Law, could a chap save himself. But (again) the point ought be raised that Jacob Bailey was trying to do good. We ought not mock his innocence.

March 27 was devoted to Art. He and Mr. Morton "took our leave of Dr. Bearcroft," but "were first shown the beauti-ful paintings of Charterhouse."

We were conducted by the Dr. into a large chamber —the walls and ceiling were of prime white marble and curiously

*covered with a great variety of figures. The walls were hung
with some of the noblest paintings in Europe. Over the fire-
place was the founder of the Charterhouse, on the right hand
Charles the Second—and on the left the Duke of Buckingham,
but our seeing this place was attended with the same misfortune that always accompanies strangers when they are shown
any curiosities of London. They are not suffered to tarry long
enough to make any particular observations.*

That evening it was off to the theatre, where he saw David
Garrick perform in *King Lear.* The next day (March 28) was
"spent chiefly at the coffee house," and the day following, he,
Mr. Greaton and Mr. Spears (presumably the officer of *The
Hind*) and a Mr. McDonald dined together, but only Mr.
Spears accompanied Bailey to the Tower, where they were
amazed at the number of arms and armaments stored there,
as well as by their arrangement in figures such as rising suns
and rainbows.

There seems also to have been something of a zoo at the
Tower, for Bailey was much taken by a creature given to Mr.
Pitt by the Nabob of Bengal. "It is reported that no more than
five of these creatures have ever been seen." The description
is that of a cat of some sort, but "if anyone even the greatest
stranger offered to stroke him he would immediately stand
still."

That evening, he and Mr. Spears "went to the play."

The 30th of March Bailey spent walking around London.

*As I passed through St. George's Fields I took great delight in
viewing the vast numbers of people that were walking back-
ward and forward and crossing each other in every direction.*

The last day of the month concludes his comments on London and, by extension, on England, and those of important society. He went to dine with one Osborn at Grey's Inn.

> *Upon my arrival he was gone to wait upon some Nobleman—but his Lady understanding that I was in his library sent for me at the house. I found here a certain Governor's Lady with a young merry creature in the bloom of age —she was very handsome—gaily dressed, complacent in her behaviour, but extremely vain.*
>
> *When Mr. Osborn came in we sat down to table, had a good dinner, but the maid was the whole subject of conversation.*
>
> *She was well dressed, beautiful and had the air of a lady but carried a visible discontent in her face. This, Mr. Osborne took notice of and made himself a great deal of diversion at the expense of the poor creature's modesty for I must needs confess that many questions put to her in a way of banter which were far from being delicate.*
>
> *I had often been informed before I saw London that many people of fashion make it their constant practice to torment their servants in this manner merely for diversion—a very cruel and inhumane kind of pleasure to make any being whatever.*

So his stay in London concludes with commentary on Britain's class-structure. The maid is beautiful and has the air of a lady. (Is she then a natural aristocrat?) But it is a diversion for the master to tease her with indelicate banter which he is free to do because of his (and her) positions in English society. Bailey sees this behaviour as a failing in his hosts because it is cruel and inhumane.

In this frame of mind, Jacob Bailey leaves London. The next journal entry finds him off the Grand Banks of Newfoundland.

What has happened to the fellow who left Gloucester, Massachusetts, walking to Harvard, to Boston, to cross the dangerous Atlantic Ocean in winter on the man-of-war, *The Hind*, on which he almost died. He had left America a prissy puritan, and landed in England a far more humane individual, fond of his profane shipmates with whom he had faced death.

In England he saw himself as English—or at least asserted that there was no significant difference between an Englishman and an American. Yet he clung to the term American and unsettled the English with his naivety—denied admission by the headmistress of a school, probably mocked by the seller of walnuts, treated rudely by servants. He acutely observed that a country can be defined by its servants. In England, he found the servants rude (and grasping) and the masters rude to their servants.

But England was heaven to a man who loved books, paintings and the theatre. Once he had some income, he was a gentleman. Yes, he liked girls and mentioned every one he noticed. He liked young girls with good manners, before they acquired passions. He was innocent of passions of all kinds. He is always ambitious for virtue—and completely out of his understanding among the young prostitutes in Covent Garden. He has no idea of the sexual imagination. He can be blinded by his own innocence.

He visits the great Benjamin Franklin and notices (or at least records) that women wear their hats while dining.

But what had he achieved in England?

He had left New England a puritanical prissy young man who wanted to be good and do good and serve the divine will. But the experiences on board *The Hind* made him more humane and generous in his judgments. Facing death so closely seems to have made him understand human suffering in a context of natural—not divine—wrath. It is especially interesting that he remains friends with Mr. Spears of *The Hind.*

Gradually, throughout the six weeks or so he is in England, he becomes the kind and generous protagonist whose descendant is Captain Absolute in Richard Brinsley Sheridan's 1775 play, *The Rivals,* who asserts (in the theatre, note, which so upset William Bartlet) good common sense in the face of dangerous romance or fantastic fashion. A man of feeling, not rules. He becomes the gentle man.

He is constant in his devotion to writing. By keeping his journal, he preserves history. In his moral fictions, he attempts to satirize foolishness (the Kissing Pickpocket) and demonstrate goodness. However ludicrous we may find his "Adventure" in the brothel, we must grant it the attempt to bring a holy light into the bordello.

As he devotes himself to the arts by which we define excellence—the paintings, the plays, the books—we see Jacob Bailey as a defender of all that is best in the past: he becomes the servant of civilization. It is indeed through the arts that we see what we mean by civilization. Not the clothes of fashion—he was apparently always somewhat careless about clothes, even while noting their power—but the arts by which we see ourselves. Not policies, or even history. But I think that he who serves civilization becomes a gentleman. You might argue that.

The Kennebec: No Place for a Gentleman

Jacob Bailey had become something of a gentleman by the time he left London in the spring of 1760. He was a man of wide reading and some sophisticated experience. He had dined with people of note and achieved, by examination in Latin and Greek, a position in the Church of England. He had seen much of high society and low. He had dined at the home of Benjamin Franklin. He often "took a dish of tea" with polite people. Moreover, he was now a Harvard graduate with an assured British income.

Bailey arrived in the Kennebec* region in the summer of 1760. It was a frontier posting—not to his surprise in the least. It was no place for a gentleman; there would be no lazy afternoons taking a dish of tea with the ladies of the landed gentry here. This was logging territory. He knew what he was getting into the moment he was offered the position by way of Dr. Gardiner's friends a year earlier. William Bartlet's title for his edition of Bailey's journals was perfectly apt. Jacob Bailey was a frontier missionary, and it meant much of what we might imagine.

In many, many ways, Bailey was the servant of his patron,

* I am using the term Kennebec to note the area in which Jacob Bailey served as a missionary chiefly because it had then and since been a confusing number of names. When Bailey came to the area it was on the frontier of Massachusetts. Maine did not join the Union until 1820. It was sometimes called "Frankfurt," and other times "Dresden." It was "Pownalborough" in 1760, named after the then governor of Massachusetts. The "Kennebec" was the name of the river which ☞

flowed past the communities to the sea.
So the larger area—which Bailey would serve by horseback and boat—was "The Kennebec." One of Bailey's poems is entitled "Farewell to the Kennebec." These days the area might be designated by the name of its principal town: Wiscasset, Maine.

✝ Ross, p. 141; Bartlet, p. 88.

‡ Ross quotes Kershaw, *Kennebeck Purchase*, p. 146.

Dr. Sylvester Gardiner. Gardiner saw him as such, as did others. And Gardiner had definite plans for the Kennebec.

Dr. Sylvester Gardiner was the chief promoter of the Kennebec Company, which in 1753 obtained a charter for a large strip of land on either side of the Kennebec River. The Kennebec Company was essentially a land company, meant to turn a profit for its proprietors. Dr. Gardiner was the most active of the proprietors, and he both encouraged and subsidized settlement of the communities along the river.

But it was a primitive place, and poor.

Julie Ross records that Bailey found that "children in rags went barefoot throughout the winter. Half the houses are without chimneys—and whole families had scarce anything to subsist upon, for months together, except potatoes roasted in the ashes."✝

Ross provides insight into the community (Pownalborough) from the first census, in 1763–4 . There were 161 houses; 175 families, including nine negroes. In 1766, Pownalborough recorded seventeen frame houses, forty-five log houses, and fifty-four one-storey houses.

> *By far the most splendid house in the area was that of Jonathan Bowman. This Georgian mansion seated by the river and warmed by its eight fireplaces (one for each room) exhibited such eighteenth century interior accomplishments as a panelled room and a superbly carved staircase.*‡

There were other marks of the frontier.

The sight of Indians in the communities made the settlers uneasy, not least because the so-called French and Indian war was still underway, and would not be settled (and then uneasily) until the Treaty of Paris in 1763. Active fighting in North

America had only recently ceased the year before, in 1760. One of the causes of disputes between the English on one side and the French and Indians on the other was the insistence of the American colonists on pushing westward and occupying the wilderness.

Later, in 1766, Bailey wrote:

§ Bartlet, pp. 83–4.

¶ Ross, p. 141.

A great number of Indians frequent this Neighborhood. They are the Remains of the ancient Norridgewalk Tribe and lead a rambling Life. They support themselves entirely by hunting, are very savage in their Dress and Manners, have a Language of their own, but universally speak French, and also profess the Romish Religion, and visit Canada once or twice a year for Absolution. They have a great Aversion to the English nation, chiefly owing to the influence of Roman Catholick Missionaries, who, instead of endeavouring to reform their morals, comply with them in their most extravagant Vices, and teach them that nothing is necessary to eternal Salvation, but to believe in the Name of Christ, to acknowledge the Pope, his holy Vicar, and to extirpate the English because they cruelly murdered the Saviour of Mankind §

When Bailey arrived that summer of 1760, there was neither church building nor a house waiting for him. He went to live with one of the Kennebec proprietors, the surveyor Major Goodwin. The next year the new courthouse was built. It also served as an inn and general store.¶ But it was what it symbolized—legal matters; commerce—that attracted professional people (lawyers like the eminent William Cushing, for example) to the area. Bailey's early Anglican services were held in the courthouse as well.

It would seem, however, that the appointment of Jacob

* Ross, p. 135.
We might recall
that, when Jacob
Bailey failed
to secure testi-
monial letters
from Harvard,
Dr. Caner had
ready a letter of
recommendation
which Bailey
was sent around
to get signed by
prominent Bos-
ton Anglicans.

† Bartlet, p. 74.

Bailey as a missionary for the Church of England was not without ulterior motives. Julie Ross (in 1976), referring to the work of Charles E. Allen, questions the request ostensibly from the Kennebec residents to the Society for the Propagation of the Gospel for an Anglican missionary clergyman. The request came through the good offices of Dr. Sylvester Gardiner, and there is some suspicion that Gardiner wrote the request himself, and may have forged the names of those who signed it, and perhaps created others.* Gardiner was ever a keen supporter of the British crown and therefore the Church of England. He had ambitious plans for the area. The Congregationalists, on the other hand, wished to maintain their church supremacy throughout Massachusetts.

But Dr. Gardiner was quick.

> *In the year 1751, a number of Germans having arrived in Boston, the Plymouth Company [another, and confusing, name for the Kennebec Purchase], as an inducement to them to settle their patent, offered immediately to give each family one hundred acres of land ... pay their passages from Boston, to advance them six months' provisions, and to build them a house of defence against the Indians. The only conditions imposed upon the settlers were, that each should clear five acres of land, and build a house, twenty feet by eighteen, within three years.†*

Jacob Bailey himself was to comment upon the immigrants some years later in a communication to the *Boston Evening Post:*

> *The first settlers of west Pownalboro' [Kennebec] emigrated from Franckfort, in Germany, but upon enquiry it appears that*

not a single family came from that city or its jurisdiction. It is true that six or seven families, chiefly of French Protestants, who had been expelled from France for their religion issued from the neighboring territories; several other dutch Lutherans were collected from different parts of the Empire to which we may add a number of families from about Mount Billard, who speak a dialect of French.‡

So the Kennebec which Bailey found was largely populated by immigrants, not all of whom spoke English. It was, moreover,

A country filled with impenetrable forest, and thinly inhabited by people of several nations each differing in their religion, manners and language this naturally threw a prodigious gloom upon, a mind lately diverted with the gay scenes of London, and used to the noble pleasures of Society and conversation.§

Moreover, Bailey was stepping into someone else's shoes. Odd shoes. His predecessor as Anglican missionary was also an ex-schoolmaster, one Mr. McClenachan, educated at Glasgow University, a convert to the Church of England in 1754, and appointed to his position by the Society for the Propagation of the Gospel in 1755. Mr. McClenachan was a man of whom it was said, "when Mr. McClanachan was in the pulpit he ought never come out of it, and when he was out of the pulpit he ought never go into it," which is a striking encomium although it raises awkward questions of possibility. It was also said of him that he "occasionally indulged in the excessive use of ardent spirits."¶

But it seems that Mr. McClenachan was itinerant by nature

‡ Bartlet, p. 249.

§ Bailey, quoted by Ross, p. 132.

¶ Bartlet, p. 254.

* Bartlet, p. 78.

† Ross, p. 85.

‡ Ross, p. 85.

§ Ross, p. 85.

¶ Ross, p. 86.

* Ross, p. 86.

† Ross, pp. 85–6.

as well as by duty, and left without telling anyone—decamped, slipped off, vamoosed—while continuing to collect his missionary pay. He was later heard to be vaguely associated with churches in New England. It was a very hard life, being a missionary.

Bailey remarked that his clerical duties covered a vast area of "one hundred miles in length by sixty in breadth."*

But for Jacob Bailey it meant a solid income for the first time in his life, and he could afford to get married.†

Sally Weeks (Bailey called her *Almira* and thought about her a great deal on his trip to England) had been one of Jacob Bailey's pupils in Hampton, New Hampshire, when he taught school there in 1756. She was fourteen, then, and the youngest daughter of Colonel Weeks, a physician—and a Congregationalist. Ross remarks that "She had been early on his favourite and he had written numerous letters to her in which he included stories with a strong moral overtone."‡ Ross notes that these were the stories which he published while residing in Hampton.§ Were some of them also the stories from the Harvard Letters of 1756? Likely.

In any event, they "traded snuff boxes as a token of our mutual regard for one another."¶ Ross adds, "Gradually … Sally became less timid and accepted a 'set of stone jewels (earrings) which she had entreated Bailey earlier on to purchase for her'."*

But Ross relates that "Sally, because of her youth, seemed to waver in her affection for Bailey. After he left Hampton, she was upset at being teased by her family about the numerous letters Bailey wrote to her and she did not seem to reply."†

Bailey continued to woo Sally by letter—moralistic letters, it must be admitted—and at last persuaded her to marry him.

... the greatest unhappiness I feel is in being separated from you—from your pleasant conversation and Innocent smiles, which always afford me the most pleasing satisfaction — Indeed when I consider the many happy moments I have passed in your company not only when you were my scholar, but ... in our agreeable journey to Cape Ann, and more lately to New Market, you must forgive me if I take a little pleasure —You are one dear Sally whom I have loved from almost your infancy with the tenderest affection.... now can you be offended if I secretly wish it were in my power to make you happy in doing for you, the most tender, generous and obliging offices of kindness—but whether you will condescend to favor me with your smiles or not, listen once more I beseech you to the voice of friendship and continue to entertain the most sacred regard for religion and virtue ... ‡

‡ Bailey, quoted by Ross, p. 151.

§ See Ross, pp. 153–7.

Sally agreed to his entreaties and they were married in August 1761. She was eighteen; he was thirty. They lived first in the Kennebec in the run-down Fort Richmond, where Bailey was allowed to farm the nearby lands—back to being the plough jogger—but, because of the "Indian menace," they moved into the Pownalborough Courthouse with Major Goodwin and his family, where they were not especially welcome. Bailey believed it was not Major Goodwin himself who begrudged them residence, but Goodwin's family and, (Ross interprets), B and C: Jonathan Bowman and Charles Cushing, Bailey's Harvard classmates.§

Responding to the energies of Dr. Sylvester Gardiner, the communities along the Kennebec River began to thrive. Gardiner provided a sloop which established coastal trade with Boston, for example, and the grand three-storey courthouse was a mark of the area's ambitions. Artisans and tradesmen

¶ Ross, p. 143.

* Ross, p. 147.

† Bartlet, p. 70.

were encouraged to settle on the Kennebec. Two of Jacob Bailey's brothers were encouraged to establish a brick-making business, and another brother, Daniel, became a carpenter in the area.¶ Farming was widely undertaken and encouraged, but perhaps lumbering was the most successful commercial endeavour. The forests provided masts for ships—and maple syrup.

The central town, which had begun as "Franckfort," became "Pownalborough," and although it might appear from its paths and buildings to be a New England community, it was not, quite. The government structure was different, for one thing. It "was not governed by a town meeting…. the proprietors ruled…. the town inhabitants had very little voice in the running of the government."* It might more accurately be described as a "company town." The proprietors kept the best land for themselves and controlled all the trade—by means of Dr. Gardiner's sloop, for example—and as a result the inhabitants earned little and purchased dear.

There was religious controversy from the beginning—or at least since the re-invigoration of the Kennebec development by Dr. Gardiner. Other proprietors of the Kennebec development were Congregationalists, and they were perhaps not pleased with Dr. Gardiner's Anglican ambitions.

It should be clear that, on both sides, religious attitudes were inextricably entwined with political views. William Bartlet, when he came to write about Jacob Bailey nearly a hundred years after Bailey's arrival on the Kennebec, is at great pains to establish an Anglican presence in the area back to the year dot—or at least to the explorations of the original Plymouth company in 1607.† By the time Bailey arrived, a Congregationalist presence had been absent for some time—

as in nearby Georgetown (which lay within Bailey's purview), ‡ Bartlet, p. 85.

for example. § Bartlet, p. 85.

The original Presbyterian, or Congregational, Society in Georgetown, was destitute of a minister for years … commencing with 1752. During that time, it had been indebted to missionaries of the Church of England for all the regular religious services which it enjoyed. Indeed, Mr. Bailey had frequently preached there. ‡

But had a dissenting clergyman been in residence and preaching, that person would have received the religious taxes of the community. This was, after all, Massachusetts. But the Georgetown treasurers

are determined to prevent us from drawing the rates belonging to the Church people, unless we can recover them by law-suit … there are £400 to £500 already in their hands. §

So to the volatile mixture of religion and politics we can add money.

But Bailey carried on with his missionary work. The intentions were noble; the conditions difficult.

While I resided at Frankfort, I observed, with concern and compassion, that the French and Dutch children were likely to be brought up in ignorance, for want of a school. This induced me to offer to instruct them gratis, but travelling was then so very difficult, and many were in such necessitous circumstances, that I had but a very few scholars, and when winter came on, nothing of this kind could be continued…. The first summer of my Mission, I officiated at Georgetown every third Sunday,

¶ Bailey, quoted
by Bartlet, p. 91.

*and was constrained to endure a great deal of hardship and
fatigue, being obliged to travel by water no less than eighteen
miles. Once, I remember, on the last of November, after being
eight hours on the water on my way to Georgetown, without
anything either to eat or drink, it was my misfortune to be lost
in the woods, where I was exposed all night in the open air to
a most severe storm of wind, rain, thunder and lightning.*¶

It was Dr. Gardiner who contributed most of the funds
required for the construction of a church building (which was
to become St. John's) and a parsonage for Jacob Bailey and his
family. The church building was available at last for worship
services in November 1770, and the house in March 1771—
although workmen were still living in the house and working on it when the Baileys moved in.

Immediately there was a challenge—in the form of a challenge to the Anglican Church's right to the land. It was almost
certainly a challenge to Dr. Sylvester Gardiner's plans for the
area, but Bailey was an agent for those plans, and thereby
found himself caught in the middle. In Bailey's mind, however, church considerations of the present took precedence over
Dr. Gardiner's intentions. When rent for the disputed land
was demanded, Bailey paid it. Dr. Gardiner was very angry
with him. On 15 October 1772, Bailey wrote to another former
Harvard classmate, the Rev. W.W. Wheeler, who had been for
a time—at Jacob Bailey's request and recommendation—the
Anglican cleric at Georgetown:

*I sincerely regret your absence from this country, which leaves
me wholly exposed to the merciless rage, I will presume to say,
of the vilest miscreants on earth. You have doubtless heard*

that I have been expelled my habitation; and with a view of preserving the church from destruction I took a lease of the parsonage house for six months. Dr. Gardiner was extremely offended at my proceedings. He wanted me to engage in a law suit with [M], but in the opinion of good lawyers, fully acquainted with the circumstances, there was hardly a bare possibility of success. There is now liberty of redemption till the last of next July, and if the Doctor would compose himself to reason, the affair might easily be accommodated. But this gentleman was certainly wrong to erect the church and house upon disputed lands, contrary to repeated remonstrances. At Convention I had a melancholy time. The Doctor made his complaint against me to the clergy, accused me of sacrilege, and, if I understand the matter, endeavoured to obtain their interest against me with the Society.... I am sorry, however, I took a lease, though my intentions were for the best. I believe it would have been better if I had wholly quitted the house and refused to commence a lawsuit about the matter; and if all should now be accommodated I am in a very bad situation, having already expended near a year's salary, and must be a slave to my successor.*

* Bailey, quoted in Bartlet, p. 342.

† He ought not be confused with his brother, William Cushing—later a justice of the United States Supreme Court—who was established as a lawyer in the Kennebec area when Bailey arrived in 1760. There is no indication that William Cushing had any animosity toward Jacob Bailey.

Matters are now about to become murky, complicated, and with several long-term effects, most of them bad for Jacob Bailey.

"M" was Jonathan Bowman, classmate of Bailey at Harvard. Bowman stood sixth on the class list, just below John Wentworth. We must remember that the list was arranged according to prominence of one's family. Bailey is dead last. Charles Cushing stands first.† Charles Cushing will be designated "N" by the biographer William Bartlet.

Why does Bartlet, in 1853, try to conceal the names of Bowman and Cushing? There is no obvious answer. One possibility which occurs to me is that their families remained prominent in Maine and Massachusetts in 1853. The more I have read Bartlet's *Frontier Missionary*, the more I have become convinced that it was censored—probably by Bishop Burgess, who wrote the Preface. But to be honest, I have no evidence whatsoever to support this interpretation. I am relying on my years of reading. I am using my intuition.

Was there any enmity between Bowman, Cushing and Bailey at Harvard? Not that I could discover. Did Bowman and Cushing dislike Bailey because Bailey sought to become a gentleman? It is quite possible that they considered him a jumped-up little *arriviste*. A ploughjogger with ambitions to virtue and excellence. Or because they thought Bailey a prissy conceited goody two-shoes, who thought to rise in the world by being better than his betters? All are possibilities.

Or was their opposition to Bailey simply an extension of their opposition to Dr. Gardiner? And was that opposition from within the Kennebec Purchase as well as outside it? Bowman was apparently a cousin of John Hancock, who was also a proprietor of the Kennebec Purchase. Was there a battle going on for control *within* the land company? There was apparently a ruling committee of ten within the proprietors, and it was there that Gardiner exercised his control. Was Gardiner in that group, and Hancock not? Was Bowman in fact living (well) in the Kennebec as Hancock's representative? Was Bowman's treatment of Bailey therefore part of commercial politics as well as Massachusetts politics? Quite probably.

Had Dr. Gardiner used his power within the proprietors

to grant land to the Church of England to which he had no right?

‡ Allen, p. 7.
§ Allen, p. 3.

In Charles Allen's view, the Revolution on the frontier of Massachusetts was less a battle of political wills than it was a war of religious denominations. The Puritans would accept no church but their own.‡ Worse, "Massachusetts Puritans cared little about religion in the wilderness except to oppose somebody who might interfere with that system of fraud which they dignified by the name of trade with the indians."§

We should perhaps remember that Massachusetts carried its theocracy into America in the years after the Revolution (in the attitudes of William Bartlet and Bishop Burgess, for example) in its famous (or infamous) Blue Laws, when "Banned in Boston" could make a book a bestseller everywhere else. After the Revolution many Americans wished to continue their Anglican worship, but the British were having none of that, and refused to consecrate any Bishops for the Episcopal Church, as the Anglicans became in the U.S. So the Episcopalians went to Scotland, since the Scots were willing to consecrate American bishops, and the Episcopal Church carried on, and carried on its influence especially among the upper classes and, perhaps, in the attitudes of Bishop Burgess and William Bartlet, in Massachusetts. And, as we know, the doctrine of separation of Church and State has been continuously challenged since by various religious denominations.

Both Bowman and Cushing arrived in the Kennebec with the Pownalborough courthouse in 1761. Both received Massachusetts appointments. Bowman became a judge of the Massachusetts Probate Court. Cushing became High Sheriff. They both owned a great deal of land and both dealt in lumber.

But the animosity between Bowman and the Church of

¶ Bailey, quoted by Bartlet, pp. 93–4. Interesting behaviour, and quite bold. He seems very sure of himself and believes he has the power to mock not only Bailey, but the Anglican Church itself. On the one hand, it seems more the behaviour of, say, an angry atheist, than a dissenting Christian, but the "corrections" would seem to indicate religious doctrinal differences.

England was by no means confined to disputes about land. Bowman sometimes attended Bailey's services, and "commonly behaved with a great deal of irreverence, especially at prayers." Moreover:

> ... *when I received a number of Common Prayer Books from the Society, he took the liberty to scratch out several sentences in all that he could procure to his hands ... he generally behaved with great indecency, contriving, by a multitude of boyish tricks, to make the women smile; and sometimes he has taken a primer, instead of a Prayer Book, and read out from it with an audible voice ... Instead of money, M [Bowman] used often to put into the contribution box, soap, scraps of paper, newsletters, and once a pack of cards ... took the liberty of dispersing several Common Prayer Books, without my knowledge, having first corrected them agreeable to his taste, and when I afterwards reproved him for the liberty he had taken with me, both in a public and private capacity, he replied that he had treated me just as I deserved, and as for those things he had erased from the Prayer Book, they ought not to be in it.* ¶

The conflicts in the community were thus demonstrated by behaviour which was at once ludicrous, childish, nasty, mean and personal. It would get worse.

For the most part, life carried on in its usual everyday way. There are problems which have nothing to do with doctrinal or political disputes. Bartlet tucks this incident away in an Appendix to *Frontier Missionary*. It is contained in a letter which Jacob Bailey wrote to his brother-in-law, Joshua Wingate Weeks, who was then an Anglican clergyman in Marblehead, Massachusetts, dated 6 February 1773:

*I lately published a young fellow to Mr. Ridley's daughter immediately after service. Another young woman forbad the banns, alledging that he was under engagements to her. The next morning they paid me a visit, and the man acknowledged that he had solemnly promised himself to both, and begged that Esther Kendall, the girl present, would release him. She declared herself willing, but was under scruples of conscience on account of her promise, which was in the following words: "I wish I may never enter into the kingdom of heaven if I marry any other man," and desired me to give my opinion. After a long dispute the fellow declared, before witnesses, in favour of the girl's character, and gave his consent that his publishment to her rival might go on, but the next day Mrs. Ridley forbad it again, and the poor fellow was left absolutely destitute, for Esther absolutely refuses to marry him, but imagines herself obliged by her promise to live single all her days. Now I should be obliged if you would give me your sentiments.**   * Bartlet, p. 344.

A fine conundrum for a pastor, to which there is no easy answer. For Esther, life today and life after death are continuous, and her vows of the present carry on into eternity. Her belief tells us something of religious belief in the era. If we need a homely example of life and religion in the eighteenth century on the frontier of Massachusetts, we need look no further. We are indebted to Jacob Bailey (again) for dramatizing the scene and quoting the girl.

Other virtues of Jacob Bailey on the frontier are perhaps best demonstrated by his devotion to his clerical duties. In his Appendix to *Frontier Missionary*, Bartlet quotes from the available Bailey journals without comment. Much that is revealed is commonplace, except that it indicates Jacob Bailey's daily life and duties. Some notes are ominous.

1774

January 13th Andrew buried.

16th—Sunday. 50 persons at church. Baptized Stephen Numphas Twyecross and David Person Bailey.

17th Married Daniel Dudley and Susy Densmore

February 1st. Set out for a journey up river. Lodged at Mr. Gardiner's. Baptized William Gardiner Warren.

2nd At Esq. Howard's. Lodged at John Gatchell's. At Mr. Hob's, Petty's and Fort Halifax.

3d. Accompanied by Dr. McKecknie five miles; arrived at Deacon Chase's a little before dark.

4th Went to Mr. Heywood's. Saw several Indians

5th Visited the Indians, Capt. Out's, and several of the new settlers.

February 6th—Sunday. 40 persons present. Baptized Eliza Pratt, Benja. Noble, Priscella Emery and Joanna Malbone.

7th. Rode to Mr. Petty's. Baptized Sarah Spencer, Amos Pochard, Abigail, Mary Isaac, and Charles Pechin, and Mary and Martha Collar

8th. At Esq. Howard's. Mr. Gardiner's. Baptized Enis, aged 128 [we may take this as a misprint], and John Thomas, Polly, Matthew, and Nelly Gaslin.

9th. At home.

21st Committee meeting.

23rd. At Capt. Callahan's. Met Dr. Hicks, from Boston.

25th. Open Andrew's grave. Find his body gone. Present, 12 persons. [A footnote is added, probably by Bartlet: "A negro slave of Major S. Goodwin. His body was used for the purposes of anatomy."]

March 3rd. Rode to Mr. Gardiner's.

March 4th. At Mr. Hankerson's and Cowen's. Baptized Polly and James Cowen. Lodged at Mr. Gardiner's.

5th. Arrived home.

6th Sunday. Cloudy and heavy rain. 70 persons at church. Contribution: 6s.

April 2. Baptized Thomas Brian. Crossed on the ice.

12th. Ice breaks up in the Kennebeck.

13th. At night. Bodfish and Mercy Goodwin come to be married, but refused.

14th. Fast Day. 30 persons at church.

24th Sunday—100 persons at church. Contribution, 16s

28th This day Peter Nephew and his wife Jenny ran away †

May 7th (Rev) Mr. Weeks and Mr. Ward arrive here.

9th. On board, Capt. Callahan. Three vessels in the eddy, loading at Dr. Moors.

11th (Rev) Mr. Weeks sets off home.

13th Mrs. Bailey delivered of a daughter, about 8 in the morning.

22nd. Sunday. 100 persons at church. Contribution £1.2.6 Baptized Mary Bailey.

30th The child dies about daylight.

31st The child buried; 36 persons at funeral.

June 10th. Mr. Gardiner's boy, Jo, suddenly killed. (Rev) Dr. Shefford and another stranger. [Bartlet adds a footnote: "A Lutheran minister, settled, at that time, at Broadbay, now Waldoborough. After Mr. Bailey left Pownalborough, Dr. Shefford was sent for and baptized the children of George and M.J. Mayer, members of the congregation of St. John's Church."]

16th. Baptized Margaret Patterson, daughter of P. Call.

18th. Rode to Georgetown. Lodged at Mr. Drummond's.

19th Baptized Patrick Drumond, Mary Pechlin [Bartlet here inserts a question mark.], Hannah Hollowell Rogers, and Elija Williams.

20th Rode home.

† Jenny and Peter Nephew were Bailey's indentured servants.

25th Sunday 120 persons at church. Contributions £2.17.0

July 24th Sunday. Showers. Warm and muggy weather. 30 persons at church. Baptized James Carney.

August 1st Baptized Jane Nephew

10th At Cobbosee-contee.

29th Abroad. brought home 12 sheep.

September 7th. Set off with Dr. Tupper, for Boston. Lodged at Stone's. Insulted the next morning.

8th Lodged at Milliken's. Ill treated.

9th Lodged at York.

10th Dined at Col. Warner's. Lodged at J. Weeks'.

September 11th—Sunday. Lodged at Newbury. The country all in commotion.

12th Arrived at Marblehead.

13th Reached Boston about sunset.

14th. Convention sermon preached by Mr. Seargent

15th Dined at (Rev) Mr. Walter's.

16th Rode to Marblehead.

17th—Sunday. Preached at Marblehead. Baptized 3 children.

18th At Salem

19th Bound homeward. Lodged at North-hill.

20th Dined at J. Weeks'. Lodged at York.

21st Lodged at Falmouth

22d Lodged at Mrs. Loring's.

23rd Mobbed at Brunswick. Got home at night. Mr. Gardiner at my house.

26th Abroad. Fled from the mob. Lodged at George Mayer's.

28th Returned home.

29th Stephen Marson buried.

Most of Jacob Bailey's days are common enough. He does his job. He marries couples and baptizes their children. He notes the attendance at church and the sum of the collection. He buries people. Quite often he travels in foul weather to perform the necessary ceremonies. He refuses to marry one couple (the woman presumably a relative of Bailey's sometime host and a proprietor), but gives no indication of his reasons. He is on the road so much and so often that he deems it worth comment when he is at last "at home." He notes the weather, the stormy days and the date the ice goes out of the river. When he goes to Boston, he stays with his wife's brother, Reverend Joshua Wingate Weeks. He visits his patron, Dr. Gardiner, often.

‡ My grandfather found a very similar story in a history of our local county in Indiana. He read it to me, punctuating with spats of tobacco juice into a Maxwell House coffee tin, and said that the local physician who had stolen the body was caught and fined ten dollars. Grandfather spat. *Ting.* "'Course, it was worth more in those days."

Necessity makes Jacob Bailey a farmer as well as Anglican priest, and he notes when he brings home twelve sheep.

But there are less common notations, too. A dead slave is buried and, when his grave is visited some three weeks later, it is found that the grave has been opened and the body taken. Bartlet (presumably) says that the body has been taken for purposes of studying anatomy—which seems at once ghoulish, educational, and scientific, and certainly of its time. It was a comparatively new way to obtain knowledge—and, if my grandfather's stories are to be credited, certainly continued throughout the nineteenth century.‡ A slave's grave could be disturbed with relative equanimity.

Indians are noted—and it is noted, too, that Bailey goes to talk with them. We get the picture of the traditional missionary among the aboriginals. We learn that Peter Nephew and his wife, Jenny, have run off. They were Bailey's indentured servants. (They have surnames; "Andrew," the slave, has none.) We might remember the incident aboard *The Hind*,

§ Bartlet, pp.
350–1.

¶ Bartlet, p. 351.

where Bailey saw a slave taken from hiding and reclaimed by his owner.

Mary, infant daughter of Jacob and Sally Bailey, is born, baptized, and buried, all in under a month.

Then, at the end of September 1774, tumultuous events even along the Kennebec. Bailey is insulted and mobbed.

Bartlet provides a letter from Bailey to an unknown person, dated only "October, 1774."

We have been in the greatest confusion and distress imaginable, occasioned by continual mobs and insurrections ... before my arrival at Falmouth [now Portland], five hundred men in arms had been to visit Mr Tyng, who was mobbed a few days before, at North Yarmouth. The country is in such a violent commotion, that my friends advised me not to lodge at a publick house.§

And,

... I was stopped at Stone's, in Brunswick, and accused of being a Tory, and an enemy to my country. They urged me to sign, and upon my refusal, protested they would visit me and Col Cushing the following week.¶

It is interesting that here the patriots consider Col. Cushing an enemy. Perhaps understandably—he is the high sheriff of the county in a colony of Great Britain.

Moreover:

I arrived at Pownalboro about dark, where I found the people in great consternation. A furious mob at Georgetown were *running about in search of tea, and compelling people, by force of arms, to sign the solemn league.* Another was raging up the river, within twelve miles. They had already destroyed one hundred and fifty pounds of tea for Esq. Hussey, and thrown his hay into the river. Mr. Gardiner had fled from their fury, and tarried with us all night, expecting every moment to be attacked, as Lovejoy had already invited them among us, and threatened the utmost revenge upon me, Ridly, Maj Goodwin, etc. Mr. Gardiner returned after service, but was obliged to fly that evening, and escape to Boston. About midnight, one hundred and fifty men, armed with guns and various weapons, surrounded his house, demanded a sight of him, and insisted upon searching for tea. Mr. Hazard, a gentleman from Rhode Island, entered into a parley with their leaders, and they firmly engaged that none, except five chosen men, should enter into the house; but they quickly broke their engagements, rushed in, rifled the house, broke open his desk, and perused his papers, and after being treated with several gallons of rum, they stole Mr. Hazard's buckles, and then inquired for Mr. Jones, the surveyor. They insisted upon his signing the covenant, upon which he stripped open his bosom, and told them they might stab him in the heart, but nothing should induce him to sign that accursed instrument. They seized him with violence and threw him headlong into the river, and then dragged him about until he was almost torn to pieces but to no purpose. †*

* The "Boston Tea Party" took place the previous year, on 16 December 1773. John Hancock was in on it up to his eyeballs, as was Samuel Adams. Purveyors of tea, even drinkers of tea, were considered enemies of the patriots.

† Bartlet, p. 351.

There is more, and all of it equally violent, and all of it tied to the tax on tea which instigated the so-called Boston Tea Party of 16 December 1773, which in popular American history is told as an evening of wild fun in which the local lads disguised as Indians made the point that the tax was resented

‡ Bartlet, pp.
351–2.

by throwing the tea into the harbour. Nothing like the rum-soaked violence noted above.

But there is something of a mystery (one among several, as we shall see) in this Bailey letter of October 1774. Before he takes up his own concerns, Bailey notes that the mob fell upon

> *Col. Cushing, returning home … They called him a—Tory, and demanded surrender of his commission. He assured them that he had taken none under the present government, and after distributing money among them, he was suffered to escape.*

Later in the same letter, Bailey notes that

> *I will refer you to Mrs. Bailey's letter … and only remark that their rage was chiefly directed against Bowman, Maj. Goodwin, Ridley, and myself, because, as they alledged, from the instigation of Lovejoy, we opposed the solemn league.*‡

Interesting. The leader of the patriots seems to be one Captain Lovejoy. His rank might be considered simply honorific, but likely was much more. He held a commission in the Massachusetts militia, and that likely meant that he had extensive military training, and even perhaps combat experience. Not a chap to be treated lightly.

Interesting, too, that Bailey refers his (unknown) reader to Sally Bailey's letter. She is carrying on their mutual correspondence. A later Committee of Correspondence will accuse her of "talking too much."

But most interesting is where the lines are evidently drawn in October 1774. The patriots are represented by Capt. Lovejoy. But considered to be on the British side are Col. Cushing,

Bowman—the chap who played the fool at Bailey's church services, and defaced the Books of Common Prayer—and Major Goodwin, one of the proprietors (with Gardiner) of the Kennebec Purchase. Very shortly there will be a somewhat different alignment, and then things will turn very nasty for Jacob and Sally Bailey.

ELEVEN

The Villains

John Adams came to the Kennebec in 1765. Did he visit his old classmate, Jacob Bailey, now Anglican cleric in Pownalborough? There is no evidence he did—although it was a very small place; it would have been easy. Jacob Bailey appears nowhere in McCullough's biography of John Adams. The correspondence between Bailey and Adams, when both were unhappy schoolmasters in 1755, came to nothing.

But John Adams might well have visited another classmate, Charles Cushing. Adams did write to Cushing, and McCullough quotes from the letter. Stirring stuff:

> Upon common theaters, indeed, the applause of the audience is of more importance to the actors than their own approbation. But on the stage of life, while conscience claps, let the world hiss! On the contrary if conscience disapproves, the loudest applauses of the world are of little value.*

Charles Cushing and Jonathan Bowman are the villains of this story. In their treatment of Jacob Bailey, and in their political lives, they have much to answer for—as Bailey attempted to ensure.

Here is what Bailey wrote of the two men, as reported by Julie Ross from Charles Allen's *History of Dresden:*

* McCullough, p. 38. Perhaps Adams was right in thinking that applause was more important than the respect of other actors in the eighteenth century, but certainly that is not true now. Theatre talk has much criticism of the actor who "milks applause," or plays the audience rather than the character. Such an actor is considered a ham, and is not respected backstage. But young John Adams undoubtedly believed that conscience was more important than public approval, and it does him credit. What's more, he demonstrated his ☞

belief by defending the British soldiers in the so-called "Boston Massacre," and even later in his career, he was willing to take unpopular stands. It is also true that many politicians since have proclaimed that it is more important to do what is right rather than what is popular, but few of them follow their conscience so carefully as they follow the polls. Today, Adams' views seem quaint, grandfatherly.

Jonathan Bowman, kinsman of John Hancock, was advanced by the interest of his uncle Thomas, Dr. Gardiner, and other gentlemen of the Plymouth Company, to a position of Justice, Clerk of the Courts, Judge of Probate, and Register of Deeds. Educated at Cambridge, he was distinguished by a subtle and tricking genius, rather than by application to study. Silent, concealed, and designing, with interest as his ruling passion, base and false in his friendships, and implacable in his resentments, he had a perfect command of himself, and seldom or never showed anger. A leader of men who generally feared but did not love him. Imperious in his bearing. As to religion, it consisted chiefly of contempt for the clergy of all denominations and inveterate antipathy to the Church of England.

Col. Charles Cushing lived about a mile from Mr. Bowman. Although educated at college, he afterwards took little pains to improve his mind by reading or study. As magistrate he was led to be closely connected with Bowman, who had a great influence over him, although there was little personal friendship. He entered warmly into Bowman's schemes, and although at first settlement in Pownalborough he professed to be a churchman, he afterwards joined Bowman's effort to settle an independent minister, as the most effectual method of lessening the influence of Dr. Gardiner, whose enterprise and influence in the country were the objects of their envy. They regarded him as a sovereign of the east, and from that libelling principle peculiar to Republicans and Independents, they determined to destroy his distinction. Bowman thoroughly understood Cushing, and used him to advance his schemes. The latter was naturally sociable and complaisant and his manners engaging, but he was haughty, proud, and imperious, with a most exalted opinion of his importance. When he once conceived an ennmity, no concession could soften him into humanity.✝

Bowman and Cushing made at least four attempts to eliminate Bailey's mission in the Kennebec—and perhaps more, depending on how one counts. Bowman's childish behaviour in church might seem like little until added to his defacing the Books of Common Prayer to suit his religious sympathies.

Bailey's church building, St. John's, was completed in November 1770, and Bailey and his wife moved into their parsonage in March 1771, but in 1772, Jonathan Bowman, Judge of Probate Court and Register of Deeds, claimed the property on which the parsonage was built for himself, and a week later, Charles Cushing, Sheriff of Lincoln County, ordered Bailey out of the parsonage. Bowman apparently purchased a previously unknown claim to the land. His judicial appointments came in handy.

William Bartlet tells the story like this:

The origin of this claim is somewhat obscure. As near as can now be ascertained, it seems to have been this: A person who had been an officer in the Church at Pownalborough, and whose general conduct, both before and after this transaction, seems to have been friendly, claimed the land, as administrator of the estates of some persons deceased … How the claim was transferred to M [Bowman] does not appear.✝

Ross notes that the administrator mentioned was Major Goodwin, the surveyor of the Kennebec Purchase, with whom Bailey had lived in the courthouse when Bailey first came to the Kennebec.§ Goodwin plays perplexing roles in Bailey's

✝ Ross, quoting Allen, quoting Bailey, pp. 191–2.

‡ Bartlet, pp. 96–7.

§ Ross, p. 182.

¶ Bartlet, p. 96.

life. Goodwin was a vestryman of St. John's, for example, but seems to have been sometimes on one side of the political divide, and sometimes on the other. Jonathan Bowman's second wife was Major Goodwin's daughter.

Jacob Bailey then agreed to pay rent to Bowman—which made Dr. Gardiner very angry indeed. Bailey insists he was acting on the advice of lawyers. A new survey was made, and, says Bartlet, "The matter was shortly after settled by the instrumentality of Dr. Gardiner, and their title to the glebe was not again disputed."¶

In 1773, Bowman made another attempt to dispossess Jacob Bailey of his church, demonstrating, as he did so, the intertwining of civic and church business, and the curious manipulations possible by those in power. Bartlet writes:

The Church was incorporated by the General Court in 1773, and a parish meeting was called in the spring of that year, by M [Bowman] and N [Cushing], during the absence of the two wardens and Maj. Goodwin. The warrant contained but two articles,—First, to choose a moderator. Second: to choose a parish clerk, assessors, and a committee for managing parish affairs. All freeholders and other inhabitants, legally qualified to vote in town meetings, were required to attend. From the titles given to some of the officers, e.g., "committee for managing parish affairs," and also from the omission of names of wardens and vestry, it is evident, that this could be no meeting of the congregation of the Church. As all freeholders, etc., were notified, the intention manifestly was, to form a new religious organization—its character to be determined by the majority of the voters present. Many Churchmen were "legally qualified to vote in town meetings," and therefore attended on this occasion, as they had a perfect right to do. M [Bowman] was the active spirit at this meeting. A moderator of his own selection was chosen, who decided that "no Churchman had any right to vote." "Our people," says Mr. Bailey, "though twenty-four to twelve, offered to withdraw from their meeting, and never more to concern themselves with any parish affairs for the future; provided, they would agree not to tax us towards the Congregational worship, but this was utterly denied us."

* Bartlet, p. 99. Churchmen were members of the Church of England.

† Bartlet, p. 99.

‡ Bartlet, p. 100; see also Ross, p. 192.

Not surprisingly, money and the power to tax for religious purposes were at the heart of the manoeuvre. In effect, this was a *coup* directed at Dr. Gardiner and Jacob Bailey.

But, upon the withdrawal of the Churchmen, and some of the others, the business was left in the hands of eight persons.

These dissenters, though so few in number quarrelled, the same evening, among themselves, about fixing the place for their meeting house; and hearing that their lumber had been seized, became wholly disheartened ...†

Bartlet concludes:

This, which was one of several abortive attempts to establish the Congregational mode of worship in the western part of Pownalborough, is spoken of here, that it may be seen how violent and unscrupulous was the opposition of a very few individuals in that place to the Church of England.‡

There was another attempt of a similar manoeuvre in March of 1776, when political controversies were roiling and Bailey was to be called before the Committee of Correspondence. At the 1776 meeting, the Churchmen were again denied

§ Bartlet, n. 4.
¶ Bartlet cites both, p. 109.

standing, and the committee of seven agreed to raise a tax upon all the inhabitants, "Quakers as well as Churchmen—toward the support of the Gospel." But, Bailey noted, local people were poor and could not afford the tax, so "the collectors are seizing their cattle by violence and selling them at publick venue for a mere trifle." Furthermore, the collectors did not hesitate "to break into barns when the proprietors were absent, taking away cattle by violence ..."§

Soon enough, actions toward Bailey were more direct.

There are two versions of the next attack. William Bartlet tells the story, which Bailey told in his journals, of a fellow attempting to fire a gun (borrowed, says Bailey, from Bowman) at Bailey's house, but it "providentially" misfired. Bailey reports that the fellow said, "This is a ... nest of tories, and I'm going to blow as many of them to ... as possible." This was probably an accurate quotation. Bailey always had a good ear for speech. Bailey's brother-in-law, Joshua Wingate Weeks, was visiting at the time, and wrote of the same incident to the Society for the Propagation of the Gospel.¶

There are two versions also of the next attempt to supplant Bailey as the religious leader of the community in the summer of 1775.

About the beginning of this summer, one Whiting was engaged to officiate at the Court-house. The fellow, now 19 or 20 years of age, had been extremely notorious for his vicious and idle conduct, having first been expelled from the college at Cambridge, and afterwards (it is reported) obliged to flee from the seminary at Providence, for stealing the President's horse. He had been employed for some time as a schoolmaster in Kennebeck, but was represented as a person disposed to ridicule both religion and virtue, yet pretending to a sudden and miracu-

lous conversion, and assuming uncommon zeal in the cause of liberty, he is conceived to be an happy instrument of carrying on the blessed work of ruining the Church.... all who were inclined to favor the present commotions attended his vociferations, and besides, some persons, who desired still to adhere to the Church, went occasionally to meeting, hoping by his seasonable compliance either to avoid the imputation of being enemies to the country, or to escape the persecution they conceived was descending on their neighborhood ...

* Bartlet, pp. 109–10.

† Ross, p. 196.

‡ Bartlet, p. 110.

Ross, citing other sources, has Whiting preaching from the pulpit of Bailey's own church. This was ordered by Bowman and Cushing "in retaliation" for Bailey's "highly criminal" omission of an "order of Thanksgiving" in a previous service. The result of Whiting's preaching, wrote Bailey, was that those "who had hitherto been very moderate and happily united fell suddenly into the most violent commotions," and "Bailey was exclaimed against as a malignant Tory and enimy ..."†

Then there was the matter of the liberty pole. It was Christmas, 1775. "Mr. Goodwin, a deputy-sheriff and jail keeper, began to spirit up the people."‡ Goodwin, if it is indeed the same as Major Goodwin, seems to have been a man set against the British, and was yet an Anglican Churchman, and having invoked a demonstration, tried to mitigate its effects. Bartlet again uses Bailey' s own words.

It was determined that a liberty-pole should be raised before the Church door "to affront" (as it was said) "the parson, and to express their defiance of the King," but Mr. Goodwin, a Church warden, the principal conductor (under the secret direction, as I suppose, of M [Bowman], being opposed by the Vestry, eight

§ Bartlet, p. 111.

¶ Ross, p. 197.

* Ross, p. 197, citing Allen, *History of Dresden*, p. 298.

† Bartlet, p. 111.

in number, induced the people to erect it on the plains. M., some days before, had engaged to give them a quantity of rum to elevate their spirits upon the glorious occasion.... Capt. Lovejoy insisted my being sent for to consecrate the pole by prayer, and, if I refused, it was proposed that I should be whipped around it, but the motion was lost by a majority of two.§

Later, as Ross tells the story from Charles Allen, the pole was cut down and Bailey was "suspected of being the instigator."¶ Bailey denied the act, but stated

*you are sensible that liberty may subsist without any pole at all ... that if all the pines, spruces, and firs were lying prone on the ground it would not elevate tyranny a bit.**

Moreover,

My Presbyterian neighbours were so zealous for the good of their country that they killed seven of my sheep out of twelve, and shot a fine heifer as she was feeding in my pasture.†

Notions of Justice

"the power of bad men to indulge their ill nature ... "

Killing his livestock was a serious attack on the life of Jacob Bailey and his family—which soon included a son, Charles Percy Bailey, born on 3 May 1777. According to an account recorded in *Frontier Missionary*, the intention was to give the boy the Christian names of Hugh Percy, after Lord Percy, who fought at Lexington. Bartlet notes this as an indication of the strength of Bailey's loyalty to Great Britain. But "Mrs. Callahan, the Godmother, seeing so many Patriots in the Church, was afraid to give his name, and called him Charles, the name of her husband. He was baptized Charles Percy, and always signed his name so."*

Because Jacob Bailey was unable to receive his stipend from the Society for the Propagation of the Gospel after 1775,† his sole means of support came from the livestock and crops he raised on the glebe lands near the church and parsonage. To attack these was consequently to threaten his life and that of his family. The intention therefore was to attack the individual through his family, and to leave them all destitute, hungry and afraid. It was a nasty business, and there was worse. By 1778:

> ... *my family severely felt the distresses of hunger and famine, and sometimes had nothing to eat for several days together*

* Bartlet, p. 112.

† Bartlet, p. 121.

‡ Bartlet, p. 122.

but an handful of vegetables and a little milk and water, and at other times they remained twenty-four hours without any sustenance at all, till Mrs. Bailey had almost determined to die rather than make her situation known, for it has long been criminal for any person in this country to afford us support, and many have been prosecuted as Tories for no other reason. Human nature cannot but reflect with reluctance upon such unchristian and cruel proceedings, neither is it possible for sufferers to love and esteem those institutions which put it in the power of bad men to indulge their ill nature, their malice and revenge, on innocent and defenceless objects. ‡

In Jacob Bailey's life during the American Revolution, chief among those "institutions which put it in the power of bad men to indulge their ill nature" was the Committee of Correspondence, which was clever in its origin, effective in its implementation, cruel in its practices—and perhaps saved the colonies from anarchy.

Christopher Moore, in *The Loyalists*, describes the origin of the "Committee of Correspondence":

Colonial government had always required an alliance between the elected representatives who formed the colonial assemblies and the royal governors who administered the colonial government. As trust between the colonial spokesmen and the royal officials disappeared, each group used its power to thwart the other's program. Royal governors called and dismissed sessions of their legislatures each year, and they could use this power to neutralize legislative criticism or opposition: a hostile assembly could be sent home, or simply dissolved to face new elections. To free themselves of this obstacle, colonial legislatures began to appoint standing "committees of correspondence," to

remain in session when the legislature was not meeting. The § Moore, p. 57.
committees' original purpose was merely to maintain com-
munications between the various colonial legislatures, but as
resistance to royal authority grew more open, the committees
quickly became independent centres of discussion and decision-
making that still enjoyed quasi-legal status as committees of
the royal legislature but could not be restrained or removed by
royal authority. By the early months of 1774 every colony had
such a committee. §

The committees of correspondence which demanded obedience from Jacob Bailey were local groups which were apparently "sub-committees" of the quasi-legal standing committees of the colonial legislature. Bailey saw the mobs which attacked individuals and intimidated, not to say starved, families and communities, as the creation of John Adams' older second cousin, Samuel Adams, and controlled to a greater or lesser extent by Jonathan Bowman's cousin, John Hancock. There were close personal connections. All had power within the various committees of correspondence.

The American Revolution had men of genius (Benjamin Franklin, Thomas Jefferson, Thomas Paine), but also others like Samuel Adams who were simply devilishly clever, and who created the means by which the fine ideas of Philadelphia were translated into power in the colonies. It is fair to say (in condemnation) that Samuel Adams created the mobs; but it is also fair to say (in his defense) that he found the means to control the mobs. Still, the cost to fine ideals was great, especially in Massachusetts. It is perhaps appropriate that his name is known now chiefly as a brand of beer. He contributed greatly to the American way of life. It was Samuel Adams out of Boston who circulated pamphlets and letters describ-

¶ See Christopher Moore, *The Loyalists: Revolution, Exile, Settlement*, especially Chapter Two, for the language of the Revolution.

* The origin of the term is obscure, but unknown before the nineteenth century. It was early applied to prison courts, which might be said to "leap to conclusions."

ing and denouncing British taxes and policies; it was Samuel Adams in his *Circular Letter* who informed other colonial assemblies of the decisions made in Massachusetts. It was Samuel Adams, founder of the Sons of Liberty, and almost certainly a planner of the Boston Tea Party, who established the terms (like the "Boston Massacre") of American history, employed to this day.

It was Samuel Adams who controlled the information which, together with cash and rum, created the mobs. This was very clever work. It is likely, in fact, that the mobs took power in Massachusetts long before the orators of the Continental Congress formulated their ideals.

Somehow or other, these legally elected committees of the colonial assemblies created local committees which may or may not have been elected. Others were self-appointed by those most fervent in the cause of the Revolution, those who were most influential in their communities, those who could read and write, those who called themselves "Patriots." ¶

As the Revolution progressed, these Committees of Correspondence took on other tasks, other names. They became the Committee for Inspection, or the Commitee for Public Safety, or all three at once. They became a quasi-judicial system which replaced the discredited British colonial courts. They were at their most effective when they persuaded community leaders—like Jonathan Bowman and Charles Cushing—to cross the street to the Revolutionary cause. But they were (although the word was unavailable at the time) kangaroo courts.*

The standards of the local Committee in Pownalborough seemed simple enough. In one case, when the judges were asked if "speaking a few exceptionable words [is] counteracting the struggles of the American States for Freedom?" the Commit-

tee agreed: that every inadvertent word, or any expression that tended to censure the American measures was certainly counteracting them, except Justice North, who added that even thinking or conceiving that the public administrations were unjust or injurious, was evidently a crime which deserved the severe sentence of transportation.✝

So, thoughtcrimes!‡ Who would have thought that its origins were so humble or so early.

In short, the Committees of Correspondence/Inspection/Public Safety provided courts without laws. Hard on those called before them. But they did have one virtue: their very existence, their very guise of legality, probably controlled the rum-fuelled mobs somewhat. The committees likely prevented anarchy. Something worse happened not too much later, in France, during the French Revolution. *Transportation*, after all, is not *execution*. And indeed, it seems that in Massachusetts, at least, rulings of the Committees had to be endorsed by the General Court of the (state) assembly. So Jacob Bailey could appeal the most egregious decisions of the Pownalborough Committee to Boston.

⌒

These were terrible times for Jacob Bailey and the other Loyalists, and it is just here that we want a clear record—and just here that the record is not entirely clear. One reason is that Bailey's journal "for the entire year of 1777" is missing.§ And Bartlet is far from clear on page 112 of *Frontier Missionary* when he notes that on 3 May 1777, Charles Percy Bailey was born, and then that on "May 23, [Bailey] was summoned before the committee," leaving the impression with the reader that we are now in 1777—which is not the case. What seems

✝ Bartlet, n. J, p. 264.

‡ See George Orwell's novel, *1984*, the appendix on NewSpeak, especially the B vocabulary where crimethink is a thoughtcrime.

§ Bartlet, p. 117.

to be happening is that Bartlet is scrambling among accounts, perhaps (and this is my speculation) because he is continuing to try to protect the names of Judge Jonathan Bowman and High Sheriff Charles Cushing. Bartlet splits the account of these crucial years between the main text, a note in the back of his book (designated J), and the Appendix (p. 353) which gives a listing of the entries in Bailey's journals for 1776 and 1778— which in some cases includes extensive quotations and notes that the journal for 1777 is missing. This is all the more perplexing because throughout *Frontier Missionary* Bartlet has been careful to note the year under discussion by printing it at the top of the page. Very handy for the reader seeking certainty—except when the Rev. Mr. Bartlet plays fast and loose with his own standard practices. (The page noting Charles Percy Bailey's birth, page 112, is headed 1776.) Confusing? Certainly. Why? Perhaps because of Bowman and Cushing, and perhaps furthermore because Bartlet was embarrassed by the actions of the mob or the behaviour of the kangaroo courts.

Julie Ross puts matters straight by quoting in entirety certain pertinent *dated* documents in the Appendices of her study of Jacob Bailey's life. We can therefore construct a chronology of the chief events which led to Bailey's forced departure from the Kennebec.

> *May 23rd, 1776. Summoned before the Committee*
> *May 24th, 1776. Examined by the Committee*
> *May 28th, 1776. Laid under bonds.*

And here, in Ross's Appendix viii, is what Charles Cushing, Chairman, attests is a true copy of the "Meeting of the Committee of Correspondence Inspection and Safety for the Town of Pownalborough May 24th 1776":

Upon the Complaint against the Revd Jacob Bailey for being unfriendly to the Cause of Liberty, Resolv'd

¶ Ross, p. 321.

1. *That the said Jacob Bailey has in diverse Instances since the Year 1774, discovered an undue Attachment to the Authority claimed by Great Britain over the united Colonies, and thereby has given Reason to believe That he does not wish Success to our Struggles for Freedom.*

2. *That he has been Guilty of criminal Neglect in not reading Proclamations issued by the Continental and Provincial Congresses, for Days of Public fasting ... and thereby throwing Contempt upon Congresses and virtually denying their Authority.*

3. *Therefore Resolv'd That the said Jacob Bailey give Bond to the Treasurer of this colony, in the penal Sum of Forty Pounds with one or more Sureties, condition'd That the said Mr. Bailey appear before the General Court of this Colony when called thereto by the said Court to answer for said Conduct , and in the mean Time That he shall not aid the despotic Measures of our unnatural Enemies, or by any Ways or Means directly or indirectly assist them in their Designs of enslaving the said Colonies, in their obtaining their Liberty & Freedom from the tyrannic Measures of Great Britain; and that the said mr. Bailey shall observe and obey all the Orders, Resolves & Laws of the said Court & of the Continental Congress and in all Things behave himself peacably towards the People and Government of this Colony.¶*

How's that for a judgment with speeches? It would reward another reading. Take note of Rev. Bailey's "unfriendly" attitude, or "undue attachment," and "That he does not wish Success to our Struggles for Freedom," or "the despotic measures

* Ross, Appendix ix, p. 322.

✝ Attitudes today are different; a Canadian Anglican congregation may decide to pray for the monarch or not, as it chooses.

of our unnatural enemies." There is no mention of laws—or of laws broken. The Committees of Correspondence took their authority from Whim—or, as Bailey was to note in the title of his play about the committee, "Humors."

Jacob Bailey, with his brother David Bailey, put up the demanded £40 to the "Treasurer of the Colony of Massachusetts Bay" on 28 May 1776.*

On 11 August 1776, the Reverend Bailey was forbidden to pray for the King. Perhaps non-Anglican readers require a note of explanation here. In the eighteenth century, praying for the King was not something which the local vicar might decide to do or not, as he felt obliged or moved to do.✝ It was not at all like the Marine Lieutenant on *The Hind* in 1760 sending for his commission so he could kiss the King's signature to demonstrate his loyalty to the monarch. No, the prayer for the King was an integral part of the Anglican service, and so noted in the Book of Common Prayer. It was required. And reasonably so because the King was the head of the Church of England. Henry viii had seen to that.

So the American rebels had a point. They saw the prayer as support of the British government. Bailey saw it as a communication with God. Charles Allen comments that Bailey might have argued (with more wit than would have been good for him), that if the King was so bad then surely the King needed all the prayers he could get. Clever advice, but not perhaps good strategy. Wit so rarely is. But Bailey continued to pray for the King.

On October 28 and 29, Bailey found himself once again before the Committee and ordered to defend himself. He was charged with praying for the King, refusing to read the Declaration of Independence from the pulpit, and preaching a seditious sermon.

Julie Ross provides (in her Appendix VII, pp. 318–20) a copy of Bailey's letter to the Committee of Correspondence, dated 28 October 1776. This was presumably his statement of defence, and it focuses on his refusal to read the Declaration of Independence from his pulpit. "Because," Jacob Bailey writes, "I am severely to examine the Solemn Oath I had taken" when he was ordained in London in 1760, and "I found I could not comply" with the demand of the Committee of Correspondence "without offering great Violence to my Conscience." Moreover, "that it is my duty to obey God rather than Man"

His position is clear. But he goes on to point out that some other clergy—including Ministers of the Congregational Church—have "neglected to read the Paper of Independency." And he asks what would be the effect if *all* oaths were to be taken lightly. What would happen, he wonders, if the Congressional Army should decide to break its oath to the Congress, and to set up their General as a King? What if they in turn ordered him to publish their proclamation from the pulpit—would it be right for him to comply?

He goes on to point out that he has never had any criminal charges of any kind laid against him. "At College I was known to two of the Gentlemen present, and defy them to charge me with any crime."

So Bowman and Cushing were both on the Committee of Correspondence. Bailey concludes his arguments:

And pray, Gentlemen, what have I done to injure the American Cause? Have I taken up arms in favour of Britain? have I gone into any publick Meetings to defend or establish the Pretensions of either the King or Parliament? have I prevented anyone from enlisting in the Service? have I by Word or Writing conveyed any intelligence to the Enemy? have I ever

‡ Ross,
pp. 318–20.

§ Ross, Appendix x, p. 324.

attempted to escape out of the Country, even when I had an Opportunity, or have I aided abetted or assisted the Enemy of my Country: what is my crime, is it those Connections I cannot dissolve: I am criminal only for acting as ever honest Man ought to act in the same Circumstances in rather choosing to Suffer the Penalty (if any Such is annexed) to an Order of Council, than to feel the External Reproaches of a Guilty Conscience—I would observe further, that supposing I was really in my heart unfriendly to the Country (which I absolutely deny) it is not in my Power to injure it. Can any Person without Money, without Influence, without Authority, without opportunity, in such a remote Corner, do any thing to obstruct the Wheels of Government, or to determine the Operations of the War?—Is it not therefore ungenerous and a little inhuman to render anyone uneasy, who has neither power nor inclination to hurt you. ‡

The argument was not effective with the Committee and certainly not with Charles Cushing. (Did Cushing realize that John Adams had written to him about the "Reproaches of a Guilty Conscience" all those years ago? Probably not.) And it was Cushing who wrote the judgment, saying that Bailey's reasons "have a direct Tendency to undermine the Foundation of the United States of America," and that if Bailey persists in praying for the King, "thereby approving of his Tyrannical Measures, against these States and of the Bloodshed in which they are involved," the Committee is resolved "That the said Jacob Bailey is in Principle and Practice, a most inveterate and dangerous Enemy to the Rights and Liberties of the United States." Bailey is ordered to appear before the General Court of the State at its next session "to answer for his Conduct relating to the Crimes aforementioned and to any other Matters that may then and there appear against him." §

But Jacob Bailey had touched a nerve. In a letter to Samuel Freeman, Cushing is beside himself with fury. It was Bailey's insistence that Oaths were eternal which enraged Cushing. He took it personally—as Bailey undoubtedly intended. "If this Doctrine be Just what becomes of all the old officers in the United States that have taken to oaths of Allegiance! Have they all incurred the guilt of Perjury!" ¶

¶ Ross, Appendix xi, p. 325.

* See Christopher Moore's *The Loyalists.*

Well … uh … yes.

The fellow who was last in the Harvard Class of 1755 had bested the chap who was first. Bailey was not likely to be forgiven.

What happened next is not entirely clear. Since Bailey's journals for 1777 have disappeared, Bartlet turns to Bailey's letters which, as often as not, refer to pertinent events —but in scant detail. Julie Ross calls on Charles Allen's "History of Dresden," which seems also to be short on details. However, as Cushing's verdict, as noted by Ross, would seem to indicate, a verdict was not necessarily a judgment. That is, Cushing found Bailey guilty of being a Tory, but seemingly had to refer Bailey to the next General Court for the verdict to be turned into punishment. If Bailey should happen to disappear before punishment was decided, then a warrant for him could be issued—a warrant for his arrest, certainly, but also perhaps a warrant for transportation. (I am speculating much here.) Transportation might mean that he would be forced to leave his home and be sent to the British lines, as many Loyalists were.* But a punishment might mean imprisonment. Many Loyalists were imprisoned, although Moore's contention that William, Benjamin Franklin's bastard son (and Governor of New Jersey), was sent to the prison in the old copper

† Black, *Peep Show*, pp. 38–9.

‡ Bailey, quoted by Bartlet, pp. 112–3.

mine at Simsbury, Connecticut, has been disputed. A pertinent observation turns up (a bit oddly) in David Black's 1986 novel, *Peep Show*.

> *... the house, an old saltbox with gray shingles and a flagstone terrace. Above the front door, stamped on a brass plate, was the date the place was built: 1762.*
>
> *"It belonged to a Tory who spent the Revolutionary War locked up in a copper mine near Hartford ... An underground concentration camp."*
>
> *She sounded outraged, although she must have told the story to every new visitor.*
>
> *"He grew to hate the light. When he was released and returned home, he boarded up all the windows.*†

Or perhaps Bailey did appear before the General Court, and was cautioned and released. Whatever the case, Bailey continued to serve his congregation. He wrote to the Society for the Propagation of the Gospel:

> *On one hand ... we were assaulted by armed multitudes, pouring out torrents of reproach and execrations, and threatening to make us the victims of their vengeance. On the other, we were besieged by the entreaties and tears of our friends to practice a little compliance (which, by the way, only made our enemies the fiercer) ... In particular, the Sunday after the news of the Declaration of Independence arrived ... besides the ravings and menaces of the wild sons of freedom ... the more moderate ... assured me that every clergyman had both omitted all prayers for His Majesty, and published the Declaration of Independency, while ... friends earnestly besought me to prevent the destruction of our Church ...*‡

By 10 October 1777, Bailey was writing to his brother-in-law, Joshua Wingate Weeks, that "I have a warrant issued against me ever since the 20th of July, and several officers have attempted to take me, but hitherto without success," and noting that he was continuing to officiate at services every Sunday. He explained that he was continuing to hold services for the sake of the Royalists:

§ Bailey, quoted by Bartlet, p. 115.

¶ Bartlet, p. 116.

> ... *our continuing to assemble for Divine Service is considered by the Whigs as the principal support of our party. They imagine that it gives life and spirit to our opposition, and besides the chief objection against me is my praying for the King. For this single offence I have been threatened, insulted, condemned, and laid under heavy bonds, and for this I am now doomed for transportation.*§

Bartlet notes further, quoting from an undated manuscript, that Bailey, "having been concealed in his own house for the space of five weeks, received information that a design was formed against his life," and escaped on the evening of October 15. It was noted that shots, were fired at a couple of young lads, probably intended for him, and but fired at the young fellows by mistake.¶ Bailey fled through the woods towards Boston, encountering celebrations along the way for the defeat of the British General Burgoyne at Saratoga (New York) on 17 October 1777. Bailey returned home just before Christmas.

Church services continued through the early part of 1778, although sporadically, and Bailey was soon in trouble with the local authorities yet again, this time for preaching a sermon which was considered treason. Bailey wrote to Reverend Parker of Boston on 1 October 1778, that

… I am this minute informed that I am presented before the Grand Jury for preaching treason on the Sunday after Easter. When I came to examine the matter I found there was nothing in either of my sermons which tended in the remotest sense to meddle with the present times; this induced me to search the lessons for the day, and I presently found that the sixteenth chapter of Numbers was the lesson appointed for the Morning Service, and that the twenty-sixth verse contained almost the very words sworn to in the deposition upon which they founded their presentment…. "And he spake unto the congregation saying, Depart, I pray you, from the tents of these wicked men, and touch nothing of theirs, lest ye be consumed in all their sins." *

Bailey does not mention that verse thirty-two notes that the earth will open up and swallow those who have not departed from the "tents of these wicked men." Did he read that, too?

"The Grand Jury, however … refused to find a bill."✝

But the summer of 1778 found Jacob Bailey in Boston again. His poverty was evident.

… an old rusty thread-bare black coat, which had been turned, and the button-holes worked with thread almost white, with a number of breaches about the button-holes, and hanging loose, occasioned by the leanness of my carcass, which was at this time greatly emaciated by the constant exercise of temperance; a pair of breeches, constructed of coarse bed-tick, of a dirty yellow colour—a perpendicular patch upon each knee of a different complexion from the original piece; a pair of thick-seamed stockings, well adapted to exclude the extreme heat of the season; a hat with many holes in the brim, adorned with much darning in other places, of a decent medium between black and white. My wig was called white in better days, but now

resembled in colour an old greasy bed blanket; the curls, alas!
had long since departed, and the locks hung lank, deformed,
and clammy about my neck, while the shrinking caul left both
my ears exposed to view.‡

‡ Bailey, quoted
by Bartlet,
pp. 118–9.

§ Bailey, quoted
by Bartlet,
pp. 118–9.

¶ Bailey, quoted
by Bartlet, p. 119.

However, one friend provided a "handsome coat, jacket, and
breeches," and Mr. Parker furnished the requisite "very elegant wig, which, though it might not furnish my brain with
wisdom, yet certainly enabled me to shew my head with greater confidence."§

* Bailey, quoted
by Bartlet, p. 123.

† Bailey, quoted
by Bartlet, p. 123.

And thus, decently clad, he went forth on July 29 to petition the Council.

Concluded this morning, notwithstanding the contempt which
is poured upon Britons from every quarter, to petition the
Council for liberty to depart for Nova Scotia with my family;
and because I perceived that our magistrates could not admit
pleas of conscience, I confined myself to the simple article of
poverty. Mr. Parker had in the morning obtained leave of Mr.
Powell, the President, to offer my petition. Accordingly, having
it prepared, I went down to the Courthouse and presented it to
that gentleman, who engaged to give me his interest. ¶

In the meantime, the dreadful duo of Bowman and Cushing were on their way to Boston with a deposition of treason
as demonstrated by Numbers 16:26, intending to stop Bailey's
petition, but "though wafted upon the wings of malice and ill-
nature, their arrival was too late."*

About the beginning of November I received a permission from
the General Court to remove with my family and substance to
Halifax. ...†

‡ Bailey, quoted
by Bartlet, p. 122.

§ Bartlet, p. 125.

So, in one way, Bailey had won. Petition granted, he was to be allowed to leave with his family and substance. He had out-manoeuvred his nasty Harvard classmates, at least in this.

In other ways he had lost. Poverty (hunger, destitution) had won, and the poverty was the result of Bowman, Cushing, the Committee of Correspondence, and the American Revolution. His pulpit was gone. Anglican services on the Kennebec seemed to be ended.

There were still some indignities.

Being afterwards at a settlement about fifty miles from my own habitation, at the requisition of the people to preach and baptize their children, I was assaulted by a violent mob armed with clubs, axes, and other weapons, who stripped me naked in search of papers, pretending that I had conceived a design of escaping to Quebeck.‡

But by the time Bailey received permission from the General Court to leave, it was too late in the season for travel—so he opened St. John's Church again, and preached.

Cushing was (perhaps literally) stamping his feet with fury. He sent a message to Bailey by one of the church wardens.

Tell the Parson that if he presumes to discharge his functions any longer, I will immediately commit him to prison, and that if he do not enter into a written agreement to forbear the exercise of Public Worship, I will myself appear on Christmas day, attended with a number of resolute fellows, and drag him headlong out of the pulpit.§

Bailey considered Cushing's request, but rejected it.

… it could not possibly injure any person alive, nor occasion any damage to my country, for which I shall always retain the warmest affection; and that it was not repugnant to any laws, since preachers of all denominations, as Ana-baptists, Separates, Quakers, prisoners, &c. are allowed to preach without either taking the oath or suffering any kind of molestation. ¶

¶ Bartlet, p. 125.

* Bartlet, p. 126.

† Bartlet, p. 128.

‡ See Bartlet, p. 177.

The drama was somewhat postponed because the weather on Christmas Day was so inclement that services could not be held.

So Cushing and fellows appeared at Bailey's house just as the Bailey family was sitting down to Christmas dinner. There was a row. Coarse language was used by the High Sheriff and his deputy—and a man servant, provoked, threatened the crude fellow with violence.*

We do not know what happened next. The story of Jacob Bailey on the Kennebec ends with a fist fight threatened, but not perhaps carried out. Well, there's a little more: Bailey continued to baptize the children, visit the sick and bury the dead, and Cushing attempted to apprehend him at a funeral, but "through the vigilence of friends, I had timely notice, and escaped the danger."†

There is a coda. Sometime in 1781, a raiding party of Loyalists led by John Jones slipped into the Kennebec, grabbed Charles Cushing—by then a Brigadier General—and dragged him off to the British camp at Castine. It is said that he was treated roughly.‡ According to the Cushing family website, after the war he relocated to the Boston area, and was Clerk of Courts in Suffolk and Nantucket Counties until his death in 1810. His family spoke well of him.

THIRTEEN

Escape to Nova Scotia

In June 1779, Jacob Bailey and his family* escaped the Kennebec. It was not that they were exiled, exactly, nor that they were banished—for Bailey had permission from the General Court of the Massachusetts Assembly to leave with his household goods, such as they were (his plea of poverty was accepted)—but they were nonetheless on the run from the enmity of Charles Cushing, who seemed to have little regard for courts, even the Massachusetts courts. Bailey and his family slipped away from the coast of Massachusetts on a schooner which they had engaged for the purpose.✝

> ... *we carried our beds, and the shattered remains of our fortune, the whole not worth forty dollars, on board our schooner, a little vessel, not more than fifteen tons, with such slender conveniences that we were obliged to make provision for lodging in the hold.*‡

They visited friends, stopped at several islands, but kept a sharp lookout for rebel ships, because "I had a number of papers on board which would have been reckoned highly treasonable against the States."§

Bailey's sensibility seems to have altered somewhat. The man who, earlier, had accepted petty doctrinal prohibitions

* There is some confusion about the number in the Bailey group. For example, Arthur Eaton, in his 1891 book on the Loyalist clergy, writes that the group included "two young girls about eleven years of age." Later we find Bailey's household contains Mrs. Callahan (Charles Percy Bailey's godmother, who named him) and quite likely her children. She and her husband, Captain Callahan, had supported Bailey throughout his troubles with Bowman and Cushing.

✝ Bartlet, p. 130.

‡ Bartlet, p. 131.

§ Bartlet, p. 132.

¶ Bartlet, p. 141. as indicative of goodness, had grown out of it. Bailey was now vexed by the petty New England notions of propriety. On one island, Sally Bailey's hairstyle apparently gave offence.

> *Mrs. Bailey was dressed with a small roll upon her head, which induced Mrs. Welch, mistress of the house, and her father to exclaim with the utmost vehemence against the wickedness of the times, and when they perceived that she was a minister's wife, they conceived the wearing of the roll to be an unpardonable crime. It is really surprising that when so many flagrant vices prevail in the country, such as the most daring profaneness, perjury, and a visible contempt for all religious institutions, not to mention the oppression, injustice and inhumanity that is everywhere practiced with impunity.... To rail against fashions has always been the employment of little and narrow minds ...* ¶

Later, on June 20, a Sunday, which turned out to be a surprisingly fine day, although they were becalmed,

> *... John Hoffman put over a line and caught two fine cod fish, one upon each hook, and continued the sport with the same success till he had procured a dozen. Upon this, the two brothers coming upon deck, reproved him sharply for his wickedness in profaning the Sabbath, and when they could not restrain him they swore a multitude of oaths! Strange, that persons who indulged themselves in the rudest conversation, and who scrupled not to take the Sacred Name in vain, should nevertheless have such a reverence for a day consecrated to His service, as to neglect all kinds of business, however advantageous and necessary. But this is just in the character of New England saints, who worship the Sabbath, while at the same time they*

*treat the Lord of the Sabbath with the most indecent familiarity and disrespect. Thus man, the most inconsistent animal in nature, often strains at a gnat and swallows a camel without any manner of inconvenience.**

It was a bedraggled family and friends who arrived in Halifax on 21 June 1779. The group's appearance attracted a small crowd to the dock. Bailey addressed his audience from the quarterdeck of the schooner.

Gentlemen, we are a company of fugitives from the Kennebeck, in New England, driven by famine and persecution to take refuge among you, and therefore I must entreat your candour and compassion to excuse the meanness and singularity of our dress.†

He describes himself:

… legs were covered with a thick pair of blue woolen stockings, which had been so often mended and darned by the fingers of frugality, that scarce an atom of the original remained. My breeches, which just concealed the shame of my nakedness, had formerly been black, but the color being worn out by age, nothing remained but a rusty grey, bespattered with lint and bedaubed with pitch. Over a coarse tow and linen shirt, manufactured in the looms of sedition, I sustained a coat and waistcoat of the same dandy grey russet; and to secrete from public inspection the inumerable rents, holes, and deformities, which time and misfortunes had wrought in these ragged and weather-beaten garments, I was furnished with a blue surtout, fretted at the elbows, worn at the button-holes and stained with a variety of tints, so that it might truly be styled a coat of many

* Bartlet, p. 151. In my copy of Bartlet, someone has underlined in pencil the words, "But this is just the character of New England …"

† Bartlet, p. 156.

‡ Bartlet, p. 157.

§ Bartlet, p. 158.

colours the waist descended below my knees, and the skirts hung dangling about my heels; and to complete the whole a jaundice-coloured wig, devoid of curls, was shaded by the remnants of a rusty beaver, its monstrous brim replete with notches and furrows, and grown limpsy by the alternate inflictions of storm and sunshine. ‡

His wife?

… arrayed in a ragged baize night-gown, tied round her middle with a woolen string instead of a sash…. bonnet of black moth-eaten stuff…. petticoat … jagged at the bottom, and curiously drabbled in the mud, for a heavy rain was now beginning to set in. §

Jacob Bailey was at once concerned about apparel, and not. He realized that clothes were important because clothes indicated one's social status and importance (or lack of it), but throughout his life he had difficulty with dressing properly.

When anonymous letters were written about him to ecclesiastical authorities in London (and letters were written; the Loyalists were a backbiting bunch), one complaint levelled against him was the poor state of his attire. A gentleman was supposed to dress like a gentleman—an attitude which says much about the Loyalists, and while Bailey insisted he was a gentleman (Harvard, ordained by the Bishop of London), he was always too poor to dress the part. Moreover, he was as often as not working in his garden to feed his family. Money was always tight; he was often in debt. When dignitaries came to town, he was expected to put them up, and he did.

One of his great detractors in Nova Scotia was a fellow Loyalist Anglican cleric, the Reverend William Clark (also spelled Clarke) who was for a time at nearby Digby. Historian Judith Fingard seems to accept William Clark's stories about Bailey at face value. Clark considered Bailey slovenly, and worse:

¶ Fingard, p. 71.

* Fingard, p. 72.

> *Jacob Bailey's unconcealed fear of death and corpses provided a deeply regretted example to his flock. He was so superstitious that he avoided funerals as often as possible, and "when he does attend, never stands within 20 yards of the Grave, when he reads the Prayers; and instances have been known, when he has been so frightened, that he has called his Servant to read the service and run off himself.* ¶

Such behaviour is not noted elsewhere, but Fingard accepts Clark's word. (Has anyone considered a putrid corpse?) She likes Clark.

> *The Loyalist clergymen from small, rural communities in the American colonies identified themselves with the pioneering, common people in Nova Scotia. William Clark, one of the best sources of information on clerical behaviour in the 1780s, was a "gentleman" cleric used to polished society, but he left descriptions of two excellent examples of men who were his opposite. Of Bailey, "The Frontier Missionary," whom he found slovenly in appearance and offensive to those members of his church in Annapolis who were urbane and cultured Loyalists, Clark wrote "I thought that when he came among so polite a people he would shake off his Rusticity and clownish manners … but instead of that it is if possible a thousand times worse than ever."* *

Clark also noted that the wife and niece of Roger Viets (Angli-

+ Eaton, p. 170.

can cleric at nearby Digby), were to be found at their spinning wheels if visitors called, and "all in a clutter."

As Fingard also notes, many of the Loyalist clergy in Nova Scotia were forced to return to America because of poverty, and Clark was among them. Arthur Eaton, author of *The Church in Nova Scotia: the Tory Clergy of the Revolution*, quotes Bailey on Clark and his wife, "who was unable to rough it as himself." +

Shortly after Bailey landed in Halifax, he was offered a position as clergyman in the Cornwallis area —in what is now the area of Wolfville and Kentville. He accepted the offer. The place was not far from a British garrison at Windsor, but the area was not considered especially loyal to the King. It was an area in which the Planters were in residence (and in control), and they had planted whipping posts and put them to use. But before Bailey could leave for Cornwallis, he was offered a (perhaps much better) place in Halifax itself, which, because he had promised the people of Cornwallis that he would come to serve them, he felt obliged to turn down. So he went to Cornwallis, where he found people of religious differences unwelcoming. But—and this was to be true throughout his life—his dedication to their spiritual needs won them over, however grudgingly. It might be remembered that in that era the need for religious ceremonies—for baptism, especially—was more important than dogma. Put bluntly: people believed they needed Bailey to get into heaven, but they had no intention of accepting the Anglican attachment to the British Crown or the House of Lords.

So Thomas Raddall in *His Majesty's Yankees* was right (and Ian Lawrence in Annapolis Royal is right): Nova Scotia at the time of the American Revolution was no bastion of support for King George III, except perhaps in Halifax—and Halifax was a British garrison town and naval base, full of military personnel and military money. Halifax looked to London for support. The rest of Nova Scotia looked to Boston.

Bailey stayed in Cornwallis for two years, and by the time he left to accept the call to Annapolis Royal, his Cornwallis parishioners had come to accept him, and possibly admire him, if not agree with him. In some ways he was sorry to leave. But Annapolis Royal, once capital of French Acadia, later capital of Nova Scotia, and administrative centre for both, must have seemed a good place for a man of learning and discernment.

Not quite.

Not for the first time, Jacob Bailey was caught in the middle. As at Kennebec, Bailey found himself in a very mixed community in Annapolis Royal. The inhabitants came from everywhere (and recently), and professed many different versions of Christianity. At the end of December 1784, Bailey wrote to Dr. Morice of the Society for the Propagation of the Gospel, in London, to describe the situation in Annapolis County:

> *The present inhabitants of Annapolis county consist of a mixture various and discordant, perhaps beyond example—as to nation, character, religion—Besides Indians, Acadians, and Nova Scotians of British extract, we find natives of England, Scotland, Ireland, Jersey, France, Portugal, Holland, Prussia, Sweden, Switzerland, numbers from almost every dominion in Germany and from all the revolted states of America. Among these we may reckon disbanded soldiers and yeoman—half pay officers, merchants, mechanicks, farmers, gentlemen formerly of independent fortunes, now reduced to poverty—persons whose birth and education ranked them among the lowest vulgar, suddenly enriched by spirited ingenuity during the late com-*

‡ As Judith
Fingard
demonstrates
convincingly,
Bailey was right
about that.

*motions—emissaries of the American republicks in disguise
to forment divisions—magistrates who here to fore served his
majesty and their country with fidelity, affection, honour and
integrity—without support—multitudes advanced in life with
large families and no prospects of obtaining subsistence—wid-
ows and orphans whose husbands and parents either perished
in the royal cause or were cruelly massacred by their treacher-
ous countrymen … besides the prevailing religions of the several countries from which they emigrated, as Roman Catholics,
protestants of the church of England, Lutherans, Calvinists,
Presbyterians, Morovians, Independents and Quakers—with
a number of nameless subdivisions….*

Moreover, it likely seemed to him that the evangelical sects
were overwhelming the more sober interests in the Church of
England.‡ In the middle of January 1785, Bailey complained
to the Rev. Dr. Breynton in Halifax that:

*We have in this county almost as many religions as there were
living creatures in Noah's Ark and numbers without any religion at all … New Light preachers are roving about and
labour with indefatigable industry to gain proselites and their
endeavours are attended with too much success—for many who
are oppressed with misfortune and soured with disappointment
countenance, entertain, and support them….*

It is a shrewd assessment, and an insight into the causes, too:
"oppressed with misfortune and soured with disappointment."
Moreover, just as before on the Kennebec, glebe lands were
in dispute.

In many ways, the conflict was understandable. Former
New Englanders were forming local government institu-

tions on familiar models. For example, they used the town meeting to establish authority—an institution much revered in retrospect, but certainly open to religious manipulation in actual practice then.§ Dr. Gardiner had probably fudged some votes to get the Anglicans established on the Kennebec in the first place, but at Georgetown (then in Massachusetts, now in Maine), which was part of Bailey's purview, glebe lands were rented out to support local dissenting clergy designated by the meeting. This was the puritan tradition in practice. The same thing was tried, using very dubious meetings, in an attempt to take over Bailey's own church lands at Pownalborough. When he came to Annapolis he found a similar attempt on glebe lands across the basin at Granville. Writing to Dr. Breynton on 17 January 1785, Bailey says that "a party of the church people at Granville with some New England dissenters are attempting to deprive me of the glebe that rented for 40 shillings per Annum ..." The people of Granville seemed unaware that (as Thomas Haliburton records in his *History of Nova Scotia*) the British colonial government had forbidden town meetings on 14 April 1770.¶ More likely, the edict was simply ignored by the people of Granville.

What seemed simple enough in British law—that glebe lands were to support the state religion—was ignored by the New Englanders.* Despite Bailey's warnings, the people of Granville accepted the actions of the local meeting, and rented out the lands for local religious benefit. Bailey wrote to a Mr. Webber of Granville, who had taken a lease from the group, that "if ... it should appear that I am in the right, you must not only lose your improvement but answer all damages which the law in such cases may exact."

§ The Congregational Church did not use "church buildings" for worship; it used "meeting houses." Town discussions and religious services used the same buildings. They of course saw no distinction.

¶ Thomas Haliburton, *History of Nova Scotia* (Joseph Howe, Halifax, 1829), p. 249.

* When the Annapolis fort fell to the British and Massachusetts forces in 1710, the Roman Catholic lands were simply taken over by the Anglicans. The chief glebe lands in Annapolis Royal, which were more or less inhabited by residents paying rents, were where the Saturday Market is in 2008—where the tourist authorities have installed the cutesy Puritan punishment stocks.

† Again it is Judith Fingard whose research into the use of glebe lands demonstrates that the glebe lands rarely raised the money which was expected, although Jacob Bailey did better than others. Local authorities often granted land to support schools as well as the church, but the land was often far from the best.

Life in Annapolis Royal in 1782–83 was tumultuous. Bailey, as one of the most educated persons in the community, and as a man of the cloth and representative of the Crown, like it or not, was called upon to organize the survival of 2500 Loyalists, and he did. He became a *de facto* administrator. He was a chief reference for many of the new arrivals, and wrote letters and testimonials for many of them as new governments lurched into being in New Brunswick and Nova Scotia.

Money was scarce and uncertain for some and not for others. The Loyalists generally received support of one kind or another from the British government, which confused the local economy. Those who had food, fuel, or especially skilled services to sell certainly benefited from the newly arrived money. Those who had to pay for that food, fuel, or skilled services without a subsidized income undoubtedly found life more difficult than before. Inflation was running at something like seventy percent a year, which was good news for people with skills to sell—like carpenters—but not for an Anglican cleric on a fixed income from London whose glebe lands were being grabbed by other denominations.†

Economist Julian Gwyn aptly titles his work on the era *Excessive Expectations: Maritime Commerce and the Economic Development of Nova Scotia, 1740–1870.* Many of the Loyalists expected a golden age, and Jacob Bailey was among them. Gwyn's work might just as easily have been titled *Unrealistic Expectations.* Over in Shelburne, the early Loyalists built fine houses on their arrival—and then discovered there was no money to maintain them or the lifestyle they represented. Shelburne was expected to be the new New York, and reached a population of some 8,000 people within a year or so of the Loyalist arrival; but within another year or so it was half that, and shrinking. The hope had been that the land around Shelburne would support the community. But it was poor land. And there was a great deal of unemployment, which resulted in the race riot of 1784, when the white workers felt the black workers were undercutting wages.

Gwyn argues that the myth of prosperity had no basis in truth, that "there never was a golden age from which they were supposed to have fallen."‡

There were not many people in the province. Gwyn's figures are similar to those of Thomas Haliburton in his *History of Nova Scotia*, which was written in Annapolis Royal, where the young Haliburton then had his law practice. The population of the province was approximately 18,000 in 1755. With the expulsion of the Acadians, it was down to 11,600 in 1771, and did not rise to 14,000 until 1781. Then the Loyalists arrived (to swamp the locals) and in 1791, there were 45,000 people in Nova Scotia. And Gwyn makes it clear that, from an economic point of view, the Expulsion was a disaster not only for the Acadians but for the population that remained. The Expulsion destroyed the agricultural economy, and the garrison—which ate up the produce and stock which had been confiscated—had no idea how to produce more. The farms were destroyed; houses, barns, and outbuildings were burnt. Gwyn notes that it was perhaps half a century before the economy of Nova Scotia reached the level the Acadians had attained in 1705. Moreover, Britain was soon weary of Nova Scotia's repeated requests for support. Edmund Burke wrote in 1780 that "Nova Scotia was the youngest and the favourite child of the Board. Good God! What sums the nursing of that ill-thriven hard-visaged brat has cost to this wittol nation."§

And Annapolis Royal had its own distinctive characteris-

‡ Gwyn, p. xi.

§ Gwyn, p. 28. Gwyn also notes that stopping the slave trade also hurt the Maritime economy. Economists note only the economy, not justice, morality, good taste, or much else.

tics, attitudes and requirements, and all of them played important roles in Jacob Bailey's new life. For example, Annapolis
was first of all a fort, and had been since the French establishment in 1605. It was a fort with a garrison, and therefore
Annapolis Royal was a military town, first French, then English—although often as much Massachusetts as English. The
soldiers were a rough lot, and it should be noted that in the
eighteenth century (and, truth be told, much later as well),
criminals were commonly sent into the army. They were
badly paid, and the bad pay was often delayed. It was expected that many of them would have jobs in town, and they did.
But others stole. Bailey was to complain that the soldiers were
responsible for most of the theft in town. On 20 January 1785,
he wrote to his friend Thomas Brown in Halifax:

> *The Regiment quartered at Annapolis are perpetually engaged*
> *in stealing and plundering the property of their neighbours—*
> *I who am seated extremely convenient for their depredations*
> *have lost in fencing, stuff, potatoes, fruit, fowls, hogs etc about*
> *twenty pounds during the last seasons … Besides these martial*
> *sons we have disbanded soldiers, sailors, free negros, sturdy*
> *villains from the continent, and even some of the pious inhab-*
> *itants of Nova Scotia—I attended last May the execution of a*
> *woman belonging to the latter description. And though she was*
> *of new light, she died the most hardened monster I ever beheld.*
> *Nine persons were tried for capital offences at the same court,*
> *four were condemned, two executed and others pardoned—*
> *But all these instances are trifling to a combination just dis-*
> *covered in Digby.… A Captain Young, whose character had*
> *hitherto been irreproachable with fifty desperate fellows at his*
> *command—had appointed to murder Justice Bunhill on the*
> *Queen's birth night, while the principal inhabitants were at*

the assembly, to plunder the whole town, to carry the effects on board a vessel and then make their escape to Boston.... Young is taken up and now confined in Annapolis jail ... The free negros are excusible than any other denomination of thieves since they are allowed no provisions, a circumstance which has reduced them a starving condition—unless some speedy relief is afforded them, they might perish by scores with hunger.

The above letter is amazingly rich in information: thieves abound, especially from among the soldiers, the population is immigrant and various, many are poor to the point of starvation, nine persons were tried for capital offences, four were condemned, and two executed—among them a new light woman who "died the most hardened monster I ever beheld"—a band of fifty (presumably ex-soldiers) planned to plunder Digby and escape to Boston, and the free negroes were "allowed no provisions." So the community was rife with crime and on the edge of anarchy—in addition, in 1783, Annapolis Royal was sacked by an American privateer.

In Annapolis Royal, life was neither safe nor comfortable but because it had once been an administrative centre, it was a small community of the professionals serving the military and the government. It was largely a paper economy. It was *not* a rural farming community, and in fact since the expulsion of the Acadians in 1755, there was likely less commercial agricultural activity than before.

Moreover, with the removal of the capital to Halifax in 1749, and with it the most of the British military force, Annapolis Royal was something of a leftover outpost, getting by as best it could until suddenly there was this huge influx of Loyalists.

But the fort and the town were in many ways one and the

¶ Dunn, p. 187. One of the more interesting of the deputy chaplains was the Rev. Cuthbert, who formed an attachment for the wife of one of the local craftsmen which became so public and scandalous that the deputy chaplain, refusing to give up the attachment, had to be confined to quarters in the fort.

* Bartlet, p. 107.

same and had been since the beginning. The religious needs of the town were met by the chaplain of the fort, for example, or, to speak more accurately, by the deputy chaplain, and since the victory of the British/Massachusetts forces in 1710, the chaplain was naturally Anglican. A chaplain might reside in the fort for a time, return to England, or not come at all—but draw a living from the position. The chaplain might then appoint a deputy who would come to Annapolis Royal to attend to the spiritual needs of the soldiers and the townspeople. ¶ It was the duty of the deputy chaplain to perform the necessary ceremonies, most commonly the burials. Services were conducted in the chapel within the fort, although by the time Jacob Bailey arrived in Annapolis Royal, a new church was being constructed, and was put to use to keep the arriving Loyalists out of the weather until other shelter could be found for them.

But if the chaplain's fees stayed in England, the deputy chaplain's fees were controlled otherwise. The Rev. Joshua Wingate Weeks, Jacob Bailey's brother-in-law, secured the deputy chaplaincy of Fort Anne from its commanding officer while Bailey was still in Cornwallis. But Weeks decided to live in Halifax. It was safer there. It was Bailey who performed the services and buried the dead in Annapolis Royal. Bailey believed that he deserved to have the emolument, but Joshua Wingate Weeks thought otherwise. Bailey desperately needed the money, but Joshua Wingate Weeks did not care.

Those who owed Bailey most, treated him worst. For example, his brother-in-law, Joshua Wingate Weeks, fled with his family to Bailey's protection in Kennebec in the summer of 1775 and received hospitality and safety.* But Weeks treated Bailey very badly when both were "safe" in Nova Scotia.

Judith Fingard (in *The Anglican Design in Loyalist Nova Scotia, 1783–1816*) points out that there were several Anglican clergyman characterized by one frailty or another (some drank to excess; others quarrelled with their congregations), but that from the point of view of the Society for the Propagation of the Gospel, Joshua Wingate Weeks was worse than most:

> *The SPG would not, however, tolerate insubordination. Joshua Weeks was sent to Nova Scotia in 1779, where he dallied in Halifax and did not even visit his mission of Annapolis until 1781. His instant dislike of Annapolis Royal prompted him to return to the capital, where he became curate to the rector of St. Paul's and arranged to pay a curate of his own at Annapolis. When the SPG insisted that he should reside in his mission, he refused with such impertinence that the Society dismissed him and appointed Jacob Bailey in his stead. As soon as Weeks heard of this appointment, he secured the deputy-chaplaincy of the garrison at Annapolis from the commanding officer, the titular chaplain being a non-resident. This proved to be a considerable disappointment to Bailey because he had to minister to the garrison and claimed he was entitled to the emolument. Nevertheless, Governor Parr refused to grant him the deputy-chaplainship and championed Weeks' cause, principally on the ground that he had nine children. Nor was the SPG able to intervene on Bailey's behalf, because it had no control over the appointment of deputies in the chaplaincy service of the British forces. The society could do no more than protest against this injustice and express annoyance with the governor, and in these circumstances Weeks was forgiven in 1785.*
>
> *Yet this was not the end of the episode. Weeks remained in Halifax and on the resignation of the rector of St. Paul's in 1790 he sought adoption as the new incumbent of the most lucrative mission in the province. The SPG refused to consider the request and when Robert Stanser was appointed in*

✝ Fingard,
pp. 58–9.

1791, Weeks retaliated by securing two chaplaincies in Hal-
ifax which by tradition belonged to the rector of St. Paul's.
He was deprived of these the following year, largely as the
result of the more cooperative attitude of Lieutenant Gov-
ernor Wentworth towards the ecclesiastical authorities, then
forced to seek appointment as missionary at Preston. On the
recommendation of the Bishop, who had not known Weeks at
his most obstreperous, he was accepted back into the Society's
service on condition that he gave up the deputy-chaplaincy of
Annapolis. Weeks complied, and was appointed in 1793, and
he remained missionary at Preston and later at Guysborough
without further trouble. Secretary Morice, however, remem-
bered the case of Weeks' insubordination as the most trouble-
some affair he ever had to resolve.✝

To be fair, Weeks' attitude was not unusual, nor was the
practice, in the eighteenth century. The great English writer
who was also an Anglican cleric, Laurence Sterne, collected
fees from parishes where he performed no duties, and thought
nothing of it. In the British system in which church and state
were allied through the gentry, an income had everything to
do with status and very little to do with the performance of
duties; more to do with family, and certainly nothing to do
with merit.

But the Anglican presence (as Judith Fingard makes clear)
in Nova Scotia was not anywhere so great as might be expected, even after the great influx of Loyalists. For one thing, not
all Loyalists were Anglicans. For another, even the Loyalist Anglicans were divided among themselves. Bailey would
point out that one Anglican group wanted services as they
had been back home; another group from another place wanted to follow their local traditions. And if the Anglicans were

the "official" church and had the perquisite of issuing marriage licences, and alliances with the British colonial government, they were very, very definitely in the minority, far outnumbered by the Dissenters of various kinds: Presbyterians, Methodists (who in America decided to send missionaries to Nova Scotia in 1782 to convert the heathen—inspiring perhaps Bailey's wicked satire, "Jack Ramble") and New Lights.

Moreover, educational practices were equally in flux. In New England, as Jacob Bailey's life demonstrates, there were private, individual schools operated individually by freelance schoolteachers. Bailey's school in Rowley had not been a success. When such schools appeared in Nova Scotia, Bailey was harsh in his disapproval. Anyone could set himself up as a teacher: there were no required qualifications, and even had there been, they could not have been verified. Co-educational schools supported by the community and administered by the "selectmen," of the kind in which Bailey taught in New Hampshire, were also not usual in Nova Scotia.

Education in Nova Scotia was chiefly that supplied by the Society for the Propagation of the Gospel in the form of charity schools—which were allowed to accept fee-paying pupils so long as they did not outnumber the charity pupils. If these schools had few enough pupils, they were co-educational until enough pupils of both genders were enrolled to justify splitting them into two groups. But the relationship between the Anglican Church and these schools was anything but clear. On the one hand, Christian values were expected, but usually there was little or no attempt to inculcate Anglican doctrine. On the other hand, local Anglican clerics were expected to be involved to one extent or another. Fingard points out that the Society for the Propagation of the Gospel considered Jacob Bailey a teacher as well as a missionary. Certainly Bai-

‡ Moore, p. 189.

ley was interested in education all his life and especially the education of girls.

Judith Fingard is especially informative about educational practices in Nova Scotia. There were two methods generally practiced in the latter part of the eighteenth century, and both (as in *The Little Female Academy*) used the older pupils to teach the younger. But one of them, the Madras method, supported the use of Anglican religious principles, and the other, the Lancaster, thought that religious instruction should be left to the family.

In addition, there were schools operated by the curiously named Associates of the Late Dr. Bray, which were exclusively for black children and taught only what whites thought necessary for blacks. They taught reading, but not writing, and were otherwise vocational. The pupils were largely prepared to be servants, and success was measured in the pupils' performance in such roles.

In thinking about the Loyalists, we might remember, in fact, the fifty-five leading American Loyalists who asked Sir Guy Carleton for 5,000 acres each in what was to become New Brunswick so that these prominent men might then establish landed estates in the new province and thereby establish a life and economy on the British model—which had worked quite nicely in upper New York state, for example, and not badly in New Hampshire under John Wentworth, until the rebels ran him out of town and province, and was certainly working well in Great Britain.‡

But it was the New England mind which won out; Loyalty did not include the British model. The 5,000-acre estates were not granted. Each Loyalist who went to New Brunswick received one hundred acres and perhaps more, depending upon military rank and size of family. But the situation of the clergy was uncertain, and in Nova Scotia, the rights of the established Anglican Church were challenged by the New England settlers. Moreover, in the case of Joshua Wingate Weeks and Jacob Bailey, the practice of the absentee cleric was challenged and eventually resolved in a North American way.

The family ties between Weeks and Bailey were severed, and the two men—who had corresponded much when they were in Massachusetts, never corresponded (nor spoke, so far as we know) again.

It was not until 1793 that Weeks was forced to give up the appointment as deputy chaplain in Annapolis, and it was given to Jacob Bailey by the governor of Nova Scotia, John Wentworth—the same Harvard classmate of Jacob Bailey in the class of 1755 who, as governor of New Hampshire, had believed absolutely in the British system of landed gentry (and established a country estate at Wolfeboro, New Hampshire), and was run out the country because of it. In 1783–84, there was a great deal of adjustment in thinking and attitudes. Many of the Loyalists may have wished to carry on as before, but it was not possible. What was happening in the Maritimes was the establishment of provinces which were neither British nor American, but something else. Eventually we'd call them Canadian.

View of Annapolis taken the 15th Sept. 1775 by Lt. Richard Williams

Who Would Have Thought It?

I t was in Annapolis Royal that Jacob Bailey the writer came into his own—although that did not mean publication. Printers were wary of him, and the province was not generally in support of his views. Bailey's best writing was likely too controversial for a province full of New Englanders, but his satires were copied and passed from hand to hand as an early-day *samizdat*.

His writing had heretofore been unfocused, as if his talent was waiting for the circumstances to call forth his best— and his best turned out to be rude. Who would have thought it? The parson had a tart tongue—and, to be honest, it was sometimes coarse when it was most witty. Nearly a hundred and fifty years later, a scholar like Aunt Minnie's friend Professor Ray Baker felt it necessary to shy away from certain quotations.

But, to look back on his writing life for a moment, the pursuit of literature was almost certainly one factor in his conversion to the Church of England from the Congregationalists. He had been a reluctant Congregationalist, as demonstrated by his "approval" by the panel of Congregational clergyman (Bailey had to be persuaded to preach), and if the opportunity to travel to London to be ordained was his first incentive, then perhaps the literary tradition found in the Anglican church was a contributing factor. The Congregational Church had the New England saints (Jonathan Edwards dangling a man's soul like a spider over a fiery pit), but the Anglicans had the great lyric poet (and, incidentally, satirist) Robert Herrick ("Gather ye rosebuds while ye may"), as well as more recently Jonathan Swift (*Gulliver's Travels;* "A Modest Proposal") and, an exact contemporary of Jacob Bailey, the great comic ironist, Laurence Sterne (*Tristram Shandy*). The Church of England may not have welcomed them, but it had room for all of them, and for Jacob Bailey, too

❧

The young Jacob Bailey had written poems to young ladies when he was at Harvard, and shortly thereafter, pious poems in response to the Cape Ann Earthquake of 1755. All of it was conventional verse in the fashion of the time, which featured literary allusions and extravagant feelings in extravagant language. If it had any literary virtue, it was that of extravagance. Big, if not precise.

But there was also the rude behaviour and its literary counterpart in "The Corn-Husking Bee," a poem full of earthy life with a thin moral—that rural people were not so innocent as we might assume (a myth that dies hard), and were in fact as likely as anyone else to roll around on the floor in sexual play. Shocking, when you stop to think about it. Ray Baker comments: "... the blunt, realistic sketches ... indicate that life in New England in the eighteenth century was neither so bleak nor so proper as it has often been pictured."*

And although some of his work was written earlier (his

geographical studies of New England, and perhaps his "History of New England") and was transported with some risk and great difficulty to Nova Scotia, it was not until he arrived at Annapolis Royal that Jacob Bailey could look back on the tumultuous times in which he lived, and take on his enemies: the Congregational Church, the evangelical sects, the deists and disbelievers, and the political combination of all of them into what became known as the American Revolution. He knew his enemies and attacked them harshly, and sometimes individually.

Bailey discovered—or uncovered—a talent for satiric verse narrative: stories told in rhyming couplets which lampooned and skewered American patriots—especially Samuel Adams, John Adams and Benjamin Franklin—and evangelicals alike, and he saw the one group contributing to the other.

Unfortunately, only a few of his shorter satiric efforts were ever completed, not least because the intentions for the others were so huge. One shorter satiric poem, "The Trimmer," was captured and published (in large part) by Professor Ray Baker, in 1929. Baker wrote that "The Trimmer" dealt with a subject which aroused "the ridicule of both parties"—the fence-sitter, the fellow who, in the end, is trusted by nobody.

> *They nicely trim, 'twixt Whig and Tory,*
> *And gravely think that honesty*
> *Is out of date in policy....*
>
> *There lived in our new-fangled nation*
> *A man of wondrous moderation;*
> *While some were eager of the laws,*
> *And others fought in Freedom's cause,*
> *Till all was madness, rage, and foam*
> *He kept himself concealed at home—*

† Baker, pp.
74–7.

‡ Baker, p. 77.

Or like a coward in a brawl
Couched close and snug behind a wall.
He was to all disputes a stranger,
And shut his eyes from every danger;
To Sons of Liberty was civil,
But shunned a Tory as a D-v-l,
And yet my authors all relate
He had for Whigs a mortal hate.

A zealous father of sedition
Took up the good man on suspicion;
Forced him without a grain of pity,
Before th' inflexible committee.
Committee men are dreadful things,
More haughty far than Europe's kings;
The latter mostly rule by laws,
The first are governed by a Cause—

The committee turns the fellow over to the mob, which tars and feathers him, and in order to escape being hanged by the mob as a spy, he must flee to the British (who also do not trust him), and from this Bailey draws a moral:

Now, neighbours, whether Whig or Tory,
Learn from this sad and tragic story
The voice of Conscience to obey,
And walk as she directs the Way. †

Baker believed that "Bailey could write easy, if not brilliant verse," but that "The Trimmer" did not represent Bailey at his best.‡

Professor Baker in 1929 provides an excellent commentary

on Jacob Bailey's early poetry and makes a very useful implicit connection between Bailey's comments on the Christian sects of his day and Sinclair Lewis's 1926 novel, *Elmer Gantry*. The American Great Awakening grinds on through the evangelical George Whitefield and the Wesley brothers to the televangelists of today. Baker quotes from a Bailey letter (which Baker does not identify further) in which, Baker says, Bailey touches on "the evangelistic fanatic," who:

§ Baker, p. 78.
¶ Baker, p. 78.

> *whispers to his female adherents, with the appearance, of great delicacy, with forced sighs, affected groans, doleful looks, and artificial tears. The progress of this enthusiasm … is attended with many pernicious effects. It encourages idleness, excites dissension, begets poverty, brings Christianity into contempt, and promotes a criminal intercourse between the sexes. People of this character delight, if possible, to assemble in the evening, and find a pretence to continue their lectures beyond the usual hour of repose …*§

Baker comments, "At such seasons many circumstances 'conspire', continues Bailey, to arouse the passions and to turn the 'meeting house' into a brothel." ¶ Then Baker quotes more, in this case from Bailey's long, unfinished, unpublished poem, "Jack Ramble, Methodist Missionary." Baker compares the performance described below to *Elmer Gantry*. I would say Baker's insight is exact.

> *Behold the gifted preacher rise,*
> *And roll to Heaven his half-shut eyes;*
> *In every feature of his face,*
> *See stiffness, sanctity, and grace.*
> *Like whipping post erect he stands,*

* Baker, p. 79.

And stretches forth his waving hands …
Observe him spring with eager jump,
And on the table fierce thump
With double fist he beats the air,
Pours out his soul in wrathful prayer;
Then, seized with furious agitation,
Screams forth a frightful exhortation …
The agonies of deep distress;
Then groans, and scolds, and roars aloud
Till dread and frenzy fire the crowd …
Some heaven extol with rapturous air,
While others rave in black despair …
Thus in some far and lonely site,
Amidst the deepest glooms of night
Where roll the slow and sullen floods,
O'er hung with rocks and dusky woods
I've heard the waves terrific howl—

Baker comments "when the enthusiasm reaches its height, and shouts of joy mingle with sobs of grief, not a few of the godly are discomfited by their excess…. religious exaltation and sexual excitement seem to merge."*

Here blue-eyed Jenny plays her part.
Inured to every saint-like art,
She works and heaves from head to heel
With pangs of puritanic zeal.
Now in a fit of deep distress,
The holy maid turns prophetess,
And to our light and knowledge brings
A multitude of secret things;
And as enthusiasm advances,
Falls into ecstasies and trances;

Herself with decency resigns
To those impulses and inclines
On Jimmy Trim, a favorite youth,
A chosen vessel of the Truth,
Who, as she sinks into his arms,
Feels thro' his veins her powerful charms.
Grown warm with throbs of strong devotion,
He finds his blood in high commotion,
And, fired with love of his dear sister,
Is now unable to resist her. ✝

✝ All poetry
cited by Baker,
p. 78–9.

Could Byron have said it better? And the alert reader will recognize the whipping post and the storm at sea.

Professor Baker quotes extensively from sources which
seem familiar but are unidentified. Perhaps (as in the letter quoted on "the evangelistic fanatic") Baker had sources
(from Aunt Minnie?) which were uncatalogued in any way
and therefore impossible for him to reference. He admits he
is unsure if the hot-blooded scene above is from "Jack Ramble" or from another source.

T.B. Vincent, in 1976, seems to have taken upon himself the
task of asserting some order to the manuscripts he found in
the Provincial Archives of Nova Scotia, and he asserts that
there are two long major verse satires by Jacob Bailey—one
chiefly on politics, begun in 1780 and ending about 1784, which
Vincent terms "America"—and a second, focused more on dissenting itinerant evangelism, called "The Adventures of Jack
Ramble, the Methodist Preacher."

The two long poems have much in common, and Bailey saw
the American Revolution and evangelical practice as equally responsible (or equally guilty) for the odious upheavals in
eighteenth-century North America.

Vincent notes, for example, that "America" begins as a con-

‡ T.B. Vincent, "Some Examples of Narrative Verse Satire in the Early Literature of Nova Scotia and New Brunswick," *Humanities Association Review*, p. 165. Butler was a Royalist—as was Robert Herrick, the lyric poet and Anglican clergyman. Both suffered for their allegiance.

§ Vincent, p. 165.

tinuation of Samuel Butler's 1663 poem, *Hudibras*. (Bailey is delighted in 1760 when he finds a descendant of Samuel Butler among the crew of *The Hind* on the way to England.)

> *In Bailey's eyes, Butler's poem was relevant because the same non-conformist religious sentiments which Butler believed had precipitated civil war in 17th century England were at work in 18th century America, pushing the American colonies into rebellion.* ‡

To demonstrate the connections, Professor Vincent has provided a very useful prose summary of "America," which I have abridged further. The story "begins with a satiric attack on Hudibras, the true-blue Protestant knight, and on the kind of moral license fostered by non-conformism."§

> *Hudibras becomes enamoured of a young lady whom he happens to see at a prayer meeting.... He propositions the young lady, who ... arranges a secret meeting for that evening ... Having satisfied himself that the Elect are not bound by the same moral rules as the Rejected, he then takes "his fill of amorous play."*
>
> *The result of this liaison is a girl, Hecka, who grows up to be a "forward creature ..." Hecka decides to emigrate to America in order to recover something of her reputation. There she is well received by her father's spiritual kindred in Massachusetts. Indeed, we find that the American "saints" are really no different from English non-conformists; they share the same religious and political assumptions, and display the same hypocrisy in morality. Hecka ... marries an American "saint," and raises a large family. Among her children is a daughter Molly.*

Molly grows up to be a girl of exceptional virtue and religious sentiment and becomes involved in the "New Light" movement. She is ... converted by Preacher Tom, is remarkably fervent in her faith, and ... is soon pregnant [by a chap named Jemmy]. When confronted with the accusation, Jemmy does not deny it, but refuses to marry Molly because he has caught her with other men, notably Preacher Tom. However, Jemmy finally complies when her father comes up with the right price. When a child is born, it is named Convert.

As a boy, Convert soon begins to reject the religious teachings of his forebears and to flout all religious rules. As a young man, he follows the lead of "modern" thinkers, rejecting established truth and developing his own "creed" through the exercising of his own reasoning faculty. He becomes an atheist, a rationalist, and a freethinker. In light of all this, it is not surprising that he should declare himself an enemy to "authority" in both Church and State, and dreams of attaining power and command for himself. In pursuing this end, he seeks the assistance of Doctor Faustus (Benjamin Franklin), a man whose background and mentality is not unlike that of Convert himself.

Motivated by arrogance and a selfish desire for power, Convert and Faustus conspire together against the established government. They call a secret meeting in Boston which is attended by two local leaders, Tony Clincum (Samuel Adams?) and lawyer Bumbo (John Adams?). Rum flows freely, and as it begins to take effect, instilling courage in the conspirators, Convert rises and urges the cause of freedom and independent government. Clincum supports Convert and asserts that independence was in fact the intention of the founders of the colony.¶

¶ Vincent, p. 166.

* Quoted by
T.B. Vincent,
"Alline and
Bailey," *Canadian
Literature*, p. 130.

At this point, Faustus suggests that they foment dissension in Quebec, Bumbo points out that the government backed down over the Stamp Act and urges independence, while Clincum notes that they need some issue to drum up support from the people. And then the manuscript ends—probably because (suggests Professor Vincent) by 1784 all the battles seemed lost.

In another article, Vincent demonstrates the power of Jacob Bailey's satire. Vincent quotes a passage from Book VIII of "America," pertinent to Samuel Adams ("who could make a T— as sweet as honey; Or cause a dungheap to excell/The pink or rose in fragrant smell") and John Adams.

> *Boston people we are told*
> *Believe his arse was made of gold,*
> *And on the credit of his Bum*
> *Borrow'ed a most enormous sum,*
> *And he employed this numerous score*
> *To cozen and to cheat them more.* *

It is almost impossible to disagree with the snap of the end-rhymed couplet. And John Adams *did* raise a great deal of money for the Revolution, and he was … well, portly, some might say fat, and notoriously vain. It is *not* fair nor balanced commentary; nor is it meant to be. It is meant to be vicious, angry and vengeful. Who would have thought it of Jacob Bailey?

Of the other long satiric verse narrative, "Jack Ramble, the Methodist Preacher," Professor Vincent writes that:

> *It was particularly relevant at this point in Maritime history because, through the late 1780s and early 1790s, the influ-*

ence and authority of the established Church of England in the Maritimes came under considerable pressure from the popularity of itinerant evangelical preachers. In Bailey's eyes, these evangelical preachers not only posed a threat to the authority of the established church, but their doctrines were inherently dangerous to political and social stability ... he linked non-conformism with anarchy and rebellion.

The intention [of "Jack Ramble"] was to articulate the danger of non-conformist religion in general and Methodism in particular ... The Methodists became Bailey's special Bête Noire because, at the founding Conference of the American Methodist Church in 1784, the American Methodists had designated Nova Scotia as a foreign mission under its auspices, and sent two American missionaries into the region. This action was viewed ... as having insidious political as well as religious implications ... ✝

✝ T.B. Vincent, *Humanities Association Review*, p. 166.

"Jack Ramble" begins (in Professor Vincent's summary) in the adolescence of Jack during the American Revolution, and finds him at the end of the war "so corrupt he cannot bring himself to pursue an honourable and decent way of life in peacetime. He decides to commit suicide," from which he is saved by Parson Og, who suggests that Jack become a Methodist and take up the preaching trade. Jack protests that he has an unsavoury past, but Parson Og says that Jack has the essential qualifications: "daring impudence" coupled with "stubborn ignorance." All Jack need do is proclaim a sudden reformation. "Which, like impetuous streams of light/ Chang'd all his soul from black to white." In short, writes Vincent, "Jack has all the makings of a consummate hypocrite, which (Og asserts) happens to be the essential characteristic of the Methodist preacher."

‡ T.B. Vincent,
*Humanities Asso-
ciation Review,*
p. 168.

§ The definition
is taken from
John Dryden's
prologue to his
poem, "Absalom
and Achitophel,"
from 1681. We'll
meet Dryden
again very
shortly.

Jack sets off to be an itinerant Methodist preacher, but it is a steep learning curve, usually involving women. He is persuaded to preach at a meeting—into which a person masked as the Devil rushes, causing Jack to "befoul himself and faint dead away." Jack later goes drinking with a friend, passes out, and is smuggled by others into the bed of a woman whose husband is away on business for the night. The next morning the husband returns, assumes the worst, and "whips Jack's hide unmercifully." In another incident (just before he is to leave for Nova Scotia), a young woman seems wonderfully moved by his preaching and asks for a private consultation: he ends up in her room in what seems to be a brothel, and is blackmailed by the madame. His trip to Nova Scotia includes a terrible storm at sea, but having survived it, Jack attempts to seduce the virginity of the lovely daughter of a generous man—but the daughter and her brother set a trap for Jack, and send him into the bed of the black maid, who does not receive him kindly, and screams bloody murder.

In short, all of Jack Ramble's preaching meetings seem to focus on women; "he exploits female converts for the sake of sexual gratification or monetary gain." ‡

In some ways, it is unfortunate that Jacob Bailey's special skill (aside from his value as a diarist) turned out to be for satire. Satire is a literary form which, all too often, has a short shelf life, not least because it is topical. In no time at all it requires footnotes and professors to explain what all the invective is about. Satire is intended to reform through laughter, but it rarely if ever does anything of the sort.§ Those at whom it is aimed rarely read it, or if they do, understand it, and almost universally deny that it is aimed at them. Moreover, it has little effect. Two of those which have survived the longest are Aristophanes' comic play *Lysistrata* from 411 B.C., which is still performed, and Jonathan Swift's prose essay, "A Modest Proposal." *Lysistrata* was intended to stop a stupid war. It did not; nor have subsequent attempts to stop stupid wars by satire. Jonathan Swift's "A Modest Proposal" (1729) suggests that the two problems of Irish over-population and famine be solved by eating the children, which some readers took as a really good idea, instead of the intended opposite.

¶ PANS, mg. 1, vol. 98, no. 16.

In fact, "successful" satire is that which gives heart to its supporters with a long, often hilarious, jeer—and infuriates its opponents if they happen to notice. Even today Christian evangelists and American patriots alike would likely be outraged by Bailey's satire. I like it, not least because I like Jacob Bailey, and because (although I am an admirer of Benjamin Franklin), I think American "democracy" deserves some sober second thoughts, and Evangelical religion of any kind is pernicious.

My chief literary interest, naturally enough, is in Jacob Bailey's single piece of theatre. The script is in the Provincial Archives of Nova Scotia.¶ It has a title and a subtitle. The title is: *The Humours of the Committee.* (At one point the spelling is *Humors;* later it is *Humours*). The subtitle is *The Majesty of the Mob.* Both title and subtitle are appropriate, and seem to speak directly to Bailey's intention. The core of the play closely follows Bailey's appearances before the Committee of Correspondence, and the third part of the play focuses on the incident in which he was accosted not far from Pownalborough, accused of being a spy, and stripped naked. Bailey—here in the role of "Parson Teachum"—is first at the mercy of the Committee's moods (there are no regulations, and "evidence"

is whatever the committee deems evidence), and then at the mercy of the Mob's curious beliefs.

But dealing with the manuscript presents some immediate problems. For one thing, the anonymous cataloguer who has done so well by curious researchers in describing Bailey's manuscripts makes a rare error. The cataloguer thinks there are two plays. The authors of the article on Jacob Bailey in the *Canadian Encyclopedia* (Julie Ross and T.B. Vincent) think the same. Yet it seems clear enough from the manuscript that it is a single play in three parts. The first four pages are missing, but there are two distinct breaks in the subsequent manuscript. One indicates that what follows is "Part the Second," with a list of *Dramatis Personae*, and the other is "Part the Third," with different *Dramatis Personae*. These are Bailey's terms.

Moreover, Bailey's page numbers on the manuscript are consecutive throughout—and some of them are quite clear; although others must be deduced. So it is definitely one play.

As usual with almost all of Bailey's surviving writing, the manuscript is a first draft of an unfinished project. At first glance, in fact, the project seems somewhat less dramatic than it is. Although Bailey uses stage directions, it sometimes seems that this was intended to be read rather than performed but, especially in the third part, the Mob is seen in full cry—and dispensed with a musket. Actions take place; personalities are seen.

But the manuscript is extremely difficult to read. Many pages are dim or illegible, and others appear to have been edited by mice. I worked with enlarged photocopies of the microfilm.

Still, much can be inferred, and usefully, from little. The

title and subtitle indicate Bailey's twin themes. The names of the characters suggest much. "Mr. Truman," for example, is a friend of Bailey, and therefore condemned by the Committee. His statements are dismissed by the Committee.* Truman himself is accused of disloyalty.

The use of descriptive names for characters was common in eighteenth-century life and literature. Bailey himself gave Latin names to his friends—as with *Fidelis* for his Harvard friend, Dr. Robie Morrill—and referred to Sally Weeks, later his wife, as *Almira*. But the use of "Parson Teachum" for himself was quite possibly more specific. The "Mrs. Teachum" of *The Governess or The Little Female Academy*, was the widow of a "Parson Teachum."

Moreover, in the first and second parts of the play, one major character is called "Achitophel," and another is "Joab," or sometimes the "Brigadier." The Colonel Cushing who was active in pursuing Jacob Bailey through the committee and even into Bailey's house on Christmas Day was later made Brigadier General in the army of the Continental Congress.

The allusion to Achitophel is at once a Biblical reference to II Samuel (13–18) and to John Dryden's 1681 poem, "Absalom and Achitophel." The story is that of the son (Absalom) who rebels against his father, King David, at least partially as the result of bad advice from a counsellor, Achitophel. Battles follow. King David, supported by God, wins, and in a wonderful scene, Absalom, riding on his mule, gets his head caught in the fork of a tree, is lifted off his mule, and dangles there until the men of David's army fill him full of darts. Achitophel goes home and hangs himself.

John Dryden wrote the long poem (in rhyming couplets) "Absalom and Achitophel" as a cautionary tale using II Sam-

* The procedures of the Committee and those of McCarthyism and the House Un-American Activities Committee in the 1950s have much in common, where to support an accused results in the supporter being himself accused. It is a curious strain in American political life. Who would have thought it began so early?

† There were
many executions
and the bodies of
the rebels were
left to rot in
gibbets at cross-
roads all over the
west of England.
Others were sold
as slaves to ladies
of the court and
were sent to the
West Indies.

‡ Lines 150–67.

uel in response to the rebellion of Charles II's bastard son, the Duke of Monmouth, to his father. The rebellion was put down easily and the reprisals by Judge Jeffrey in the Bloody Assizes were arguably the most savage in British history.† In the third part of Bailey's play, the character of *Zimri* appears, taken almost certainly from Dryden's poem.

Dryden's poem contains some of the most misquoted and mis-attributed lines in English literature. He describes Achitophel. (Otherwise called "Ahitophel," which is the spelling used by Bailey.)

> *Of these the false Achitophel was first;*
> *A name to all succeeding ages cursed:*
> *For close designs and crooked counsels fit;*
> *Sagacious, bold, and turbulent of wit;*
> *Restless, unvixed in principles and place;*
> *In power unpleased, impatient of disgrace:*
> *A fiery soul, which, working out its way,*
> *Fretted the pygmy body to decay,*
> *And o'er informed the tenement of clay.*
> *A daring pilot in extremity;*
> *Pleased with the danger, when the waves went high,*
> *He sought the storms; but, for a calm unfit,*
> *Would steer too nigh the sands, to boast his wit.*
> *Great wits are sure to madness near allied,*
> *And thin partitions do their bounds divide,*
> *Else why should he, with wealth and honour blest,*
> *Refuse his age the needful hours of rest?* ‡

It is not difficult to see how Jacob Bailey would find "Achitophel" a suitable model for Jonathan Bowman.

So "The Humours of the Committee" is in some ways a dramatic continuation of Dryden's poem, in much the same way that "America" continues Samuel Butler's "Hudibras." The American rebellion was the eighteenth-century mistake demonstrated in the Old Testament and in John Dryden's seventeenth-century poem. At once the name suggests Biblical knowledge and literary tradition.

There is some possibility that the play was initially intended to be a fable, a form of allegory in which animals lend their personalities to characters (see Ben Jonson's *Volpone*) as the first line of the surviving first page (page five in Bailey's numbering) reads: "the thief in the Mill, the fox in the trap. Enter Toby Wriggle."

But very quickly we are into the moods of the Committee: "The instruction we received from Mr. Hancock and Adams, require that we put the very worst constructions upon everything that is said or done by an obnoxious person ..." and "It is only a trifle in itself, yet we can work it up into a most heinous crime and hereby expose him to the fury of the Mob." The reference is to Bailey's apparent unwillingness to read (from the pulpit) a proclamation for a fast day in support of the Continental Congress. Moreover, "he has always received a salary from England." He is "unfriendly to the cause," "having an undue attachment to Great Britain," and "being disaffected to the noble struggles of America for freedom." When Parson Teachum attempts to reply that he is only following the practices of his church, it is pointed out to him that "every indifferent thing of practice in England becomes a crime when performed by an American." Moreover, "he never gave any rum towards rasing the liberty pole, nor attended to offer a prayer of consecration." Such are the accusations.

Further, it is remarked, "if you suffer a Tory rascal to preach any longer, I must be obliged to inform my cousin the Great Hancock." Later, "speak reverently of the great Mr. Hancock, the worthy, the immortal Mr. Hancock, my cousin." Another (apparent) member of the Committee comments, "I could even hang myself for the good of my country or to oblige you, Mr. Justice," and, "if he attempts to preach any longer, we will tear down his church, burn his house over his head, hang that tea-drinking tory bitch his wife by her heels upon the tallest pine or the liberty pole, and send him headlong to the devil."

It must be remembered, of course, that Bailey is writing his account of his trials, and, as with his satires, he has no intention of being kind. But in this play, we see not only the accusations and his replies to the Committee, but the witnesses and their testimony.

Three Evidences are called by the Committee. The first fellow is told: "It is well known you are intimate at his house … if you would escape suspicion and consequently punishment answer me." When the fellow replies that "I cannot pretend to know what is in his heart," Achitophel responds: "You won't … it is plain gentlemen this fellow is either a tory or a friend of the parson."

The Second Evidence is simple enough. The witness affirms that Parson Teachum is a Tory "because everybody says you are a Tory." Moreover,

> *Sam Saunter says … that he had it from Sarah Gadabout, that she heard a certain young woman declare that she overheard Granny Fetchum inform somebody, that Parson Teachum's wife told her husband … had received a letter a different account of Lexington battle than that published in the newspaper.*

And more about the parson's wife: "Another evidence is that he allows his wife to talk more than becomes her." Further: "I have heard several women say she is a plaguy Tory for her nurse or granny I forget which told them that she always drank tea when she can get it … damn her blood I wish she may be drowned in the tea kettle."

Act Two features a scene in which two members of the Committee uneasily discuss their roles:

Hezekiah Lumber remarks:

> *I am surprised at your conduct, Mr. Driver, did we not promise each other last time not to meddle with the minister again, we were both convinced you know that it was all a matter of spite, the justice and Brigadeer forced to sign the paper to punish him against our consciences, and besides all this Mr. Twyblade our representative refuses to go.*

Gabriel Driver replies that well, uh, but "these committee meetings make us look big," and Hezekiah has to agree, "Nothing in the world makes my wife so mortal proud … after committee meetings when I return all my neighbours treat me with as much respect as if I was the King." And besides,

> *Twyblade says all things are uncertain in this changeable world now I was thinking as the Parson lives in the woods, out of sight of any neighbours, we had better call slyly to see him and make some apology to him before we go to meeting for he may possibly have it in his power to plague us hereafter … I have heard my grand-mother say every dog has his day, and to prevent his growling and snapping it will be proper to give him a crust.*

Hezekiah and Gabriel go off to see Parson Teachum in private, out of sight of observation, but find him not at home.

Parson Teachum faces more accusations in this second appearance before the Committee of Correspondence. He is charged with preaching a seditious sermon, with failing to read the Declaration of Independence from the pulpit, and for praying for the King. In fact, as Joab remarks,

> *I wonder, Mr. Teachum, to find you standing up for a government, which is already demolished or keeping to a religion which shortly be put down, for if we Americans prevail, there will not be a churchman allowed in the country.*

The alleged seditious sermon is seemingly that which threatened an earthquake, and a fellow named Firebrand says it was "something about a parcel of fellows who were punished for rebellion, the ground or the devil I cant tell which swallowed them up."

Parson Teachum protests that the sermon was written nine years ago. And protests that he is following the dictates of a higher power:

> *I could not comply with the requisition to read the declaration without offering the utmost violence to my conscience and solemnly declare in the presence of this assembly that my refusal did not proceed from any contempt of authority but from my sacred regard to my former engagements and for fear of offending that God who is so infinitely Superior to all earthly power.*

Moreover, when Joab (the Brigadeer, Cushing) queries, "are you obliged by your allegiance when the king has broken his coronation oath," Teachum replies with a comment on the duty of oaths:

> *treachery of one party can never justify the … of another. For instance … marriage vows. That the husband commits adultery the wife cannot take the same liberty without … of her nuptial obligations.*

And would the Parson "condemn as perjured villains all these gentlemen who formerly took the oath of allegiance to the King and have since taken it to the present government?" Apparently, yes. It's an awkward moment. And what about praying for the King? Teachum replies that:

> *We are requested to pray for our enemies, and when we consider the King of Great Britain as an enemy pursuing our destruction, it cannot be any crime to pray that the Supreme ruler would turn his heart and incline him to pity and spare us.*

But Joab indicates that Parson Teachum does not understand. All this talk of Truth is beside the point.

> *You will find that Truth is not to be spoken at all times. Abundance of mischief has been done in these times by speaking the truth. Lying has been vastly more to our purpose … when they [the people] have truth it discourages them greatly, they sink into despondency and will do nothing for the good of their country. Therefore upon the whole gentlemen he that speaks the truth freely upon all occasions is a professed enemy to our cause.*

§ Lines 544–54. The Third Act begins in the committee room, but soon moves elsewhere. Achitophel sends a message to a revolutionary group in another community that Parson Teachum is to travel in their vicinity. Achitophel says,

> *I am informed that you have no committee men among you now there can be no liberty where there are no mobs and committees and consequently no tories ... [when] Parson Teachum comes to preach among you and then give him a devilish mobbing if you kill him in the Squabble so much the better.*

So the central incident of Act Three apparently takes place somewhere north of Pownalborough (Wiscasset) near Winslow, and follows the incident where Bailey, responding to a call for religious services some distance from Pownalborough, is grabbed by a mob and, accused of being a spy, stripped naked. The leader of the mob is Zimri, who seems to be taken from Dryden's "Absalom and Achitophel," where there is a most excellent description of him.

> *A man so various, that he seemed to be*
> *Not one, but all mankind's epitome*
> *Stiff in opinions, always in the wrong;*
> *Was everything by starts and nothing long;*
> *But, in the course of one revolving moon,*
> *Was chymist, fiddler, statesman, and buffoon;*
> *Then all for women, painting, rhyming, drinking,*
> *Besides ten thousand freaks that died in thinking*
> *Blest madman, who could every hour employ,*
> *With something new to wish, or to enjoy.*§

In fact, the Zimri associated with the Mob near Winslow seems nothing like so interesting.

But Bailey's depiction of the Mob is valuable for its characterization of their stupidity, ignorance, and violence:

> … *why mother says a tall girl of fourteen, he looks just like other folks   I thought Tories were dredful looking creaturs worse than bears or wolves with teeth and claws as long as my fingers   father when he went into the army told me that the tories would kill folks but I am sure he wont hurt a mother   while they were talking great a boy threw a stick torward him. I will kill him   dont whispered another let him alone for if you provoke him he will tear us in pieces we had better coax him a little. Mrs. Rattlefire tells us that the tories are bloodthirsty creatures and have already devoured great numbers whole nations of our people   I always found it not to matter   shake a surly boy that he main't bite me. Mr. Softly invites his neighbour to meeting, and assures them that the parson is going to preach at Deacon Doubtful's   what cries a number go to hear a damned tory preach I will sooner hear the devil   a fellow that wants to cut our throats let us kill his horse and force him to go home on foot   one clap[s] his backsides kiss my A-ce Mr. Tory   I wonders says an old woman the ice don't break under him and let the monstrous wretch into the river   If I was a tory I expect to be struck dead on the spot. At length they approach the house of Mrs. Rattlefire who seeing the parson bawls out a Tory a Tory the great Tory of Pownalboro is come to play the devil with us   we fastens to the door then seeing a number of people going to attend divine service she ran out among them with her stockings about her heels her hair hanging over her eyes and her bosom naked. Stop Stop*

you are no better than a parcel of cursed tories   won't let my husband go I swore to him he should never kiss me again if he did. I hope no person will dare to entertain him. If my own father should be guilty of such a heinous crime I will set fire to his house with my own hand and burn it over his head and the old rascal in it. Mrs. Rattlefire continues to run backwards and forward in a perfect frenzy and by her threatenings and exclamations prevents a majority of people from hearing divine service.

... get this damned tory parson to baptize my child no I had rather he shouts be ducked in a mud puddle. I would sooner let him die and go to the devil if I knew it would save my childs life and even his soul, the creature should not do it.

be glad to peep at one if I thought it would not leave me out of my senses ... wish they would take him and carry him about for a shew baboon some years ago

if they would I vow you I would give a good continental dollar to see him but I hope he will be confined in a cage that he maint not hurt us.

damned Tory let us dash his brains about the woodpile oh how I long to wash my hands in his blood.

the deacon smacked down his loaded musket and vowed he would blow out their brains if they advanced any further   the mob stood gaping ...

The deacon (and his loaded musket) seemingly carry the day, and although the Parson is told to give up his papers he refuses, not least because the Mob here seems to be asserting an authority (and power) it does not have—or against the deacon's musket, at any rate. (Nor did the Committee of Correspondence headed by Bowman and Cushing have the power it claimed beyond the local community.)

The Humours of the Committee: the Majesty of the Mob is a far more impressive piece of work than it at first appears. It shows promise of becoming a very good little play. Jacob Bailey's apparent intentions are admirable, too. On the one hand, he wants to demonstrate that the local Committee for Correspondence has chiefly the power of intimidation. It has little legal power, if any, even under the administration of the Continental Congress. Its only standards are whims, or humours; consequently, logic in response is of no use whatever. The Committee's only weapon is the mob—so rule, such as it is, is mob rule, and keeping in mind that one of the aggrieved—Bailey—is writing the play, it depicts the mob as a conglomeration of stupidity, ignorance and violence. And show it he does—in the picture of Mrs. Rattlefire, for example, rushing out of her house half-naked and hair flying, stockings around her heels. In the comments of the mob—not only its expectations, which take metaphor for fact (the British, they think, devour nations, which they do and of course do not), but its imagination: Tories have long claws like bears; teeth like wolves. The Mob is ignorant entirely of metaphor. The moral is that stupid people are dangerous. And they are.

What offended Bailey most, I would guess, was that the Committees and the Mobs assaulted Reason. Neither would listen to reason.

The Man Who Said No

There are several strands in Jacob Bailey's life, all of which are important to our understanding of him, and some of which (inevitably) seem contradictory to one another. History is like that, untidy. Biography is the most untidy form of History.

In Jacob Bailey's life we see a young puritan—a man who wanted to be good and do good and achieve excellence. He achieved a kind of excellence by attending Harvard and becoming an educated man, which meant that in certain terms he was a gentleman, even though he never achieved the independent income of a gentleman, nor ever dressed fashionably. Indeed, he was poor and poorly dressed most of his life. "Friends" and foes alike sought to take away what little income he had. Those who treated him worst, who treated him most unfairly, were his brother-in-law Joshua Wingate Weeks—a fellow Anglican cleric—and two of his Harvard classmates.

But he was a puritanical youth. As he recorded in his journals, he was tormented by sexual yearnings which conflicted with his desire to be good. The corn-husking bee and something very like "bundling" raised terrible temptations. He believed the earthquake of 1755 was punishment for the bad behaviour of people who ignored the clergy, did not respect

Harvard graduates, and let their children play on Sunday. He was especially annoyed by the local people who believed that the earthquake was the punishment and now that the earthquake had passed, so had the punishment, and they could resume the lives they lived before it shook them. He, on the other hand, believed the earthquake was a warning of something worse to come.

Jacob Bailey believed that education was achieved by a mastery of ancient languages (Latin and Greek), a knowledge of the ancient worlds of Athens and Rome, and the Bible. We know that as a Harvard student he was four years older than most of his classmates, but we do not know if he was a brilliant student, a mediocre student, or a bad student, because class rank was determined by prominence of family. It had nothing to do with merit. It's fair to say, in fact, that in the eighteenth century in North America and Europe alike, standing of any sort depended upon family, friends and wealth. Breeding counted; individual ability did not. We know that Bailey's family had no social standing whatever. His father was a farmer and weaver; one of his brothers was a carpenter; two other brothers started a brickyard. The possibility that he was a brilliant student might possibly explain the enmity he invoked at Harvard, from President Holyoke and the head of the class, Charles Cushing, when Bailey opted for the Church of England—which required his education in Greek and Latin—over the Congregational Church—which did not. Paradoxes abound.

Bailey made some decisions which define him forever. For example, Bailey decided against the Enlightenment which was taking place at Harvard even while he was a student there. *Excellence* for Bailey was moral excellence, not scientific truth. Bailey makes no mention of Harvard Professor John Winthrop's scientific explanation of the Cape Ann Earthquake of 1755. Benjamin Franklin receives an honorary degree from Harvard in 1753, and Bailey visits Franklin's famous London residence in 1760, but makes no mention of talking with Franklin, and later characterizes Franklin as Dr. Faustus in the satires written in Annapolis Royal. Bailey does, however, notice that the women in Franklin's entourage keep their hats on while dining.

For Bailey, knowledge was that of the classics and literature, not science, but it would be inaccurate to suggest that for Bailey only the past was true. If he ignored the Enlightenment in its scientific aspects, he explored the new thinking. He owned David Hume's essays; he ordered Lord Kames' *Elements of Criticism*. He was always thoughtful, and came to conclusions about the origins of the American Revolution which were perceptive—if unwelcome by American patriots of the ilk of Bishop Burgess in 1853.

But for Bailey, education was not only in the skills of reading and writing, but in morals. And if, to the disapproval of his biographer William Bartlet, Bailey performed in Moliere's *Scapin*, and attended David Garrick's performances in *King Lear* and the moral tragedy by John Home, *The Siege of Aquillea*, he was also reading the moral works for children by Sarah Fielding and the essays of Joseph Addison and Richard Steele, as well as the riotous imagination of Laurence Sterne in *Tristram Shandy*. It's fair to say that Jacob Bailey's reading was usually more adventurous than his writing—although that is not always true. His youthful poem about the corn-husking bee is a depiction of earthy rural life which likely still has the power to unsettle those city folk who cherish a belief in pastoral innocence. His satires are suitably vicious and true. Bailey hated hypocrisy.

It is also fair to say that Bailey's writing usually had a moral purpose, even in the brothel story from 1760—which I find smarmy and Bartlet found (I'm guessing) apoplectic, but its intentions were to shine a holy light into the dark behaviour of the human heart. You have to give credit for good intentions. Bartlet's omissions, concealments and shiftiness, it might be noted, tell us almost as much about the nineteenth century as Bailey tells us about the eighteenth.

But it was the trip to England in 1760 which changed Bailey's sensibility. It demonstrated his decision to say No to his puritan upbringing and Yes to the traditional Church of England. I would argue that chief among his motives for leaving the Congregational Church for the Church of England was the Church of England's requirement that he visit London for ordination. He wanted the trip. In that outpouring of autobiographical writing which marks Bailey's arrival in London, he notes that even as a boy he wanted to travel. London gave him the world of art, theatre and literature. He was never to see its like again, but he stayed true to his decision. London was more important than Boston had ever been.

Women? He liked girls, but grown women frightened him, as he notes in the same autobiographical essay. As a boy, he would hide from them. Sexual girls (as found in the "Corn-husking Bee") were seriously unsettling for a young fellow who wanted to be good and do good according to the strictures of the puritanical church in which he was raised. He liked girls who were polite and modest. His wife was much younger than he, and had been his pupil when he taught at Hampton, New Hampshire. Sally was articulate, forthright, and courageous, as some later evidence would suggest. At one point in his correspondence, Bailey refers the reader to his wife's letter on the demands of the Committee of Correspondence. In the uncompleted play which he wrote about an appearance before that kangaroo court, one of the accusations against the preacher is that he allows his wife to talk too much. But Bailey's attitude toward girls was not at all that of (my favourite) Anglican poet, Robert Herrick, who was much less interested in girls' modesty than in their animal high spirits. Bailey believed very strongly in curtsies.

When he arrived in London, Jacob Bailey wanted to be an American Englishman. Like many others of his era, he saw America as part of Britain. The innocent honesty of his journal entries (in the walnut incident, for example) is sometimes embarrassing. Later, his experiences in London with rude servants and their rude masters, and the knowledge of his own heart, invoked some second thoughts. The landscape to which he was attached was North American. One of his better poems was the lament, "Farewell to the Kennebec." He wanted the excellence of British art, theatre, literature and education, but he made no attempt to live in England after the Revolution, and many other Loyalists did.

We should be careful, however, not to raise false distinctions. Jacob Bailey wanted to be a gentleman, but that did not make him any less the dedicated Christian clergyman. All his life, he performed his Christian duties. It would be false, in fact, to see his desire to be a gentleman as the same thing as a desire to be a port-sipping vicar among the ladies of the gentry. That life (you'll find it in the writings of Jane Austen and Anthony Trollope), was nothing like the missionary work along the Kennebec, and we should remember that Bailey was recruited specifically for the post on the Kennebec. He had no illusions about what his life would be there. He was a gentleman who rode through the mud to baptize children and solemnize marriages in cabins on dirt tracks in the woods. What may have surprised him was the animosity of his Harvard classmates, Charles Cushing and Jonathan Bowman.

To his other virtues, we must add those of duty and courage.

But for a literary wanderer like myself, the great virtue and great value of Jacob Bailey is that *he wrote everything down*. He gives us pictures of a tumultuous time. Nothing like the official pictures from the fine speeches of Philadelphia, nor the heroics of the battlefield. In Bailey we find neither the ideals of the American Revolution, nor the murals of which came afterwards. Bailey finds himself through no fault of his own (see his speech to the Committee of Correspondence) at the mercy of kangaroo courts and the mob on the Kennebec. His view of the Revolution is not that of the political theorist. Bailey decides that he will continue to pray for the King; he decides not to read the Declaration of Independence from his pulpit. He says No. His life and that of his family are put at risk. It is messy out there on the frontier. There is neither natural justice nor theoretical justice. There is only a court with one verdict and a mob to carry out the sentence. This was the Revolution as rum and looting. No wonder that William Bartlet tried to conceal the identities of the villains. Cushing and Bowman were traitors who betrayed their oaths of office, and who behaved like jackals. Patriots? They are not people the American Revolution wants to remember, but they were the cost of changing governments.

It is one of the little ironies of history that Jacob Bailey won't let us forget them. He wrote everything down.

All History is Revisionist

A n event happens—but if there is no record of it, the event is meaningless. It never happened. So *History* is less the events than the records of events. This is why Jacob Bailey is so important to us: in the middle of tumultuous events, he kept the records.

But the keeper of the records is therefore important, and the historian as important as the events which he or she records in one way or another. So Bailey's point of view of the American Revolution is important, and that point of view is influenced by the ideas he inherited as well as his experiences. Every historian requires a biographer. And the biographer in turn requires examination.

Jacob Bailey's first biographer, William Bartlet, in the curiously-named *Frontier Missionary: the Memoirs of Jacob Bailey*, tells us something about himself, perhaps inadvertently. For one thing, William A. Bartlet, describing himself on the title page ("Rector of St. Luke's Church, Chelsea, Mass. and Corresponding Member of the Maine Historical Society") makes clear that he is interested chiefly in the missionary work of the Rev. Jacob Bailey. For another, he is unusually humble for a biographer. He knows perfectly well that he is chiefly editing Jacob Bailey's journals and letters—rather than examining his life—and therefore Bartlet is quite right to call his book the "Memoirs" of Jacob Bailey. Moreover, we have the word of the Right Reverend George Burgess—Bishop of the Protestant Episcopal Church in the Diosese of Maine—who provides the Preface, that in Bartlet, Jacob Bailey's writings were in the "hands of one [for] whom to examine, to study, to arrange, to digest with scrupulous accuracy and indefatigable attention, was a labour of love." Also, Burgess says that he can testify to Bartlet's skill in dealing with the "vast extent, various contents, and discouraging aspect of that sea of documents, out of which these facts have been rescued." So the Right Reverend Burgess gives us a picture of Bartlet. It seems an accurate assessment of Bartlet.

Except of course for some puzzling omissions. Bartlet has clearly read the Bailey journal of 1759–60, but has left out a great deal which I think is important. Moreover, there is the very curious business of the cover-up of the names of Jonathan Bowman and Charles Cushing, the villains who tormented Bailey on the Kennebec. If Bartlet was a man of "scrupulous accuracy," why did he omit much and conceal (not very well) the names of two significant players in the drama on the Kennebec?

The answer would seem to lie with the personality of the Right Reverend Burgess. I think he censored Bartlet's writing. Why do I think this?

First, because (in my opinion, mind) he did not approve of Jacob Bailey. Oh, he approves of the Jacob Bailey who might help "trace the early annals of the Episcopal Church in America"—although, to be accurate, all that information is provided by Bartlet, not Bailey. Was that information provided at Burgess's instigation or insistence? Burgess is quick to note that in establishing the Anglican church in Pownalborough,

> *There was no encroachment on sectarian ground: it was a simple work of charity; and the time may come when even this*

*seed, which appeared to be quite trodden down in the struggle
of revolution, will be seen to have borne its fruit after many
days.*

Burgess is careful not to use the terms *Anglican* or *Church of
England*. No mention of Dr. Sylvester Gardiner's plans for
the Kennebec.

There then follows Burgess's position:

> *That a considerable portion of the clergy maintained their alle-
> giance to the British crown, may be remembered with regret,
> but not with shame. There is no cause to blush for a mistaken
> conscience, or for sacrifices to principles, the highest in them-
> selves, though erroneously applied ... knowing, as we do, the
> great designs of Providence for our Republic, and the bound-
> less blessings which its establishment has shed abroad, we must
> lament that good men should have shipwrecked their temporal
> fortunes, and, for a time, the interests of their communion, by
> their too tenacious adherence to obligations which the nation-
> al will dissolved. We can read of the sufferings of the loyal-
> ists without danger lest our sympathies should persuade us to
> forget the preciousness of our political heritage, or the great
> deeds by which it was purchased; and this book will cast some
> light over that painful story.*

It is an amazing statement. Were the "great deeds" those of
Bowman and Cushing? Is that why their names must be concealed? No, it's clear to a careful reader that Burgess thinks
Bartlet is treading on dangerous ground with these memoirs
of a man with "too tenacious adherence to obligations which
the national will dissolved ..." God, in the form of Providence,
blessed America. Burgess not only disagrees with Jacob Bailey; he is embarrassed by Jacob Bailey.

Moreover, Burgess, in the middle of the paragraph quoted above, reveals one of his central worries—

Should a crisis arrive, when the citizen of one of the United States shall be compelled to choose between the commands of his own State and those of the Federal government, the position of those clergymen may then be appreciated.

In one sense, the Right Reverend Burgess is prescient: as early as 1853, he sees the Civil War coming.

So to evaluate Jacob Bailey's writing, we must evaluate William Bartlet's positions in 1853, and to understand them, we must look closely at the Bishop Burgess's Preface. Close reading, if not necessarily scholarship.

My attitudes, too, require some examination: I term Bowman and Cushing "villains." A scholarly study would not be so bold. I clearly disapprove of Bishop Burgess. Moreover—if the alert reader has not already learned this, I am a Freethinker, an adherent of no church but the mind of the Enlightenment. I like Ben Franklin. I am very wary of organized religions.

Each person who writes about events has a very complex point of view, as does the person who writes about the writer. *History* is constantly revised by Historians. William Bartlet is seemingly horrified that Jacob Bailey performed in a play. I think it is a very good thing that he performed in a play; while admiring William Bartlet's industry, I disapprove of William Bartlet. I actively dislike Bishop Burgess.

Sometimes these feelings collect themselves in what might be called a "Prism." (It's only a metaphor; don't get excited.) This prism is a collection of attitudes—which may be focused on a particular historical event—through which we see other events. For example, I see much of *History* in light of the photographs (probably in *Life Magazine*) of the liberation of the Nazi death camps in 1945. In 1945, I was nine.

Even Charles Allen revises the History of Jacob Bailey. Allen harbours a deep resentment toward Massachusetts Puritans—and Massachusetts young sparks who treat Maine as their private hunting reserve.* But Allen also raises the importance of the Salem Witch Trials.

I have the feeling that Jacob Bailey saw much of his life through the Salem Witch Trials, and if so, it would explain why he was so concerned about the emotional responses of pubescent girls; why he so distrusted religious ecstasy; why he rejected the Congregational Church which hosted the trials and the executions; why he mistrusted the entire evangelical tradition; why he hated the Mob.

Jacob Bailey, in common with many other writers of his time, did not restrict himself to diary-writing or satiric poetry, or the theatre. A writer was a writer who explored all manner of writing. Jacob Bailey also wrote history: he wrote "A History of New England," still unpublished and available in manuscript form in the Provincial Archives of Nova Scotia—although, to be fair, he might simply have been writing a textbook for his own use.✝ A great deal of Bailey's "A History of New England," is what we today might call Geography. He describes the physical landscape as well as the events of the past.

A major chapter in Bailey's "History" is devoted to the Salem Witch Trials.‡ Bailey does not claim to be original in his research. He uses the work of Thomas Hutchinson, the last royally appointed civilian governor of Massachusetts, who left office in 1774, and was succeeded by General Gage. The publishing history of Hutchinson's historical work is somewhat cloudy, but it seems to have been written after Hutchinson fled to England shortly after 1774. So Bailey *prob-*

* Allen, p. 12.

✝ A number of Bailey manuscripts in the Provincial Archives of Nova Scotia are termed "textbooks," but are simply Bailey's teaching notes—for arithmetic, for example.

‡ PANS, mg. 1, vol. 98, no. 3.

§ "Truth" can be Revealed Truth (in which God speaks to the Believer) or Observed Truth, in which the observer deduces certain facts. But the Observer has doubts; the Believer has none.

ably (there's no proof) read it after Bailey was ensconced in Nova Scotia after 1779. But it is clear from Bailey's comments on the Salem Witch Trials that he is seeing them through the eyes of a man who has some experience with the theocracy that was Massachusetts and the effects of that theocracy on the American Revolution.

The Salem Witch Trials of 1692 are one of the most shameful episodes in American history *and* the history of the Protestant Church. They are frequently, and rightly (Bailey does so), compared to the Spanish Inquisition. Both these horrors of Christianity were created with the support of Faith, with which there can be no argument or debate.§

In one significant way, we have the advantage over Jacob Bailey. If we wish to understand the Puritan mind of 1692, we can read Nathaniel Hawthorne's masterpiece short story, "Young Goodman Brown," published in 1836. I recommend it, especially if you wish to know something about Bailey's youth and, yes, his soul. Bailey was born in 1731 at Rowley, some fifteen miles from Salem Village, the site of the witch trials and the home of Nathaniel Hawthorne. One of Hawthorne's ancestors was a judge in the witchcraft trials. There is a Bailey cited by Bailey among the justices who reject John Proctor's appeal. Jacob Bailey quotes the appeal in his chapter on the Witchcraft Trials in his "A History of New England."

What makes Nathaniel Hawthorne's story especially unusual and possibly unique is his understanding of the mixture of faith, fear, belief, doubt and savagery which characterized the Puritan mind in the 1690s.

In the story, young Goodman Brown leaves his lovely wife, Faith, to whom he has been married for only three months, to attend a convention in the forest. No reason is given for the purpose of this journey. Along the way he meets an older man (who seems to have a common aspect with Goodman Brown's father and grandfather) ¶ who serves as his guide. Goodman Brown comes on a piece of pink ribbon, exactly like that which adorns Faith's cap. The meeting seems to be a gathering of Satanists; in attendance are even some Indian ritualists. What shocks Goodman Brown is that he recognizes most of the people there as people from home, from Salem Village. For example, there is Goody Cloyse who taught him his catechism. (A Goody Cloise appears in Jacob Bailey's history.) Outwardly the people seemed strong Christians. Inwardly, they are beyond hypocrisy. They are not only less than they had appeared, but worse: committed to wickedness. Then somehow Faith is by his side and young Goodman Brown looks to heaven and cries out to resist the evil one, and Poof! he is back on the streets of Salem village as if he had never left. It is suggested that what he has seen might have been only a dream.* Except it changes him ever after: he becomes a sour man and dies so.

This was the mind of Salem✝ which made the Witchcraft Trials possible. The good folk of Salem were quite willing to believe in the Devil. Did they not believe wholeheartedly in God, and fear God? Was there not a sense of evil always tempting them? So when a few young girls (and then more young girls, and then others who were not so young) fell mysteriously ill, a physician pronounced them bewitched and they agreed. Bailey quotes from Hutchinson:

> *In 1692, a daughter and niece of Mr. Parris, minister of Salem village ... of about ten or eleven, and two other young females in the neighbourhood, began to alarm their friends ... with uncommon complaints.... Phisicions were consulted who immediately pronounced them bewitched.*

¶ Goodman Brown's grandfatherly guide carries a walking stick with aspects of a serpent. My grandfather had a walking stick with aspects of a serpent, and a head which could bite a small boy, too.

* The actual pink ribbon in what may be a dream, which seems to validate the experience, is much debated in studies of American literature. It floats out of a dark cloud. But it is much the same technique of verisimilitudes Jacob Bailey was using in his stories of 1759–60, in the letter which seemingly validates the seduction story of the young officers while *The Hind* is anchored off Nantucket, and the cost of the frolic in the London brothel: £1.19s.

✝ The place name "Salem" is commonly held to be a shortened version of "Jerusalem." There are scores of "Salems" in the United States. I graduated from Salem High School in one of them.

Bailey remarks that "the female mind even at the earliest period of life is open to the attacks of *emulation and vanity* [my italics]." Neighbours who were in league with the devil were hurting them: pinching them, pricking them as if with pins. Mysterious figures of friends appeared with a book, urging them to sign. If they signed, presumably, they were henceforth devotees of the Devil.

Proof was not required. Ann Putnam was asked by the examining magistrates (who judged the cases together with clergymen) if "this woman hurt you?" The reply was "Yes, sir, a great many times," and then, when the accused looked upon the girls, the girls fell into fits. On other occasions the girls stuffed their fists into their mouths and appeared speechless, which was also considered proof of torment by the devilish powers of the accused.

One clergyman was among the accused, a Rev. Mr. Burroughs. Against him were five women who *pretended* (Bailey's word) to be bewitched by him, and "eight confessing Witches." "Another said he carried her to the top of a high Mountain and shewed her glorious kingdoms, telling her he would give them to her if she would sign the book."

Jacob Bailey suggests that there were sectarian influences on the courts.

Mr. Burroughs was certainly unfortunate in concluding his devotions with the Lords Prayer since it is frequently used in the common prayer book, which both preachers and Magistrates at that day held in the highest detestation and contempt. And it is remarked by a grave author of prodigious influence in the government a prophet among the people and a leader of these dreadful prosecutions, that though the possessed were unable to peruse the bible or any other godly writer, yet when the common prayer book was offered they could read it with great facility.

Others who were accused confessed under the belief that they could thereby save their lives, or accused others with the same hope. Recantations were no good. One young woman who, together with her mother, accused her father of dealing in darkness, attempted to recant and thus save her father, but the mother was given no second chance.

Others were tortured, tied heels and neck until blood gushed from their noses.

The writer (quoted by Bailey) noted, "These actions are very like the popist cruelties: they have already undone us in our estates, and will serve their turn out in our innocent blood."

Bailey opened his chapter comparing the witchcraft mania to the "fire of enthusiasms thro every rank and order" (the comparison is to the evangelicals), and toward the end of his commentary writes:

these pious clergymen were so deeply engaged in the overthrow of Satan's kingdom as to be insensible to all the feelings of humanity.... The most savage and untutored tribes of America have more rational notions and act in such cases with less inhumanity.

And then:

It is somewhat curious that twenty-two persons out of twenty-eight were females. It must have been, I conceive, a prevailing article of faith in those times that women are more easily seduced into a correspondence with the malignant spirits of darkness, than men.

So we should not be surprised that Jacob Bailey devoted a lifetime to education, and especially to the education of young women. Had not the infamous Witchcraft Trials been instigated by girls of ten and eleven years old? Enough snickers, then. Given the right kind of community beliefs, ten and eleven year old girls can be extremely dangerous.

And given the right kind of community beliefs, what kind of laws, what kind of punishments, can we expect? In the "evidences" brought to the Witchcraft Trials, we see the "evidences" brought into the hearings of the Committee of Correspondence during the American Revolution. The tradition of guilt by accusation returns to American life from time to time.‡

Jacob Bailey and his family arrived in Annapolis Royal probably on 1 August 1782.§ His family consisted of his wife, Sarah (known usually as Sally), son Charles Percy (born 3 May 1777) and daughter Rebecca Lavinia (born 1780). Shortly thereafter, according to Bartlet, a Captain Mowat of the Royal Navy (reviled in Maine, writes Bartlet) sent his son to Annapolis Royal to be educated by Jacob Bailey. Mowat was reviled because he had burnt Falmouth (later Portland) to the ground during the American Revolution. Mowat sent a black slave to accompany his son to Annapolis Royal, with orders that the slave should obey Bailey as if he were the master. In addition, Bailey had permanent house guests—the widow of Captain Callahan and her children who had been his loyal friends on the Kennebec.

Bailey was scarcely settled in Annapolis Royal in the summer of 1782 before some 600 Loyalists arrived in October. He found shelter for them. As many as 2,000 more arrived in the spring of 1783. There was scant help from the "Bluenoses" already ensconced in the Valley. The animosity between the two groups was never solved (not least because of the religious differences between the evangelical sects and the established church), but more or less dissipated when the Bluenoses and Planters were outnumbered—and outvoted—by the Loyalists.

As usual, Bailey performed all his religious duties, and more. He served as deputy chaplain to the garrison at Fort Anne with no reward but a fuel ration until 1794, when at last his brother-in-law accepted a position with the Church of England in Preston, Nova Scotia, which in turn enabled John Wentworth, Harvard classmate of Jacob Bailey in 1755 and now Lieutenant-Governor of Nova Scotia, to award the Annapolis Royal position to Bailey. Bailey was also Rector of St. Luke's in Annapolis Royal.

He wrote poems, satires, parts of novels, an unfinished play, history.

There were family crises. Daughter Rebecca Lavinia ran off in 1801. A man was involved. It is not clear where she went or with whom, but she returned unmarried and became the schoolmistress in Annapolis Royal for many years.

Son Charles Percy became part of the Duke of Kent's entourage and was killed in the Battle of Chippewa in 1814. The other sons came to no good—according to my favourite local historian, Aunt Minnie. On 13 December 1925, Aunt Minnie wrote to Reg Woodbury:

Sally. I was told when I visited Mr. Allen that she was rather a gay lady for a minister's wife. Miss Sarah Bailey that you remember was a daughter of Thomas Bailey. He did not marry his wife until all of the children were born. I have heard my mother say that he always promised to marry her when she had a boy. The boy never arrived. However, he married her before he died. The girls never knew it until they were young women when it was thrown up to them. They felt it deeply, that is why they were a little peculiar and Martha never went out after she knew it. His other son, William, was even worse. He was married but he was running around with other women and had several children by them. Mrs. Peter Bonette was his daughter. His wife was Col Delancey's daughter. I don't think they got their badness from their father, but the Weekses had quite a name. People were disgusted with the wild behaviour of … two sons, Thomas and William, who I don't think were much like their father, because from all accounts he was a … hardworking Christian missionary. But his wife's family, The Weekses, were very different. If I ever see you again I will tell you some stories about them. I think Mr. Bailey's sons took after their mother's family.

And on 1 January 1926:

Charles Percy had two brothers, William and Thomas, but Charles Percy was the only one that the Duke of Kent had trained as a soldier and bought him a commission in "The King's Own." He was a Captain, he was very fine-looking which attracted the Duke's attention. William was Barracks-Master here in Annapolis and he was the father of Mrs. Peter Bonnett. He also had two illegitimate children and the Baileys at R.H [Round Hill] are descendants of one of those.

Rumour dies hard in Annapolis Royal. It is still said that Bailey was fond of girls. And so he was. But the rolling of eyes which responds to that statement might mean something else if the listener is thinking of Jacob Bailey's sons. Aunt Minnie has raised a new possible interpretation. If rumour refers to a naughty Bailey, it was more likely one of his sons than the clergyman himself.

And that's History for you: Gossip, Fact, Opinion. It's always being revised: I revise it; Aunt Minnie revises it. It carries on.

Jacob Bailey died in 1808. His bones are buried in the burying ground at Fort Anne—no one knows exactly where.¶ There is a monument to him at the corner of the burying grounds nearest St. Luke's Church, but, to my mind, this is a monument to the First Rector of St. Luke's. I am here to praise the diarist, writer, and survivor of the Committee of Correspondence who was Jacob Bailey.

His real memorials, I think, are in the words of Charles Allen, William Bartlet, Julie Ross, and Aunt Minnie.

¶ Jacob Bailey's bones are interred somewhere in the Fort Anne burying ground, but no one knows exactly where. The memorial to Bailey was erected by the parishioners of St. Luke's Church in 1922. Conversation with Alan Melanson, Parks Canada, on 18 July 2006.

Acknowledgements

The preparation of this book has been aided by many people in ways both great and small. Among them are the directors of the Annapolis Heritage Society (O'Dell Museum), John Kirby, Ryan Scranton, Ian Lawrence, Lois Jenkins, Jim Lannon, Lorraine Slopek, Father Wayne Lynch, Reverend Ruby Todd, the staff at the Harriet Irving Library of the University of New Brunswick in Fredericton, the staff at the Vaughan Memorial Library of Acadia University in Wolfville, the staff of the Provincial Archives of Nova Scotia in Halifax, Julie Ross, Tom Vincent, Jim Tillotson, and of course my editors, Kate Kennedy and Andrew Steeves. All errors, mistakes, opinions, and stupidities are the sole responsibility of the author. Thanks is also due to Millie Hawes who provided the costume for the author photo.

The portrait of Jacob Bailey reproduced as the frontispiece was among the documents and artifacts donated to the O'Dell Museum, Annapolis Royal, in 2001 by Bailey's descendent George Woodbury of Osoyoos, BC. The artist is unknown. The image on page 13 is the title page of Jacob Bailey's journal dated 1759, covering his trip to England for ordination. The image on pages 40 & 41 is a letter dated 29 December 1755, to John Adams, a classmate at Harvard and later second President of the United States, recorded in Jacob Bailey's letterbook of 1755. These three images are courtesy of the Annapolis Heritage Society Archives, O'Dell Museum, Annapolis Royal. ¶ The image on page 81 is *An Attempt to land a Bishop in America* (London, 1769). Courtesy of the John Carter Brown Library at Brown University. ¶ The image on pages 232 & 233 is *View of Annapolis taken the 15th Sept. 1775* by Lt. Richard Williams (c. 1750–76). Watercolour with ink border on laid paper, 25.0 × 42.2 cm. Collection of the Art Gallery of Nova Scotia. Purchased with the assistance of a Movable Cultural Property grant accorded by the Minister of Canadian Heritage under the terms of the Cultural Property Export and Import Act and funds provided by the Historical Association of Annapolis Royal, 2005. Photograph by Shannon Parker.

Sources Cited

Two main archival collections were used in researching this book. The Jacob Bailey Papers, including Bailey's 1755–56 letterbook and journal of 1759–60, are at the O'Dell Museum, Annapolis Royal, Nova Scotia, as are Aunt Minnie's letters and Charles Allen's essay. Materials were also consulted in the Jacob Bailey Collection, Provincial Archives of Nova Scotia, Halifax (see The Bailey Papers, mg. 1, vol. 98, Nos. 3 & 16). Published sources cited by the author are listed below:

Charles E. Allen, "The Rev. Jacob Bailey, His Character and Works, Read Before the Lincoln County [Maine] Historical Society, 13 November 1895." Printed by the Society, 1895. Available at the O'Dell Museum, Annapolis Royal, NS.

Ray P. Baker, "The Poetry of Jacob Bailey, Loyalist," in *New England Quarterly* (Cambridge, Mass., 1929, pp. 58–92).

William S. Bartlet, *Frontier Missionary: A Memoir of the Life of the Rev. Jacob Bailey* (Boston: Ide & Dutton, 1853).

Ambrose Bierce, *The Devil's Dictionary* (New York: Dover, 1993 [1911]).

W.A. Calnek & A.W. Savary, *History of the County of Annapolis* (Toronto: William Briggs, 1897; Mika Facsimile).

Arthur Cash, *Laurence Sterne*, 2 vols. (London: Methuen, 1986).

John Cleland, *Fanny Hill: Memoirs of a Woman of Pleasure* (Los Angeles: Fitz, 1964 [1749]).

David Cruise & Alison Griffiths, *On South Mountain: The Dark Secrets of the Goler Clan* (Toronto: Viking/Penguin Canada, 1997).

Brenda Dunn, *A History of Port Royal/Annapolis Royal 1605–1800* (Halifax: Nimbus, 2004).

Arthur Wentworth Eaton, *The Church of England in Nova Scotia and the Tory Clergy of Nova Scotia* (New York: Thomas Whitaker, 1891).

Sarah Fielding, *The Governess or The Little Female Academy* (Kessinger Reprint; original probably c. 1749).

Judith Fingard, *The Anglican Design in Loyalist Nova Scotia, 1783–1816* (London: SPCK, The Church Historical Society, 1972).

Benjamin Franklin, *Autobiography & Other Writings*, ed. Jesse Lenisch (New York: Signet Classics, Penguin, 1961).

Julian Gwyn, *Excessive Expectations: Maritime Commerce and the Economic Development of Nova Scotia, 1740–1870* (Montreal & Kingston: McGill-Queen's University Press, 1998).

Thomas Haliburton, *History of Nova Scotia* (Halifax: Joseph Howe, 1829; Mika Facsimile).

Rod Horton & Herbert Edwards, *Backgrounds of American Literary Thought* (New York: Appleton Century Crofts, 1952).

David McCullough, *John Adams* (New York: Simon & Schuster, 2001).

John S. Moir & D.M.L. Farr, *The Canadian Experience* (Toronto: Ryerson, 1969).

Christopher Moore, *The Loyalists: Revolution, Exile, Settlement* (Toronto: McClelland & Stewart, 1984).

Samuel Eliot Morison, *Three Centuries of Harvard* (Cambridge: Harvard University Press, 1936).

Thomas H. Raddall, *His Majesty's Yankees* (Toronto: McClelland & Stewart, 1942; New Canadian Library No. 133, 1977.)

————, *The Path of Destiny* (New York: Popular Library, 1957).

————, *In My Time: A Memoir* (Toronto: McClelland & Stewart, 1976).

Julie Martha Ross, "Jacob Bailey, Loyalist: Anglican Clergyman in New England and Nova Scotia" (M.A. dissertation, University of New Brunswick, Fredericton, 1975).

T. B. Vincent, "Alline & Bailey," in *Canadian Literature* (Vancouver, No. 68–9, Spring–Summer 1976, pp. 124–33).

————, "Some Examples of Narrative Verse Satire in the Early Literature of Nova Scotia and New Brunswick," in *Humanities Association Review* (Kingston, No. 27, 1976, pp. 161–75).

Typeset in Bell by Andrew Steeves & printed offset at Gaspereau Press under the direction of Gary Dunfield.

1   3   5   7   6   4   2

Library & Archives Canada Cataloguing in Publication

Thompson, Kent, 1936–
The man who said no: reading Jacob Bailey, Loyalist /
Kent Thompson.

Includes bibliographical references.
ISBN 978-1-55447-055-6

1. Bailey, Jacob, 1731-1808. 2. United Empire loyalists—
Nova Scotia—Biography. 3. Anglican Communion—Nova Scotia—
Clergy—Biography. 4. Annapolis Royal (N.S.)—Biography. I. Title.

BX5620.B34T56 2008   283.092   C2008-900979-7

❧

GASPEREAU PRESS LIMITED
Gary Dunfield & Andrew Steeves · Printers & Publishers
47 Church Avenue Kentville, Nova Scotia, Canada
www.gaspereau.com